A Memoir

M.J. WALLRICH

ISBN 978-1-956010-95-4 (paperback)
ISBN 978-1-956010-96-1 (hardcover)
ISBN 978-1-956010-97-8 (digital)

Copyright © 2021 by M.J. Wallrich

All rights reserved. No part of this publication may be reproduced, distributed, or transmitted in any form or by any means, including photocopying, recording, or other electronic or mechanical methods without the prior written permission of the publisher. For permission requests, solicit the publisher via the address below.

Rushmore Press LLC
1 800 460 9188
www.rushmorepress.com

Printed in the United States of America

PART ONE
A HIGH DESERT TALE

CHAPTER 1

They were two hours late when Betsy called us and said she couldn't get Christopher to get in the car. It was a Sunday afternoon four days after Christmas in 2002. Sandy and I were waiting for our tall nephew Christopher and his new girlfriend to show up for dinner at our place outside of Prescott, Arizona. They lived in Cornfield, a small town forty miles away. Betsy asked if our daughter, Hedy, was going to be at our house and when I said no, she said they were on their way. The two showed up after dark; Betsy was apologetic and Christopher was quiet. He was a foot taller than Betsy, and she was eight years older than him. He had a tortured look on his face most of the evening. They weren't hungry. We shared drinks and talked and played a few rounds of draw poker. Christopher didn't laugh when we laughed; he was on edge, miles away in his mind. I figured he was going through a blue period. I asked, "Work been keeping you busy, Chris?"

    He said, "Sort of." Christopher was a sheetrock taper.

    Betsy said, "Things are going to pick up soon."

    I said, "We're swamped at our shop."

    "Well, good for you," said Betsy. I understood by her tone that we should talk about other things. And we did. They stayed less than two hours. About eight o'clock, we walked them out to their car; Betsy and I got to their car first, while Sandy and Christopher lingered on the porch in a conversation. Later, Sandy said that he whispered to her, "If I go down, I'm taking everybody with me." Neither of us could figure out what he meant by that. It would be another month before the answer came and when it came, it hit like a meteor.

In early February 2003, the space shuttle Columbia exploded, killing seven sky travelers and scattering debris from Nevada into Texas. I wish we had paid more attention to the part about picking up the pieces. A week after the Columbia went down, our daughter Hedy, who was living in Prescott, phoned on that Saturday morning and asked if she could come by after she got out of work that evening. She had something important to tell us, and it had to be face to face. Sandy set up the meeting for that evening.

Hedy shared a house in Prescott with five young people, one of which was the bass player of their punk rock band. She was twenty-two years old, worked three part-time jobs, and sang her did and danced her didn't. Hedy had stopped going to college classes a year and a half earlier. She had a boyfriend named Chuck. Sandy and I tossed ideas about the meeting. Had Chuck asked her to marry him? He had an eight-year-old daughter—was Hedy scared of being a mother to the girl? Was Hedy adding another tattoo? Was it purple hair this time? Was Hedy going to finally embrace her first love—music? Go back to school—let her voice take her around the world. Hedy had the voice to do it. We were told by an excited college professor who chased us down in a parking lot that Hedy was a coloratura soprano. They need voices like hers in punk rock, too, Hedy said.

It was a sunny winter day in central Arizona and the air was brisk. The mile-high city of Prescott, perched in the high desert above the Mogollon Rim, has a lot of frosty winter mornings. The city of Phoenix, where it seldom freezes, sprawls on the valley floor one hundred miles to the southeast. I finished some chores that afternoon, and then played tennis ball fetch with Woody, our Cocker Spaniel. To end the game, I ducked into the garage. Sandy's car was parked on one side of the garage, and Betsy and Christopher's furniture and boxes were stacked on the other side. The two were still trying to find an affordable rental in Prescott after five weeks of searching. They only needed our help a couple more days.

We had an acre and a half lot. Our garage sat about a hundred feet from the ranch-style house nestled into a hillside. The lot was covered with live oaks, pinion pines, and the usual high desert shrubbery—creosote bushes, sage, a few prickly pear cacti, and wildflowers. The bark beetle was chewing up Arizona that year. An apricot tree behind the house had died for lack of water the previous summer. On the east side of the property, a split rail fence ran along the county road and a dry wash bordered the west side. A live oak held a treehouse Hedy and Peter and I had built years earlier. Pete, our son, was away at college at Northern Arizona University studying engineering. From our yard, we had a grand view of the east summit of Granite Mountain. Our mountain, we called it. Native Americans who had lived in the area for thousands of years had left gifts of petroglyphs along the Mint Creek trail at the base of the mountain. It was an ancient trail.

Our property was an ideal party place; we had space enough to park twenty cars, and we designated a spot by the wash for bonfires. We bought the place from the original owners, the Hewitt's, who built the house. Old Mr. Hewitt was a retired accountant, handyman, packrat, and penny pincher. He buried a lot of junk on the flat land beside the wash. We found it futile to dig there because chunks of rusting iron stopped our shovels. The neighborhood was designated as horse property; the street names had equestrian and cowboy themes like Bridle Path, Spur Drive, Lone Pine, Saddle Horn, Lariat Lane. It was a quiet place. Williamson Valley Road had a lot of traffic but we didn't notice the noise most of the time. The coyotes were the loudest disturbances. They lived in synch with the moon and when they came serenading, they called sharp and loud. Coyote banter heard late in the night can set your hair on edge, but it is exciting at the same time. A grey fox came through our yard every now and then. We had a cat named Cindy when we moved there and she wouldn't go outside for four months. The first day she did, she disappeared.

I was in the garage that day when a car pulled into the yard. Betsy, Christopher's girlfriend, had come to look for some important papers. She smelled of alcohol. I helped her move a few things to find what she needed and invited her to come to the house to have coffee, to sit a spell, and talk with Sandy and myself. Betsy accepted, but first, she needed to smoke.

We sat in chairs beside the big window that overlooked a small, attached yard, bordered with concord grapes that entwined along a pine pole fence.

"I'm sorry for the mess we've left with you, but we're running short of cash," Betsy said. "When construction picks up, Christopher will find work. It shouldn't be much longer."

Betsy and Christopher had been together for six months. "I specified in my ad," Betsy said, "that I was looking for a female roommate to share my house in Cornville. But Christopher showed up and talked me into giving him a try. Next thing I knew, we were a couple." She laughed. She had left Indiana for California to escape an abusive ex. When her car broke down on the Interstate outside of Flagstaff, she ended up in Sedona, working at the Safeway store. She said, "I'd been sober for over ten years till I shared a bottle of whiskey with Christopher one night. Now I have to start over again."

"Oh, no, that's too bad," Sandy said. "Well, start now. Start today."

I mentioned the impending war in Iraq but Sandy begged me not to go there.

Sandy asked Betsy if she had found a place to keep her dogs. "Yes, Chris's mother took them," Betsy answered with a far-away look, then added, "When Christopher was sheet-rocking in Sedona, he was making good money. I lent him some money at first and he always paid me back. Soon, I was handing him wads of cash from my savings and not expecting it back. We blew through my whole savings since he's moved in. I'm worried about what we are going to do." Then she slapped her knee and laughed, "But the sex is great."

Sandy and I exchanged frowns. Betsy continued, determined to tell us about her sex life with our longhaired nephew. "Have you ever heard of Christopher doing weird sex things?"

"What do you mean?" Sandy said.

"Well, he does these weird *things* with the dogs. He lies down on the floor with them, on his back and, you know, he does weird stuff with them. You haven't heard of him doing weird things, you know, like that?"

"No, I haven't," Sandy said. "I don't know what you mean." Sandy looked distressed. We both were uncomfortable with the direction this conversation was headed, but we didn't stop her. "And he likes for me to wear sexy clothes, you know, sexy teddies and panties. And then he chases me around the house and tackles me. He rips these things off me; rips them to shreds. And they're not cheap. You haven't heard of him doing rough things like that?"

"No. Not really. Not at all," Sandy said and looked toward me like someone was standing on her toes. When Hedy and Peter were young and we watched movies that had racy scenes, we made them hide their eyes and cover their ears. We did that until they were into their teens. One time, when we forgot to give Hedy the okay to open her eyes, she fell asleep and woke up twenty minutes later, asking, "Can I open my eyes now?" And we didn't allow slash-and-maim movies to come into our house either.

Betsy said, "Christopher scares me sometimes. He's a strong guy, you know. He can hold me down with one arm. He tosses me over his shoulder and carries me and throws me on the bed. I mean, he like throws me seven feet through the air. I thought he was like going to break my neck once. He wants to take it further now. He wants me to let him choke me while we, you know, while we're, you know—and I'm, well, not ready for that."

"Oh, my," Sandy said. "You shouldn't let him."

"And he's been bugging me to help him buy a gun. He's cooled lately about the gun because we've run out of money. But when I asked him why he wanted a gun, he said he wanted to go to the dump and shoot rats with his friends. And I said, 'Christopher, you don't have any friends,' and he got mad. I was like making a joke, see, and he like threatens to punch my teeth in. I tried to talk to Wendy about him and the rough things he does but Wendy refuses to hear a word of it."

Wendy was Christopher's mother and Sandy's youngest sister. Betsy was one distraught lady telling her worried tale. Sandy looked just as troubled at the end of Betsy's tale. Betsy let out a sigh of relief.

We told Betsy that things always worked out for the best—that Christopher would get his act together soon. But Betsy's soul seemed to drag in the dirt as we walked her out to her car. She never did ask to borrow money but I think she was hinting at it. Bob, Christopher's step-father, had been telling me for years to never give or lend money to Christopher. With the odor of alcohol dissipated, Betsy left just after it turned dark. We readied ourselves for Hedy's arrival and had little time to contemplate our meeting with Betsy.

We lit the porch light before Hedy arrived. Our screen door opened out against the firewood stacked there. Behind the stack of wood, an old five-foot diameter timber mill saw blade was bolted to a rough post. Old Mr. Hewitt had taken the blade from the old abandoned sawmill at Big Bug Creek at Spud Mountain near Spring Valley about the time he built the house. Hanging from the rafters on the other side of the door was a swinging pine log bench that I had built soon after we bought the place. When I stepped out to grab wood for the heater, I saw the headlights of Hedy's Volvo coming around the garage. We called greetings to her as she sauntered across the flagstone walkway. She had gotten away from her dreadlocks and she was wearing her hair in an uncombed bunch with a tie at the back. Her rosy cheeks matched a maroon winter hat. "Hi, guys," Hedy said with a nervous smile. She plunked piano keys as she walked by the piano.

"Hey, you," Sandy said.

Hedy sat on the loveseat, Sandy on the edge of the sofa and I, on the edge of the recliner. Sandy and I were like two smiling dogs waiting for treats from a master. But Hedy didn't have any treats; she had a bowl of bitter reality, and she didn't quite know how to dish out. She bit her lip, sighed, wet her lips, and flexed her neck. We watched her and waited. I glanced at Sandy and she rolled her eyes. Hedy fanned her face with an envelope as if the room had become terribly hot and said, "Gosh, this is so hard." Her eyes filled with tears. "I didn't think this would be so hard." With a worried face, she glanced up at the ceiling.

My grin melted, as did Sandy's. In the adjoining den, a log in the wood heater shifted and clunked. Our grey and white cat, Booger, walked between us, trying to decide who at the moment had the most inviting lap. When he chose Hedy and hopped up beside her, she pushed him away, "Not now, Booger." To the ceiling, she said again, "Oh, why is this so hard." She rocked on her folded legs and tried to sit higher. She massaged a thigh with her thumbs for a moment and fanned her face again. "You need to know this. I told Chuck two nights ago. He was the first person I ever told. I should have told this a long time ago."

Sandy said, "It's okay, honey. Take your time."

Hedy cleared her throat. "There is a someone you know. I'm going to tell you about this someone you know and when I tell you about this person, you're not going to like this person very much. It's someone you've known a long time." She took another deep breath. "Here goes: when I was six years old, I was raped." Hedy drew in some air and sobbed. She exhaled. She said, "When I was six years old, I was raped by your nephew Christopher. My cousin Christopher."

CHAPTER 2

I was only partly conscious of my jaw resting on my chest. I thought of Christopher chasing Betsy around the room of their old house. I thought of Chris as a boy, standing by lakes and fishing, casting, throwing. I saw a two-year-old Christopher letting a tetherball smack his face again and again until we stopped him. When I came out of my psychic retreat, Sandy had moved to the loveseat beside Hedy, who sobbed, "It's true. I'm sorry but it's true. I had to tell you."

In my mind's eye, Hedy had transformed into a giant six-year-old girl. Physically, she was still her 5'9" self, but her demeanor and anima were that of a wounded child, a six-year-old with giant rubbery features. Sandy said later she had also seen the giant child, and we would comment many times about that phenomenon we had witnessed. I scooted across to Hedy's side and we embraced in a three-sided hug.

After a few minutes, Sandy left the room to make tea. Hedy said she didn't want to say any more until Sandy returned. So, I sat there awkwardly trying not to say small stuff. Hedy breathed heavily with her eyes closed and her face tilted toward the ceiling. What Betsy had described to us earlier that day, what she was going through with Christopher, was part of this nightmare arising. I had a quick image, another little daydream, of our tall nephew towering about me, his face white with sheetrock mud, his green eyes locked onto me, glaring at me. Sandy returned with the tea and broke the spell.

Hedy told us the story of how she came about telling her boyfriend. Chuck worked in town and was raising his eight-year-old daughter while living at his father's house. (Chuck was seventeen when he became a father and started raising a child by himself after the child's mother didn't want to be a mother after all.) Two days earlier, Hedy had spent the evening with Chuck and as they sat talking in his car parked on a side street by a park, they swapped stories about their lives. Hedy said, "He told me that if we were ever to have a relationship, we would have to be patient with each other. Then he told me that he was sexually molested when he was a little boy. As I listened to him tell about it, I couldn't help it, but I burst out crying, uncontrollably. I couldn't stop myself. I was hysterical. We cried together for a few and he asked me, 'What was that all about?' Then, I told him that I had been raped when I was six, and the boy who did it was my cousin. I told Chuck that he was the first person I had ever told." She reached for another tissue.

"In his car, after we had run out of tears and calmed down, Chuck coaxed me to tell you. He said I had to tell you—that I had no choice. If I wanted to start my journey to healing, I had to tell you and to tell as soon as possible. He made me promise him that I would tell you. So here I am."

Hedy then described the rape to us. [Background history is needed. I will be going back and forth between the two time periods: (1) the rape assault in March 1987 and (2) that February in 2003.]

In 1987, we lived in the border town of Nogales, Arizona. Sandy taught elementary school music classes and I worked as a carpenter with a homebuilder. The first weekend during spring break that year, Sandy's sister, Wendy, and her new husband, Bob, along with Christopher, age fourteen, came from Truth or Consequences, New Mexico to visit us in Nogales. They were on their way to visit families in Tucson and Phoenix. Hedy gave up her room for the adults and she took the top bunk in her brother's room, while four year-old Pete slept where he usually did: on the bottom bunk. Christopher was okay with sleeping on the couch and we made it ready for him; he even got under his blanket and teased he was snoring. Then, Wendy suggested that Christopher sleep in the room with his little cousins, "Have a slumber party," she said. "That would be fun." Everyone was okay with that, so we padded the floor by the bunk bed with a couple of sleeping bags and we patted Christopher on the head, the teen who we'd known all of his life; and we kissed our precious tots goodnight and closed the bedroom door on the three of them. Sandy and I had held Christopher in our arms when he was a two-day-old baby. When he was age eight, he held Hedy in his arms when she was a month old; we didn't think we had anything to worry about. Family will protect family.

When Christopher was almost three, he stayed with Sandy and I in Arkansas for two weeks while Wendy, at age twenty, gallivanted across the southern states with a forty-year-old man named Glen. When Wendy and Glen came back, Christopher wanted to stay with us; he didn't want to go back with them to Tucson. He fretted and hung on to Sandy until Wendy pulled him away. At first, we wondered if Glen had done something to Chris, but guessed it was more likely that Glen had tried to introduce discipline into the boy's life—something Wendy was coldly against. Even as a toddler, if he ran toward a busy street, Wendy would have been hard-pressed to use the word "no" with her son. She thought that saying no would somehow stunt his creativity—something she repeated often.

That night in March 1987, we failed to recognize the danger that lurked in our children's room in our own home—that the teenager on our floor was a smoldering time bomb. "Stranger Danger" was what the media preached in the news in the 1980s. No one said beware of the squint-eyed family members pretending to be a real family. A high-profile case in Tucson at that time involved an eight-year-old Vickie Lynn Hoskinson, who was abducted from her bicycle in broad daylight on the northwest side of the city. Six months later, a hiker guided the police to the girl's bones in the Tucson desert. Stories that said danger lurked within families were nearly non-existent. The real monsters, the media said, were scheming in the shadows. Maybe someone should have told us that Christopher had spent months at three separate times in juvenile detention centers in T. or C. and Tucson for assaulting children and he had just been released from his latest incarceration before they drove over from T. or C. to Nogales.

(2003) That evening in Prescott, Hedy described the rape: "During the night, Christopher woke me up, whispering my name. I had been sound asleep and it was hard to wake up. After I finally was fully awake, I looked down on him in the dim light as he lay on the floor under his blanket and asked him what he wanted. He said, 'Come down here, there's something I want to show you.' So, I climbed off the top bunk. When I got next to him, I found he was naked. He slammed me onto the sleeping bag, put a hand over my mouth, and pulled off my panties, and laid on me. Put his whole weight on me. It hurt so bad. I tried to scream. It hurt so bad. He got off me and he sat on the floor and before he took his hand away, he said, 'This is our secret; you can never tell anyone.' I understood what a secret was, and I knew by his tone I had better keep quiet. I climbed back onto the top bunk. It took me a while to get back to sleep; I was so confused. The next morning when I saw that my panties were bloody, I hid them between the mattress and the wall."

"I wasn't sure what had happened. I even wondered: Was it some kind of ritual that adults sanctioned? I wasn't sure if that was the way it was supposed to happen; you guys put him in the room with me after all and I wondered if it was supposed to happen. I didn't know what to do. I was so confused. I didn't know how a marriage happened. I knew nothing about sex. I didn't know there was such a thing as sex. I remember though, I was sore for days."

The floor was turning white with the tissues we used to wipe away the tears. Booger the cat lay blissfully in the middle of the sea of white tissues.

(Nogales, March 1987) The morning after the rape, Sandy said she remembered an angry Christopher crossing the kitchen without saying anything and slapping the heavy double glass on our sliding glass door, then banging it open and going out to sit in Bob's truck parked in the driveway. Minutes later, Sandy stepped outside the house and saw Wendy and Christopher in the front seat of Bob's pickup. An angry Wendy was shaking her fists and screaming at Christopher. Sandy couldn't hear what was being said in the vehicle but it was all one-sided. Wendy was soon pommeling her son as she screamed at him. Christopher had his arms up protecting his head. Then, he bolted out of the truck. Sandy watched him run out of the yard to the gravel road where he ran down the hill. Sandy went inside and later, she asked Wendy if everything was all right. Wendy abruptly said, "I don't want to talk about my conversation with her son. That's our business." Bob, Wendy, and Christopher readied themselves to leave Nogales immediately; Tucson would be their first stop. Wendy was in a hurry to get away from our house. Sandy had prepared a breakfast that they didn't eat; she asked them why they had to leave so soon. Wendy said, "Mom is expecting us to be there in an hour." Sandy and Wendy's mother, Ches Mitcham, lived in northwest Tucson, near Orange Grove Road and the Oracle Road area.

(Prescott 2003) As we sat together on the loveseat sixteen years later, Sandy said to Hedy: "That first doctor we took you to was really upset after she examined you, and she said, 'Someone has been messing with this girl.' Why didn't you tell us then? The doctor asked you and then she had me ask you if you were molested and if someone had touched you down there. The doctor was sure you had been. You were lying on the doctor's table after she examined you and I leaned over you and took your hand and I asked you, 'Has anyone hurt you down there, or has anyone touched you and you shook your head *no*. You had closed your lips tight. I asked again and you shook your head again. Why didn't you tell me?"

"Christopher had made it clear it was to be a secret. I was so confused. I guess I took it upon myself to protect the secret. I didn't want to betray him if that makes any sense. But at the same time, I wanted to tell you. I knew it was a serious thing. I was really scared. I didn't know what to do. I even thought if you had sanctioned an illegal wedding to happen, then I was protecting you, too."

(Nogales, March 1987) A couple days after their visit to our house, Wendy called from Truth or Consequences and asked with a soft voice, "Is Hedy okay? She looked like she was getting sick that morning we left." Sandy said Hedy was okay. Wendy said she was busy and couldn't talk any more and hung up. When Sandy did laundry that next weekend and pulled the sheet off the top bunk bed, she found the bloody panties. The doctor said to bring Hedy to her office immediately. The doctor asked if Sandy knew any men who could have done something to Hedy. Sandy said no. (Bob and Christopher were not even considered because they were trusted family members.) The doctor helped schedule an appointment with a endocrinologist in Tucson. Sandy called her mother that same evening. Sandy told Ches that she had found a pair of Hedy's bloody panties. Ches said, "It's not that unusual that some girls start their periods earlier than others. Ten years old is not uncommon."

Sandy said, "But Hedy's only six."

Ches said, "Well, I bled at age six."

Every evening, for the next two or three weeks, Wendy and Ches took turns calling our Nogales home to see how Hedy was, to see what Hedy was doing and to see what Hedy was saying. That they called in tandem fashion should have triggered some suspicion in us, but in our busy lives, we lost track of things in plain sight, and things got stepped over, and things got missed. We thought they were truly concerned for Hedy. They were deeply concerned about something.

We soon started our fifteen-month odyssey to the medical specialists in Tucson, prompted in large part by Grandma Ches implying that it must be hereditary, this precocious puberty. "It happened to me," conveyed that she had all of a sudden started bleeding herself into womanhood when she was six. That's what Ches led us to believe. The totally clueless will believe anything; will trust any advice from schemers in the family. Looking back, I can see that we should have started a list of males who might have been in the area, acquaintances, strangers, and especially relatives. And Christopher and Bob would have been on the top of the list. Think the worst of young men; think the worst of your relatives; make sure they earn your trust. Your family's interests trump theirs every time. Keep your daughters and sons safe, and don't expect anyone to protect them for you. We bought into the "family first" doctrine. "The world is a tough place with all its setbacks, and criminals turn it into hell," Jordan Peterson said. If someone says "It's precocious puberty," it should be a red flag.

(2003) As we sipped our way through cups of tea and tossed more tissues on the purring Booger, Hedy wanted to make it clear that it wasn't the rape that had caused her the most grief over the years, but her major angst was created by the stunt her Aunt Wendy had pulled seven years after the rape in an attempt to silence Hedy at age thirteen. This malicious act that we referred to as the pantry scene also happened right under our clueless noses.

Wendy, who we had nicknamed Miss Me-Me-Me two decades earlier, had over time, become quarrelsome with everyone around her during the decade. We wondered time and time again what could the reasons be for her unhinged displays of aggression. Looking back, we can guess that Wendy's mood swings were caused by the foul taste of deception she was chewing on and the fear of being found out. All the clues that we missed back then were presenting themselves on that night in 2003. Another of the clues had happened one year before Hedy breaking her silence: In early February 2002, a year before, Hedy came back from Bend, Oregon, after spending seven months working in Bend and exploring the area. On the drive back from Oregon, her Dodge Shadow caught on fire in the drive-through lane at a Taco Bell in Burbank, California; we drove over to the coast to get Hedy. Later that month, Sandy, Hedy, and I went out to a restaurant. During dinner, when I mentioned that Catholic priest child molesters were once again in the news, Hedy burst out crying. Hedy said the pantry incident where Wendy accused her of child molestation had affected her life in the most devastating of ways. That accusation had stopped Hedy from pursuing a career in education or any other career involving children. Hedy refused babysitting jobs during high school—which we wondered about at the time—and any situation where she would be in the proximity of little children. Hedy said she could never trust people and especially children because of what Wendy had proclaimed had happened in the pantry on a spring day in 1984. With warped audacity, Wendy used her little boys, Nicki and Patrick, ages five and three to create an incident for the purpose of silencing Hedy about the rape. Hedy said the effects of the rape were minor in comparison to the damage to her self-image at age thirteen caused by Wendy's blackmail scheme.

Thirteen was the age we were told Christopher was molested by a predator woman in Silver City, New Mexico in the summer of 1986—something no one told us about until two and a half years after the affair. That affair was when Wendy lost the battle to protect Christopher from the at-large predators of the world. Thirteen was the age that Wendy was watching out for in Hedy, the age Hedy might have realized that the story of her rape was something she needed to share with the world. Wendy knew that Hedy had the power to disclose that secret at any time. Wendy in a way had been biding her time and biting her lip for all those years, waiting for an opportunity to blind-side Hedy. This false accusation undermined Hedy's every thought at age thirteen and her teen years and though Hedy was able to carry on and even thrive in her high school years, the thought of the accusation stayed with her, like a bad ache in her bones, in everything she did.

At age six, Hedy had not fully understood what the rape was all about. It was mentioned earlier that she thought that it might be an adult ceremony involving children—her own parents had been present when the tall boy was escorted into her room. Before the rape, she had only seen Christopher a couple of times every year. Had her parents selected her husband and was that brutal attack the ceremony that consummated the marriage? These are questions that no six-year-old should have to contemplate. The tone of Christopher's threat told her that she better keep the secret or face consequences. Fourteen-year-old Christopher, six feet tall at that age, loomed as a powerful giant. Hedy's aunt Wendy was a tall, big-boned one-hundred-and-eighty-pound giant of a woman, too.

(Prescott, 2003) Before we turned in for the night, Hedy asked us if we remembered a Christmas when we all came together and spent a night at Grandma Ches's townhouse in Tucson. It was the first Christmas after we moved to Prescott, two and a half years after the rape. Hedy was nine years old, Peter was seven, and Christopher was seventeen. Nicki, a one-year-old, stayed with Wendy and Bob in one of the bedrooms. Hedy and Pete and Christopher slept in sleeping bags on the living room floor. Hedy said, "As I was drifting off to sleep, I heard Christopher whisper from across the room, 'Hedy, come here, I want to show you something.' I didn't answer him. I heard him snicker. I had an uneasy time sleeping that night."

CHAPTER 3

Sandy and I slept not one wink through the night. Hedy went to her room about one o'clock Sunday morning and slept soundly. Sandy and I spent the night whispering, trying to remember more of the clues that the PACT, Wendy and Ches, had been dropping on us over those sixteen years. As it turned out, there were many clues. We never thought of ourselves as mentally impeded when it came to figuring things out, but we obviously had blind spots.

"Oh, my God, remember when so and so said this or that and did that or this?" How could we be so stupid? So blind? So trusting? So gullible? As the long sleepless night unfolded, the insights kept coming. We weighed each item, threw it on the pile. Then, the next arrived in a blast of trumpets. And the next. The question loomed: How were we going to announce this news to Ches and Wendy—that their game was up?

Wendy was her bossiest as we entered the new millennium. Miss Me-Me-Me had become so demanding and was so easily angered over the small stuff, and we still couldn't figure out what was happening with her. We wondered if she and Bob were having marital problems. Or was Christopher driving her completely mad? He had turned into a tumbleweed, rolling in and out of town after his divorce with Amy and after Amy fled to Texas with their child. We were used to Wendy bursting into our house, steaming mad, lashing out at us about some imagined slight or for not backing her in an array of plans that she was demanding the entire family to implement. Why wasn't the family better at jumping to her wishes? What a disappointment to her we had become. Sandy and Wendy spent half of each of a dozen years not talking to each other. Weeks passed, then sometimes months passed before they reconciled—usually as holidays or birthdays neared. That quiet time free from Wendy was a nice break. Whatever baggage Wendy was dragging around, the fabric was growing thin on the bottom.

In the fall of 2001, we told Wendy and Ches that our family would not be participating in the traditional exchange of Christmas gifts anymore. We didn't want anyone giving us gifts and we would be purchasing only a couple of gifts: for Nicki and Patrick who were twelve and ten. We wanted to continue with candlelight mass, feasting on Christmas Day, and donations to church and charities, but no gifts, please. The whole idea of gift exchange felt wrong. Gifting had turned into a worldwide circus, our family turning into serious clowns at Christmas. We suggested this bold plan in previous years, but Wendy and Ches, drunk on the notion of Christmas gifts, laughed at our ideas. Gifts trumped the true meaning of the season. We told Ches and Wendy to count us out of the gifting that year. The announcement drove Wendy into anger city. She gave gifts that we returned to her unopened. She steamed about it all year.

In November 2002 with Christmas-goodwill-to-men-on-earth approaching, Wendy wrote a hateful letter to us expressing her vehemence. This would come to be known as the hate letter. Once again, as we'd done over the years, we made excuses for Wendy. She must be just having a bad day. Let's not hold this against her; after all, she's the dear baby of the family. Rule: Never write a letter when you are angry. Let yourself cool down. Think twice. And always hang onto an angry letter you receive. It tells more about the writer than any sweet letter could.

The odious letter consisted of two single-spaced densely typed pages (approx. 1,200 words) that showed the mind of a madwoman, an angry woman, sure, but a truly crazy woman right out of a Dostoyevsky novel. In the letter, Wendy gave Sandy a scolding for being a terrible sister. Wendy wrote in detail how all of her sisters were messed up, but that she, Wendy, was the only one of the five with a heart, a soul, and a brain. She said that Christopher had been diagnosed as a paranoid-schizophrenic by his early teens. She ranted about the years of turmoil he had put her through and she doubted that we even knew about her problems, his problems, his months and months incarcerated at the detention centers and that we never cared enough about her and her son to find out. She accused us of being mean to Christopher when he was a little boy (a complete falsehood). She wrote, "He was happy when he found those arrowheads on the reservation and it devastated him so much when he found out that you guys had planted them just to fool him." (We did not do that; I was cleaning out boxes weeks earlier and had tossed broken flint pieces along the fence behind our apartment under some trees and had forgotten about them.) She wrote, "When you gave him odor-eaters for his foot problem, you hurt him deeply. It was after what you did to him that he started acting violent." (It was her idea to get him those shoe liners. She suggested it right in front of him just an hour before we bought them and he laughed and she laughed; we all laughed about it. She didn't mention either of those incidents for twenty years.) She said Christopher never got over giving up his dog, his big husky, Cody, when he was twelve and that we should've taken the dog for his sake. She said we didn't have a clue how hard life was for her and her son, that we were selfish in so many ways and especially selfish to take Christmas from her children. She raged about the fact that her three-year-old grandson, Cody (from Christopher's short marriage to Amy), was in Texas and that she, Wendy, might never see the child again and that we never lifted a finger to stop that tragedy. She warned us, as she had many times, that we should read *The Left Behind* books. "But too bad for you, guys, it's too late to start reading those books after all the hurt you have caused me and my family."

(February 2003) We wondered about that letter as we sat that night flushing out the clues: Was Wendy angry with us for not seeing the secret so clearly laid out? How many clues did we need, for Christ's sake?

After each round of trying to guess the minds of the schemers and discussing each clue, we'd relax a moment and then we would sit up quickly in bed whenever another revelation struck us, like: "Remember when Ches tried to talk us out of moving to Prescott? That we might be opening Pandora's box? That we're not going to like living with Wendy? What exactly did she mean? And why did Ches think it was not wise to be living in the same town as a beloved sister? Why would Ches want to stop us?"

During the sixteen years of the secret, Ches had been dropping clues on us as much as Wendy had been. Ches's conscience was like a big ripe pomegranate squirting ripe clues. At one point, it must have turned into a game for Ches and Wendy, a game they apparently never tired of. The clues raced through our thoughts like dominos. Were they laughing at how trusting we were? Equating being trustful with being dense? Equating clueless with being out of touch? Did they snicker and laugh together in their mendaciousness?

Sandy said, "Remember when mom didn't want me and Wendy going to counseling together—that we might be opening a can of worms? What was that about? Can of worms and Pandora's box pointed to one thing: Ches knew about the rape from day one. Mom knew the next day when Wendy was so anxious to hurry from Nogales and get to Tucson. Ches might have coached Wendy to get Christopher away from our house as fast as she could."

I said, "Remember that one Christmas at your sister Patty's apartment when Patty said, 'If Christopher were here, I bet he'd molest Hedy and Peter'? And Ches shushed Patty and shooed Patty out of the room and when we asked Ches, 'What was Patty talking about?' Ches said, 'Ah, you know Patty. She says things she doesn't mean.' Stupid us, why we didn't follow up on that?"

"Remember when Wendy took Hedy and Peter out in a boat on Lake Patagonia and the big storm came up and almost swamped the boat?" I asked. It was right after Wendy and Bob got married, six months before the rape. "Oh, my God!" Sandy said, "Why would Wendy want to terrify our children?" Wendy had spun the incident that Christopher had saved Hedy and Peter when the storm came through. Christopher never talked about it; he just stared at the ground when Wendy boasted of his heroics. We wondered what really happened. We started a list of questions to ask Hedy in the morning.

We discussed Wendy's accusation in the hate letter that it was our fault that Christopher had to give up his dog when he was twelve and he was still bitter about it years later. Was Wendy implying that our daughter might not have been raped if we had taken their big dog into our tiny cottage in Oracle those many years ago? I had written about it in a journal shortly after it happened.

In June 1985, Ches called Sandy one evening, "Sandy, I'm calling to ask you, if you could take Wendy's and Chris's dog, you know, Cody, and keep him at your house, for a while."

"That big husky?"

"Yes, that's the one. She's moving to another apartment this week and they can't have pets."

"No, we can't take on a dog. *We're* going to be moving. We can't take a dog. We have no backyard, no fenced yard. You've seen our house; I mean our cottage. It's a very small place. No, we can't take a dog."

"Chris really loves that dog. He'll be very upset if he has to give it up."

"How is it our problem?"

"Wendy was hoping you could step up for her and Chris."

"Ha! No! Step up? I offer help to her all the time, but not this time. It's just impossible."

Ches said, "I would take the dog, but I just can't."

"You shouldn't worry yourself about it. It's Wendy's problem. She should have thought before she got that big dog. It was a year old when she got it. She knew better."

"Chris is going to be bitter if he loses that dog."

"He'll have to get over it."

"I don't know what to tell Wendy."

"Tell her the truth."

"No, I can't do that."

Sandy said, "Have Wendy call me. I'll tell her no. I'll tell her no for you, too."

"She's not going to like it."

"Tell me one thing she ever likes. Mom, you're worrying yourself sick. A big dog is a big commitment. Wendy has to fix this."

"You know, Sandy, Bob moved to New Mexico. I told Wendy to see if Bob would take the dog."

"There you go. I'll mention Bob to her, too."

"There are summer classes starting this week," said Ches, "but I'm not teaching summer school this year. Is Mike done at his school?"

"The teachers are turning in their keys today. He's got half a day. Oh, we might be going to Nogales for interviews. Can you watch Hedy and Peter?"

"Of course, honey, any time. Well, I'll tell Wendy to call you. And good luck," Ches laughed.

"We'll survive, mom, and so will Chris and Wendy."

A few days later, we were back in Tucson after interviewing for jobs in Nogales and we stopped at Wendy's apartment after picking up Hedy and Peter. Wendy lived near Ina Road and Oracle Road. It was already dark when we got there. Her apartment was a mess, but not any more than she was that day. Wendy had lost her job in Durango, Colorado seven months earlier when an elderly man, died during her watch and the company she worked for blamed Wendy. She felt she was scapegoated. It was her first job after graduating from nursing school at the university in Tucson. On returning to Tucson, she started working for another nurse-for-a-day type company. Sandy had brought paper and pencils for Hedy who was four and Peter, three, and they kept themselves busy drawing at the coffee table. Wendy drank coffee laced with Kahlua non-stop as she talked about herself. The bottle of the chocolate liquor was on the counter by the stove and Sandy got up to taste it. "Where is Chris?" Sandy asked.

"He's staying at a friend's house."

"How did he take losing Cody?"

"It was so cruel. It was just so cruel. You guys could've taken Cody. He says he never wants to see you guys again."

"We could not take a dog. You should not have gotten that dog."

"That's neither here nor there. I don't know what I'm going to do with Chris. He's sneaking out at night. The screen is off in his window. He's running with these older boys. Every night. They're going to get him into real trouble. It's scary. There are so many ways he can get into trouble here. I don't know what I'm going to do with him. He challenges everything I say. I've got to get him away from these delinquents."

When we drove back to Oracle that night, we drove past a Juvenile Detention Center for Pima County. Chris must have gotten a ninety day stretch in one of the facilities in the county. We never suspected our nephew might have been an inmate at that moment. As we neared Oracle, we saw a wildfire raging in the foothills below the Catalina Mountains. Hedy in the backseat said, "Maybe somebody started a fire so they could see." All along the ridgeline, the crown of fire danced. The smoke was in the air as we drove into Oracle where the smell of the town's sewer system also greeted us. Sandy teased, "Pugh! Daddy, did you do that?"

"No, I didn't," I said.

"Yes, you did," said Hedy, teasing.

Peter said, "Maybe Hedy's moth poided." Poid was a word for fart that Sandy and her siblings made up when they were kids.

While we were standing on the stoop of our tiny house waiting for me to unlock the door, three-year-old Peter shouted for the neighborhood to hear, "Hey, I've got a so-so disease!" He had been shouting that in public for the last month, and it sure got our attention that night. He and Hedy listened to West Side Story all year and he'd picked it up from the Officer Krupkee song. Hedy said, "Don't say that, Peter, that's not nice." So, of course, he shouted it again.

A month later on the Fourth of July, Wendy came to Oracle by herself. Sandy had baked a chicken and its aroma filled the cottage. We were getting ready to move to Nogales where we'd both gotten jobs. Wendy came by herself. Hedy ran up to her favorite aunt in the whole world and showed her a pet moth. Pete showed his aunt the horned toad of the day with a dot of red fingernail polish on its back. Sandy, Hedy, and Peter took a walk every day and if they found a horned toad, they brought it home and took it back and let it lose the next day.

"Where's Christopher?" Sandy asked.

"He didn't want to come; he's at a friend's house. He's still mad at you."

"Well, that's too bad," said Sandy. "I hope you're not making us into the bad guys to him."

"You've got room here; you have pets." She pointed her mouth at the moth and horned toad. We laughed at her and she didn't laugh back. Sandy showed off the cake she made with red, white, and blue frosting. While we ate, Wendy talked about herself. "Do you like my blouse? Mom got it for my birthday. I'm thinking about taking a job in Silver City, New Mexico."

I asked, "How close is that to Truth or Consequences?"

"About fifty miles."

"What's Bob say about that?" Sandy asked.

"He wants me to come. And I need to get Christopher away from Tucson."

"That's always a good reason to get married," I said. "And Richard may like Christopher being closer to Texas."

"Screw Richard. I should move to Hawaii just to piss him off. I should ask Bob to get a job in Hawaii. Hey, Hedy's getting fat." The comment hurt Hedy.

Sandy said, "No, Wendy. Hedy is not fat. She is a healthy, normal growing child. And you should apologize to Hedy."

"I'm just stating a fact. I'm not going to apologize. She looks like Patty."

Sandy said, "Look at her! There's nothing fat about her. If you call that being fat, then you're fat. Look at your thighs, your butt, Wendy. Really gaining weight."

"I'm not fat!"

"You're fatter proportionately than Hedy."

"Okay, maybe I am. Okay, Hedy, I'm sorry I said that about you."

That same summer, my sister Sharon and her son Jeff came to Oracle a couple of days later. We went hiking at Aravaipa Canyon and brought a picnic lunch. Sharon had been dating a guy in Tucson. When Jeff was splashing in the water with Hedy and Peter, Sharon told Sandy and me that a new guy had raped her.

CHAPTER 4

Hedy had exhibited healthy self-esteem throughout her growth years by keeping herself busy with activities: singing, dancing, viola, piano, slumber parties, hiking, biking, video games, soccer, softball, basketball, cooking, art, and more. She didn't have time to dwell on the past. She pushed the rape aside. But at least, now we knew why Hedy had been spinning her wheels since high school and not taking college seriously. She wanted to tell and she didn't know how.

In 1994, when Wendy found her chance, she turned an innocent incident into a blackmail scheme to prolong Hedy's silence about the rape. The stunt Wendy pulled we refer to as the pantry scene. It happened on a rainy weekday in mid-March 1994—seven years after the rape—and again, during spring break. We had been living at the Bridle Path house for a year and a half. Hedy was thirteen and Peter was almost twelve; Nicki was five and Patrick was almost four. Bob and myself were working that day, so I've set down the incident as told by Sandy. Our pantry storage room was a deep step-in closet with a wide door and was just one step off the kitchen on the right side of the hallway.

The Pantry Scene:

Sandy said, "Wendy called in the morning and asked if she and her two boys could come over with some videos and watch them with me and Hedy and Peter. After she arrived with her boys, the kids watched a movie while Wendy and I talked. We took a break for lunch. I was in the kitchen getting some snacks together on trays when I heard Wendy pounding on the pantry door. Wendy shouted, 'Okay guys! Open this door. Open the door now!' Wendy really sounded upset. The four kids were laughing and giggling and would not open the door. Wendy continued to pound on the pantry door, demanding they open it. When I asked, 'Wendy, what's going on?' Wendy ignored me and shouted again, 'Come out of there! You need to open this door now!' The kids only laughed and giggled more. They were just playing but I saw how stressed-out Wendy was, so in a calm voice, I told the kids to open the door. They unlatched it and when I slid it open, they were still giggling. Wendy quickly ushered her two boys down the hall, saying, 'We're leaving, boys! I think I know what was going on in there!' Wendy quickly gathered their things together and headed out the door to their car. I said, 'What's going on, Wendy? Why are you leaving?' Again, she said, 'I know what was going on in there.' 'What?' I asked. She wouldn't answer me but got her kids in the car and drove off. I asked Hedy and Peter if they knew what was going on. They were still laughing. Finally, they said that they had gotten into a quart jar of sesame seeds and were pouring them into their mouths and into the mouths of the little boys and as they all tried not to laugh—which was impossible when your mouths were full of sesame seeds—they about choked on their laughter and the seeds at the same time. I got on the phone with Wendy and asked her to explain herself. Wendy said she asked Nicki if something happened in the pantry and he said, 'Yes.' He told her that Hedy had lifted her shirt up to shake out the seeds and he saw a glimpse of her bra. I told Wendy she needed to come back and explain to Hedy and Peter why she had left in a huff. It's not right to leave someone's house in anger and not explain yourself."

We thought we knew what might have set Wendy off that day. Christopher was seduced by an older woman in Silver City when he was thirteen. Her first son was molested under her watch and she wasn't going to let that happen again. We tried to understand where she might be coming from. We didn't realize it really was: a scheme she had cooked up and she was actively looking for a place and time to make it happen.

Two days later on Sunday, when Wendy came over to explain herself, she brought Bob and the two boys. Sandy and I and Hedy and Peter were waiting when they drove into our yard. We thought Wendy was going to explain why she was so worried and apologize for over-reacting. Instead of explaining herself for her abrupt exit, Wendy skipped the apology and turned the visit into an interrogation. It happened before we realized what was happening. She brought Peter into our bedroom and interrogated him, shouting at him, accusing him of trying to molest her boys, using tactics only a seasoned interrogator would know. She sounded like a Gestapo guard upon finding food in the bunkhouse. "Did you touch my boys?"

"No!" shouted Peter.

"Have you ever touched other children?"

"No!"

"Do you get off on touching children?"

"No!"

"Did you see Hedy touching my boys?"

"She didn't!" Peter yelled.

The door was locked and I couldn't intervene. Enraged and distraught, I paced back to where Bob sat on the sofa with his two young boys and told him he needed to stop Wendy. He said, "It'll be all right, Mike. Nothing happened, so it'll be all right." Bob had gone along with that to appease Wendy. I believe she had misled Bob as to what she saw and heard. Bob never heard the facts from Sandy. He only heard Wendy's lies about the incident. Not one of us, not even Bob, was able to say no to Wendy. Bob's job that day was to stay with the boys as she had instructed him to do. That's all he would venture. "For Christ's sake, Bob, they were just into the sesame seeds. This is crazy. Your wife is out of control, Bob! Speak up, man."

"Nothing happened so don't worry. It'll be all right," he said again.

But Wendy was saying something did happen. And this became her mantra: *"I asked Nicki, 'Did something happen in the pantry?' and he said 'yes.'"* That was her defense for pursuing the matter. But she wouldn't clarify what that meant. She was out to manipulate the truth. Something always does happen. Nicki said, "Yes, something happened." He saw Hedy's bra. Ask any five-year-old if something happened somewhere and the answer is always yes. Always. She had her veiled truth; that's all she wanted. When pressed to explain, she would repeat that statement: "I asked Nicki if something happened and he said 'yes.'" A five-year-old doesn't know he's being manipulated. He's simply stating a fact. It was beyond belief that Wendy thought she was above reproach.

Sandy pounded on the bedroom door saying time was up and got Wendy to open it. Peter was crying when he came out of Wendy's torture chamber. He slammed the door to his bedroom.

Wendy said, "I need to talk to Hedy."

I said, "You're not talking to Hedy without me present."

Sandy led me aside and said, "Nothing happened; it'll be all right. Wendy's not going away until she hears Hedy say nothing happened."

"She can talk to Hedy right here," I said.

Sandy told Hedy, "Honey, Wendy says she needs to talk to you and she isn't going away until she talks to you. I know you didn't do anything wrong. I was right there. I saw everything. You guys were into the sesame seeds and nothing else. If you talk to her, that should put an end to it."

Stupid us for capitulating to Wendy's demands. We closed our thirteen-year-old daughter into a room again, only this time to be emotionally raped by the mother of Hedy's rapist—the rape that only Hedy, the rapist, Wendy and Grandma knew about. I saw Hedy on the edge of the bed ready to face Wendy as the door closed. I heard Hedy say no, no, no, firmly and repeatedly and I heard Wendy's angry, accusing voice, using the same questions and tone she must have used when Christopher was running wild. I paced the hall with my fists clenched as Sandy pounded on the bedroom door and shouted, "That's enough, Wendy. You need to stop now." Through the door, Hedy talked back against Wendy's accusations. Hedy was fighting for her very soul and Wendy was getting frustrated. Sandy got a small screwdriver and we opened the bedroom door. "Time's up!" I said. Hedy escaped down the hall and into her room. Wendy came out with a hateful snarl on her face.

I said to Wendy, "I need to talk to *your* boys."

Wendy said, "You're not going to talk to my boys!" Wendy called down the hall, "Bob! Bob! We have to go. Now! Go!" Bob, as if on a planned cue, shuffled the boys out the side door of the living room, past the firewood stack, and ran them out to the car. Wendy joined them, fleeing directly out the kitchen door. As their car sped away, Sandy and I were left staring down the driveway. Peter came out of his room and asked, "What the heck? Why didn't you stop her? Why did you let her do that to us?" Hedy said, "You shouldn't have let her do that to us." Hedy knew instantly why Wendy created the pantry scene: to keep her quiet about the rape.

Hedy said she was over the trauma of the rape to a large extent when the pantry incident happened; she may not have exposed Christopher if Wendy had left things alone. We feel Wendy, Christopher, and Ches were driving themselves to the verge of insanity by the gnawing guilt from the cover-up and the lies they were feeding us. Wendy and Ches fueled each other's anxiety over the sixteen years of the secret. They must have constantly looked for ways to make sure the secret was held tight to their bosoms and not be allowed to come into the light.

As the long night continued, we had the next thought at the same time: Betsy's visit that afternoon and Christopher and Betsy's visit a month earlier. "If I go down, I'm taking everybody with me," Chris had said. "Go to the dump and shoot rats with my friends." Christopher was acting deranged and he had put us in his gun sights. There was no doubt that he was obsessing about the secret. He was probably contemplating killing Hedy or all of us and was struggling with himself, with the devil whispering in his ear. Unless he was born a psychopath and then all bets are off on what he was thinking.

Sandy said, "We have to get the police involved. If Christopher gets wind of this, he's bound to flee."

We figured that Bob wasn't part of the pact. Anything seemed possible, but we didn't believe Bob would have gone along with keeping such a secret. If Bob knew the secret, he would have realized the underlying truth of Wendy's scheme in the pantry incident. We compiled a list of our revelations. In the morning, we discussed some of the questions with Hedy. She went back to her place in town.

On Monday, Sandy took the day off from work to make phone calls. She made an appointment for us to meet with a therapist that afternoon and she contacted her brother John Timothy in Tucson and made plans to meet with him at the end of the week in Phoenix at a Burger King restaurant. She didn't tell Tim why. Sandy called the hospitals and specialists where we had taken Hedy in 1987 until the summer of 1988, but all the records had been expunged. In our boxes, we found an envelope of Hedy's X-rays that were taken then and the names of the specialists she had seen.

I worked at the cabinet shop that Monday and met Sandy after work at the counselor's office. Nancy, the therapist, led us on an enlightening path into the world of childhood sexual molestation. For our assignment, we were to read on the subject as much as we could; as much as we could stomach. Nietzsche said, "A man's worth is determined by how much truth he can tolerate." The underlying message: Wake up, it's everywhere, you can't hide from it. It has been around for centuries and hidden well, and it's still growing. One in three women in the United States will be raped during their lifetime. 85% of the rapes are committed by acquaintances of the victim. All of a sudden, it was right there on our table next to the saltshaker. We visited Dalton bookstore and bought a number of books on the subject. Thank God, we didn't have a working computer at that time, or we might have been sucked down a never-ending hole.

In the evenings, we read as much as we could. Our minds and faces twisted in shock about the dark world we had entered. The week passed quickly and before we knew it, Thursday evening was there, the day before the meeting with Tim. Ches called us that night and asked what the meeting was about. Sandy told her we had some business with Tim that didn't concern her. Before leaving for Phoenix the next afternoon, we called the Santa Cruz county courthouse in Nogales where the crime had taken place and found out there were no statutes of limitations on rape in the state of Arizona.

The sun was low to our right over the Bradshaw Mountains as we drove south off the plateau of the high desert into the valley of the sun where Phoenix sprawled. The desert flora changes as you drop over the rim. Palo Verde and mesquite trees appear, as do sagebrush, tumbleweeds, denser populations of creosote bushes, ocotillos and the cacti, giant saguaros, barrel, prickly pear, and their jumping cousins. We passed Bumble Bee and Black Canyon, Rock Springs, and New River. The flatness comes upon you like a skinned knee. As we drove into the parking lot of Burger King off Interstate 17 on the north end of that sprawling city, Tim was coming out of his car. We ate before getting down to business—a kind of a last supper. This was how we spent the eve of Saint Valentine's Day.

When Sandy and I first met in 1971, Tim was in Vietnam. A year later, he was at our wedding on the west slopes high on Mount Lemon overlooking Tucson. Before he went to Vietnam, he had finished a pre-med program but postponed medical school; like a lot of young men, he felt compelled to help out in the war effort in Vietnam. Tim signed up to work as a medic in Vietnam but they put him peeling potatoes, made him a cook, which was a slight and a blessing; it kept him out of the firefight. Though he was disappointed they had lied to him, he worked hard in the kitchen and soon was helping to supervise. Tim came back from the war disillusioned with his head stuck deep inside the bible. He carried a bible with him wherever he went and would read from it to anyone who he could corner. In 1973, just a few months after returning to the states, he caused a head-on collision while reading the bible to three of his sisters as he drove down Orange Grove Road in Tucson. Patty, Wendy, and baby Christopher in the backseat survived with minor injuries but Jolie was hospitalized with a concussion, lacerations, and bruises on her face. Tim suffered a severe head injury, a cracked skull, and had a plastic plate put in his head. After a year of rehabilitation, he spent a decade working as a sheet rocker until he paid back all the debts that resulted from the mishap, a considerable sum. No one had died in the accident.

Tim later landed a job at the City of Tucson water treatment plant because of his biology background. When he was throwing sheetrock around, he became thick-necked and muscular but since those days, he had shrunk back to a slightly less normal physique of a five-foot ten-inch man by 2003. In the mid-1990s, he bought a house in Tucson; Ches had sold her townhouse and was living in an apartment and she went to stay at his house. He never married or had children but seemed to know how everyone else should be raising children. Over the years, he seemed especially fond of telling Wendy that Christopher was out of control and she better wake up or he was going to hurt somebody or himself. Tim spent many weekends at the Pima county jail reading the bible to the incarcerated men there—trying to change lives. He won certificates of appreciation from the offices of Pima County for his commitment to community volunteering. He had his bible with him as he sat with Sandy and myself in the booth at Burger King.

As we finished dining, he said, "You know, when I was getting ready to leave the house and come see you, mother said, 'I know of something horrible that has happened but I can't tell you what it is.'

I couldn't get her to tell me more about it. Do you know what was she talking about?"

Sandy glanced at me; a glance that said a thousand words. We told Tim about the rape, and that we believed Wendy and Ches knew about it from the day it happened. I said, "We haven't said anything to anybody and now, Ches already knows about it. What is more telling than that? She's known for a long time, and we're guessing she has known about the rape for *all* those sixteen years. Wendy went running to Ches the same day."

Tim leaned back in his seat with a dazed look on his face. Finally, he said, "This is going to devastate Christopher. I feel bad for Christopher. Oh, man, I have been making progress with him, getting him to give his life to Jesus, you know. But this is going to set him back."

"What about Hedy's feelings?" Sandy asked him.

"Well, yeah, sure, it's terrible. She had to suffer with that secret for all those years, but poor Christopher—what is he going to do? He is now just learning the bible. You know, it's almost like Christopher is like one of those biblical characters, like Saint Paul, who used to be called Saul and was a persecutor of Christians. God struck Saul down and changed his life. I've been praying for and working to help Christopher turn his life around. Goodness, this is just like a story out of the bible. Oh, I tell you, God works in mysterious ways. Goodness, think of it. The bible is full of murderers and thugs who God chose to turn their lives around."

"This isn't the bible, Timmy," Sandy said.

"That's not the point," he said. "If we all work together and with God's help, we can get Christopher turned around."

"What about Hedy?"

"Oh, Hedy is going to be all right. She has all kinds of support. She's got you two guys. Christopher has nobody on his side. Christopher is the one who's all messed up and needs our help. If we don't help him, we're going to regret it later."

"You keep giving him money, Tim," said Sandy. "Do you really think he appreciates what you do for him? Aren't you just enabling him?"

"I haven't given him much money. What I have, he's promised to pay me back." He shook his head. "I only give it to him when he's desperate."

"Which is all the time," she said.

Tim was starting to get angry. "Look, this is really going to mess Christopher up, you know," he said. "It's all that pornography he was into when he was a kid. He was only twelve years old and into all that gross pornography. He was over-sexed at such a young age. He was molested when he was a kid, you've heard the story. He was just a boy, thirteen. Wendy had so many men around her all the time. Christopher's father, Richard, didn't help Wendy with any bills. She was working and going to school and running from man to man. She was messed up and Christopher became sexually precocious because no one was watching him. He was locked up a lot when he was twelve, thirteen, fourteen. The devil got a hold of Christopher at an early age."

"That's true, but you do believe Hedy is telling the truth. You do believe Christopher attacked Hedy during those wild years?" Sandy asked.

"I can't say I believe that. I don't know what to believe. I'll pray for you two, to take Jesus into your hearts. You need to take Jesus into your hearts."

This story may have seemed right out of the bible for Tim, but for us, it was coming straight out of a Hans Christian Andersen fairy tale. Wasn't there a story where an evil woman tries to poison the newborn princess so her own son can become king? Or a psycho aunt whose jealousy and revenge warp everything?

It was dark when Sandy and I walked Tim out to his car. We regretted not talking to the brick walls of Burger King, for they would have been more receptive and understanding. Tim drove away still shaking his head over the dilemma, which to him was *one more obstacle in the life of Christopher.* We did come away with a couple of thoughts as we drove back to Prescott. When Wendy was being so insistent about Christopher having a slumber party and sleeping in the room with Hedy and Peter on the night of the rape, she must have been using it as a test for Christopher, to see if he could cure himself of being a sexual predator by spending a night in the same room with children and maybe he could stop himself from raping a child that night. Wendy used our children as his test. He had just spent months in a detention center right before they left Truth or Consequences that weekend in 1987. Another thought was to move Betsy's stuff out of the garage as soon as possible. Another thought: Tim was playing us. He and Ches were on the same page all along. Ches had probably told him shortly after Wendy had told Ches.

CHAPTER 5

The next afternoon, Dennis, a neighborhood friend, helped move Betsy's boxes and furniture; he drove the U-Haul truck to Sedona. Betsy still had her job at the supermarket there. Betsy said Wendy had told her that Christopher had left town abruptly for a job in Colorado. It was doubtful that Christopher had fled to Colorado for he had told us that there was a warrant out for his arrest in that state. "For late car payments." Wendy would not have volunteered to give what direction he had fled. When we unloaded the truck in Sedona, Dennis flirted with Betsy and she flirted back. I should have warned Dennis on what was going on. If Betsy knew anything about a rape, she didn't say and I didn't tell her what we had learned. Betsy seemed relieved that she was shed of Christopher. She was still alive, no broken neck, and she had all her teeth. She wasn't flying as much, maybe, in her quest for Mr. Right, but she laughed with ease. When Dennis noticed an open box of torn undergarments, he teased her about them. She laughed and giggled.

Detective Small of the Prescott Police told us that they believed Christopher had fled the state, but he guessed to Nevada. It wasn't the first time Christopher had toured the southwest. He had left Arizona numerous times since he dropped out of school in the spring of 1990 in the middle of his junior year at Prescott high school. He was on the varsity baseball team and was warned he needed to stop smoking cigarettes and honor his contract. He couldn't stop and the members of the team voted him off. Every player had signed a contract at the beginning of the season to abstain from tobacco, drugs, and alcohol during those months. His teammates reported Christopher's indiscretions to the coach. The coach held a team meeting and the team voted. Wendy was shocked that Christopher should be held accountable for anything and she launched a campaign to smear the coach. She spoke out against the coach at a school board meeting. She tried to get us to join her in her protest of the coach but we declined. Sandy worked at the same middle school where Coach Cordes taught social studies; I had subbed in his classes. He was a fair and a much-respected coach and teacher. Coach Cordes said he was teaching the boys life lessons, to be responsible, to live up to their agreements. The school board agreed with the coach. Christopher dropped out of Prescott high at the end of February. Wendy took her anger out on us for not showing up to support her and Christopher. Our punishment: she cut off contact with us for months. We only got back together for the birth of Patrick.

Christopher had played baseball for two years at the high school in Truth or Consequences and at the end of his sophomore year, he made the New Mexico's all-state baseball team as one of the area's outstanding players. More importantly, he had stayed out of Juvenile detention for two straight years. Getting into baseball was a big thing in his life. Baseball was saving him from himself and saving him from his mother. Pete was just starting little league 1990 and I was looking forward to taking Hedy and Pete to Christopher's games.

All of a sudden, Christopher was a dropout of Prescott High, cut loose from baseball, with no direction and no plans. He had been talking about playing in the majors, and as good as he was, it wasn't that far-fetched. Wendy couldn't get herself too worked up because she had a one-year-old Nicki scampering at her feet and was five months pregnant with Patrick. Christopher worked at a half dozen service-industry jobs in Prescott that spring and summer. Money had a way of disappearing from the cash registers when he was working;

he was let go so many times that he ran out of places to look for work. Wendy had Patrick in mid-June about the time Christopher left town. He wandered through the western states with a carful of fellow high school dropouts as they made their way through California, Oregon, Washington, and Idaho doing more partying and sightseeing than job hunting, and returning when they ran out of money. One time, he returned from Utah and left for Colorado a week later after pawning Bob's tools.

Wendy had a nervous breakdown when Christopher left Prescott when Patrick was one year old. Part baby blues and part Christopher blues, she locked herself in her bedroom for two weeks not talking to anyone and seldom coming out to eat. Bob was worried and called Sandy about his concerns; he thought Wendy might be suicidal. Sandy went by Wendy's house one evening after work but she and Bob couldn't get Wendy to open her bedroom door. "Go away," was all she would say. Sandy said, "Come on, Wendy, nothing can be that bad. That's what families are for." A day later, Sandy and I tried to get her to talk to us, to open the front door of the house, but she stayed locked up. On Saturday, we visited again. When no one answered the front door, we went around to the sliding door off the deck. The curtain was open. Wendy ventured out of her room on her way to the kitchen smoking a cigarette. She looked disheveled and washed out as if something inside her had died. In the dim light, her eyes were dark echoes. Worry lines ran her face. Like a zombie, she glanced over at us as we knocked on the glass. She walked toward us like she was floating, her housecoat reaching the floor. As she pulled the curtains shut, the heaviness of her whole being seemed about to topple the house on its side. And it wasn't a mobile home.

(February 2003) We helped Hedy move from the house she shared with others in town to our house. It was a circling of the wagons, anticipating the attack that we felt was sure to come. If Tim's cold reaction was any indication, we needed to start sharpening the long poles. Wendy knew the house where Hedy lived with her friends and also where Hedy worked. There was no telling what Miss

Me-Me-Me might try. We were coming to grasp just how dangerous Wendy was. Hedy was working at New Frontiers grocery store two days a week, two graveyard shifts at the C-Stop convenient store, and weekend evenings at the movie theatre at the mall. We had always thought of Wendy as "a caring aunt" for she always wanted to know where Hedy was, what was new with Hedy, what was Hedy planning, and what was on Hedy's mind. One morning, Hedy and I were sitting at the kitchen table eating some of my homemade pancakes when she said, "In the movie La-La Land, the main character, Mia, credits her loving aunt as being her inspiration to follow her dreams. But in my life, my aunt is just the opposite of loving and caring; she is a vengeful and scheming witch." Wendy had been plotting against Hedy for two decades, and not just to hold her back but actively trying to destroy her. When Christopher dropped out of high school, he was stuck in his life and all the while, Hedy was developing into a creative and talented girl and young woman she would become. Wendy lashed out at everything about our family. We ignored her and kept living. But we ignored Miss Me-Me-Me at our own peril.

Wendy was jealous that our marriage had lasted so long while her first marriage had fallen apart in the first year. Sandy and I were married in July 1972 and six weeks later, Wendy married Richard Johnson. A year later, she was a single mom with a one-year-old.

(2003) Hedy worked that Saturday night and returned from work Sunday morning on a snow-laden Williamson Valley Road. It had snowed about five inches that Sunday morning. She was the first to leave tire tracks on the snow on the paved road. The rest of the week, we saw more snow flurries and some thawing during the days, followed by freezing nights. Williamson Valley Road was an icy mess by the weekend. That Sunday, I called Bob and asked if we could meet on Saturday night to discuss an important matter, and he said yes.

Tuesday morning, Wendy called Sandy in the choir room at Granite Mountain Middle School. Every morning, Sandy worked at the middle school for two hours before she moved to Taylor Hicks

Elementary for the remainder of her day. Wendy asked Sandy, "I hear Bob is meeting with Mike on Saturday evening. Can you tell me what it's about?"

Sandy said, "I can't talk to you, Wendy."

Wendy said, "I bet it's something about Hedy, isn't it?"

"I can't talk about it, Wendy."

"Come on, Sandy, this is what families are for. Chris has a good heart."

"I'm busy. I can't talk to you. I've got to go. Goodbye." Sandy hung up.

My meeting scheduled with Bob was a cloud of anticipation. We didn't know how to confront them, without it blowing up into a bloody fight. Keep them guessing. But, alas, we were too predictable. Tim and Ches were discussing the situation, obviously, and contacting Wendy.

Friday night, Hedy drove her car on the icy road to work at the C-Stop. We knew convenience stores attract crime and we knew Wendy knew that. Our daughter had a target on her back. Sandy and I, on a hunch, decided to drive into town to guard Hedy from a distance. I put chains on the Ford Taurus and we headed into town just before midnight.

A mile down Williamson Valley Road, we came to an incline on a curve that had a large patch of ice. I had slowed to a crawl. When the front tires touched the ice, the Taurus swerved and began to rotate clockwise. There was a rock-strewn cut hill on our right and to the left was a ten-foot drop-off into a ditch. At the base of that drop-off were a horse corral and a pond. On the top of the rise, the car seemed to move sideways in slow motion on that sheet of ice. Like a slow merry-go-round, we spun. The lights of our car panned out in front of us, turning everything silver and gold (colors associated with heaven). Our headlights lit up the scrub cedars and creosote bushes on the hillside, splashed light on the fence, a telephone pole, the void over the edge of the road, the drop-off, and the tops of trees. By the time our tires contacted asphalt again and stopped, we had rotated

360 degrees. It was an abrupt stop, and we bounced for a moment. Luckily, there were no other cars on the road, so we had a moment to grasp how fortunate we were. We could have easily flipped upside down or hit the hillside. It was a metaphor for our lives: everything spinning around and around, everything in flux. Slowly, we moved forward off the ice patch and made it into town without further incidence. We sat in the shadows and watched the front of the store, watched our girl. We took turns nodding off in sleep. Hedy, inside in the bright lights, seemed too animated, too happy as she greeted her late-night customers, many of them in dark hoodies and with their hands in their pockets. Just before sunrise, we drove back home.

We had gotten a little sleep that night, taking turns. During the week, Sandy and I had been like two sleepwalkers rising from our bed at the same time and heading across the dark house, until we drifted toward each other—an accident waiting to happen.

My older sister, Eva, who lived in Maine with her husband Jim, called that week to say that they were flying to California for Jim's handball tournament. They wanted to drive over to Arizona to say hello to us in Prescott and then go on to visit our sister Sharon in Tucson. I told Eva that it wasn't a good time; we were having a family emergency and didn't really want visitors. Eva pried, but I wouldn't tell her what it was about. She got on the phone with my other four sisters.

I got a call Saturday morning from my sister Madonna. She asked about our emergency, and after a bit of stalling, I told her what was happening.

I had called Donna, Mom, for seventeen years. This is how Donna became my mom: At my mother Katie's funeral in Iowa in 1986, at a reception dinner at the Cedar nightclub in Ashton, I had a glass of wine and being a little buzzed, I asked my two oldest sisters, "Which one of you is my real mother?" It got a lot of laughs. Katie was in her mid-forties when she gave birth to me and I said, "It all seems suspicious." Arlene and Marlys, quickly denied being my mother, but you could tell they were glad I asked. Eva and Sharon were too young. Donna, the middle sister, had just told a story that evening about sneaking into the old farmhouse late one night when she was fifteen and getting caught by father because of a squeaky staircase. Because of this story, I put my arms out to Donna and said, "Mom!" and Donna, also a little heavy on the wine, said, "Son!" We hugged. For seventeen years, I sent her "Dear Mom" letters and birthday cards and she sent me "Dear Son" correspondence.

Donna relayed the news to my other sisters and they called one after another with their condolences and advice. We had some support. My sister Sharon, who was only two years older than me, had known Christopher, Hedy, and Peter all their lives. "It's a bewildering world," Sharon said, "and then you die." Sharon's son Jeff was a few months younger than Christopher, and the two boys played together when they were young, but they hadn't seen each other in more than a decade.

On Saturday, Sandy went to Flagstaff for regional tryouts with her middle school choir. When she came back, she was shaking. She was worried about the meeting with Bob scheduled for that evening. "All we can do is all we can do," I said. "Be careful. And mind everything you say."

Saturday night, I picked Bob up at his house. We rode my pickup into the hills above the high school and parked on a side street. Bob was in a jovial mood and joked about what was up much the way Sandy and I had joked about our anticipated meeting with Hedy two weeks earlier. The weight of it all brings everybody's party to an end. I told him about the assault on Hedy and that we believed Wendy and Ches and Tim knew about the rape from the beginning. I told about the bloody panties we found at the time. Bob was stunned. I'm sure he wasn't acting. Wendy had not shared anything with him all week.

Bob said, "I know Christopher was a real pain in the ass for a long spell and I know he's done some crazy things, but I don't know if I can believe he would rape a little girl."

I said, "Better face it, Bob. He's been enabled his whole life. Enabled by Wendy and Grandma Ches and Tim, and actually, by all of us. You told me he'd stolen and pawned away every tool you ever had and your electronics and everything he could get his hands on. Years ago, you told me never to lend money to Christopher. He was a terror before he was a teen. Nobody was sharing that information with Sandy and myself. Tim knew what was going on. He knew Christopher was into sex and pornography, early. That crap Christopher pulled last year when he was coming back from Florida shows he's still in the same rut. He's never grown up. He's thirty years old now. Everybody makes excuses: it's the drugs, he never had a father, and so on."

That Florida incident occurred three years after Christopher's wife, Amy, left with their baby and went to Texas. Christopher flew to Florida for the winter, for a sheetrock job where he reportedly saved $5,000 in two months. He left Florida for Arizona by bus with a wad of cash in February 2002. In New Orleans he disappeared into the Marti Gras crowd. He told Bob and Wendy on a phone call that he was carrying cash. Christopher's friend made it to Prescott on the same bus. On the third day of Christopher's disappearance, Bob and I looked into booking a flight to New Orleans, when suddenly, Christopher resurfaced in Baton Rouge. He'd blown all his money but still had his bus ticket and was heading home.

That evening in my truck, Bob said, "I know he's been all over the board. I should know because I'm right in the middle of his crazy ways. But I can't believe that Christopher would do something so base as rape a child."

I said, "He did this, Bob. You need to ask Nicki and Patrick if Christopher has touched them in any way; he's had access to them for years now. He's come and gone so often there's no telling what he's done. Or what disease he's brought home. I heard he's fled the area. Is that true?"

"I don't know where he is," Bob said. Bob was surprised when I told him I had moved Betsy's things to Sedona. Bob said, "Mike, you need to call the police."

"We've been there, done that," I said. "The detective said Chris is keeping one step ahead of them."

Bob and I talked for over an hour. I told Bob that Betsy seemed genuinely happy that Christopher is out of her life. He was shocked when I told him what Betsy said about the little hell she was living with Christopher, the rape scenarios, and the violence she described. Bob and I shared some of the stories we'd heard of Christopher's sexual activities as a youth in Tucson, Silver City and Truth or Consequences. Bob said, "I knew Christopher had been in detention before we got married. He was a couple of times after we were married."

I said, "When Christopher was twelve and living with Wendy in Tucson, she told us he used to sneak out of his window at nights and run the streets with other lost boys. The pornography and drugs started there. Wendy took that job as a nurse in Silver City, I believe, to get Christopher away from Tucson."

Bob said, "You've heard the story about the older woman in Silver City, Wendy's neighbor in an apartment complex?"

"Yeah, I have," I said.

I had heard about that incident when we came together at Thanksgiving at Bob's house in Truth or Consequences after Nicki was born. At that visit, Tim started to tell us about the incident involving Christopher and that older woman, but Ches overheard Tim and came from the other room and told Tim he shouldn't repeat that awful story. After making sure Wendy wasn't in earshot, Ches sat down at our table and whispered the story to us, mustering up every nuance she'd learned in dramatic arts. Ches was still angry with the woman. This is the story she told:

"For crying out loud, Christopher was only thirteen years old. He would sneak out of his window at night and that horrible woman would be waiting in her bed for him to climb through her window.

She was a thirty-two-year-old divorcee, and he was just a child. Can you believe that? That horrible woman, taking advantage of Christopher like that. It went on for months, all summer. Wendy had no clue. Wendy sometimes worked late shifts as nurses do and she asked that woman to look out for Christopher. At first, Christopher thought he was too old for a babysitter, but after a while, I guess, he didn't mind. And sometimes, when Wendy was home, she would send him over to borrow, I guess, eggs or sugar or milk and whatnot. And even when Christopher didn't come back for an hour, Wendy never suspected anything. Can you believe that? Who would believe it? When he came back, Wendy would ask him how Jen was and you know how Wendy teases. She would ask, 'Did Jen give you some sugar, Christopher?' That stupid girl! It made Christopher angry and he would go to his room and slam the door and Wendy would tap on his door and ask 'Honey, are you alright?' And Christopher would say 'Go away.' She still didn't catch on. Or she'd ask him, 'Did Jenny make some cookies for you? I'll make you some cookies if you want me to.' Stupid girl. When it warmed up and Wendy would leave her windows open at night, she heard noises of people having sex, you know, moaning and cooing and such. It turned out to be Christopher and that woman making those noises. And they were laughing! And Wendy still didn't know! It's beyond belief, I tell you. That woman should have been arrested for what she did. And get this: when Wendy accosted that fiend, that low life, that scum of the earth, that woman offered to marry Christopher. Have you ever heard of such a thing? Offering to marry a thirteen-year-old boy? That horrible woman! Someone should have strangled her. Someone should have shot that woman in the head." Ches was red in the face and exhausted just from talking about it, and she put her face in her hands.

 I told Bob that night in my truck that I remembered Ches telling that story and added, "It was a year and a half after we found bloody panties. I can't believe it never dawned on us that Christopher could have hurt Hedy. How stupid of us. We didn't put a simple two and two together. But everything was so hushed; his running around and his dark side. We'd been lied to for so many years."

Bob said, "Too bad they didn't tell you. I thought you knew about Christopher and that woman. I guess I assumed you would know. I knew it, and I knew Ches knew it. Tim and Patty knew it, so I thought you had been told about him. Wendy signed him in and out of detention and left me out of the loop."

"So you don't know what he was in lockdown for?"

"No. There was this time that Christopher got into trouble. He was with a girl after school and they were making out behind the high school gym and after a while, the girl wanted to stop. But he didn't want to stop and when she pulled away from him, he tore her blouse. She went and told her father who came over with the police to our house to talk to Christopher. They talked outside by the curb for a while. Left him off with a verbal warning. He got into baseball shortly after that."

I had Bob sign a letter stating that we had talked about a crime that was committed and that Bob and his family and Christopher were not to make contact with our family unless we initiated the contact. Bob said that it might end up being a valuable lesson for Nicki and Patrick, who were fourteen and twelve.

CHAPTER 6

The next morning, a Sunday, Ches called about nine o'clock.

"How are you doing, Sandy?" she said.

"Okay."

"Are you sure you're okay?" Pause. "Wendy called me. I know what's going on. Honey, don't be making such a big thing out of this. Hedy will be alright. That same thing happened to me when I was six and I'm fine."

"What are you saying?"

"It happened to me when I was six."

Sandy tossed the phone across the kitchen and the battery flew out. I was in the den reading one of our newly acquired books: *I Never Told Anyone*. I was reading it for the hard-knocks class: "Learning About the Devastation of Sexual Abuse in Your Free Time." My hair was already standing on end because of that book when Sandy said to hurry to the kitchen. She told me what Ches had said. I put the battery back in the phone and it rang. Sandy grabbed it out of my hands and spoke into it: "What?"

Ches said, "Listen, Sandy. Just listen to what I'm saying. You're going to ruin Christopher's life if you go around blackening his name. We need to stop this now. He may have fooled around with Hedy but molestation happens in a lot of families. You're not the only one that's hurting here."

"It was rape, mother, it wasn't fooling around. She was six years old; there was no fooling around. Was it rape that happened to you? Who raped you? What exactly happened?"

"Auk, I don't remember. Six-year-olds don't remember those things. He was an older cousin, too, is all I want to say. You're being hateful and mean for what you're doing to Christopher."

"What was your cousin's name?"

"It's none of your business. I don't remember. And Hedy doesn't remember. I tell you, she doesn't remember. We need to end this now. Six-year-old children can't remember things back then. And stop saying that word—rape."

Sandy said, "Rape, rape, rape! Goodbye, mother. If you're going to attack us, I don't want to talk to you. I love you. Bye." Sandy hung up on her. "You won't believe what my mother is saying—what she wants us to do."

The phone rang again. We looked upon the off-white, shiny object ringing on the wall like it was a ticking time bomb that we had no idea how to defuse. Sandy answered it. She didn't say a word but listened to Ches. Sandy lifted the phone from her ear and pointed to the receiver and I came close enough to hear the screaming woman on the other side: "Sandy! It never happened! It never happened!"

Sandy said to the receiver, "Bye, mom, I love you," and hung up again. Ches called again but we didn't pick up. Five minutes passed and again it rang. We watched it until it rang its last. Sandy said, "Maybe she hasn't taken her meds this morning." Ches was on a regiment of eighteen pills a day; we had witnessed her morning pill ritual at her kitchen table in Tucson. She lined up the pills like a young child sorting out M and Ms by color. One by one, we watched her wash them down with sips of coffee.

What could we do? We pondered that question for a moment and thought about what Ches had said: *None of your business.* So, we brought out the family genealogy folder that we had compiled over the previous decade. We found a family tree that Hedy had made in the sixth grade with the help of a certain grandmother named

Chesna Mae. Also, Ches in her later years had written and compiled 500 pages of memoirs and photos that Ches gave to Sandy and her siblings in four or five installments. Ches had hoped to have it made into a book. The tentative title of her book about the history of her life was: *Tell Me More, Grandma.* It would have turned into 2,000 pages if she had been truthful to the grandkids.

Her maiden name was Chesna Mae Dillinger. One family story: her father, William Dillinger, was the same height and same complexion as the infamous outlaw John Dillinger. William was detained once and spent a night in jail in western Kansas until authorities confirmed he was *not* the fugitive desperado. William walked away from his family, a wife with four small children, when Ches was only five months old. Though she rarely spoke about him, Ches was bitter toward her father her entire life because of his desertion. William never remarried and died in an auto accident in 1935 when Ches was fifteen. Her mother, Sylvia, raised the two boys and two girls and she, too, never remarried and struggled to keep food on the table. According to Ches, Sylvia was "a very pretty woman, who had turned down numerous marriage proposals from many, many very, very nice men who would have made very good fathers." When Ches, in her sixties and seventies, made statements like that, you could envision her sitting as a six-year-old with her teddy bears at a small table staged with a tea party. Another giant six-year-old? No one helped Ches move from victim to survivor, an all-important step in the evolution of overcoming sexual child abuse from over-sexed cousins.

In the family history folder, we found four older male cousins of Ches's who were between twelve and fourteen in 1926 when she was six. We focused on one cousin, Allen, the oldest of the group. It was this Allen that Ches had mentioned who sent her money to help her get through college. Ches also got extra Christmas cash every year from her sister Neva. Ches went to college from 1938 to 1942. She told us that an older gentleman friend of hers sent her money to help with her expenses—out of the goodness of his heart. It sounded creepy to us. Swap *goodness* for *the guilt of his heart*, and it's a better fit.

Sandy and I agreed we'd never know for sure who her molester was unless Ches told us. As I've mentioned before, Ches liked to toy with you with her half-truths. I can still see her eyes set inward as she would say things and roll the things around in her mind and the smug little smile curling up at the edges of her mouth that seemed to say: fooled them again. She had been talking to herself since she was six, I bet. Ches acted in numerous plays in high school and college. She quipped that she was once serious about running away to Hollywood during the war when she was in her early twenties. Ches was also on debate teams and bestowed that talent for argument on Sandy and her sisters. Her girls thought they could bend rusty nails with their skills as spin-doctors. Marilyn Monroe was molested at age seven and Monroe had that same playful psychotic demeanor about her that Ches had. Ches got a job after college as a stewardess for a pioneering airline company. Her pin-up photos from the beginning of WWII show Ches as a beauty. She had an alluring yet distant smile not unlike Monroe's—like it was forced, and behind it, the little girl was saying to herself, got to fool 'em; my future depends on it. Marlene Dietrich said of acting: "It's all about honesty; if you can fake that, then you have it made." Ches was six years old in the summer of 1926, the summer she was raped, the summer that Monroe was born.

We told Hedy about Grandma's phone call. Hedy responded with anger, "I was expecting that." She grasped the harshness of Ches's betrayal. "Well, that's her problem. I'm glad it's out there. I didn't ask for this. Why didn't the adults in my life protect me? Why didn't she protect me? Why didn't she step up? What does she want me to do about it? Why didn't you protect me, Dad? None of you protected me. Why is she laying this on me? I never asked for this. No one protected me! There were plenty of adults that could have stepped up, but no one did!" She slammed the door to her room and then came right back out. "Why did you ever let Christopher sleep in the room with me and Peter that night? What were you thinking?

He was a teenage boy! What were you thinking? He was a warped teenage boy!"

"Not all teenage boys are warped," Sandy said.

"Yes, they are. You let Wendy tell you what to think; you let Wendy tell you how to think, what to do, and I got raped."

"I'm sorry. You had slept in rooms with Christopher since you were a baby and Peter, too. No one warned us that Christopher had turned into a sick-o. They all knew by then but no one informed us. Tim knew for years and never told us. Patty knew. Ches knew. No one told us. No one told us he had spent time in lock-up just before he came to visit us in Nogales."

"Well, you should have known. That was your job. It was your fault!" She slammed her door again.

Through the door, Sandy told Hedy, "Aim your anger at the perpetrator and his enablers. Chris, Wendy, Tim, and grandma, they are the guilty ones here."

"Ah!"

Sandy started taking the sleeping medication that week. She also found out that she had a case of diverticulitis, which the doctor told her could have been caused by diet and stress. Sandy's father, Tom, and his identical twin brother, Robert, when they were in their fifties, had diverticulitis during the same week, almost to the day. They were living four hundred miles apart from each other. They were in their community hospitals the same week. Sandy said that after her inflammation passed, a bowling-ball-sized ball of tears appeared in her gut.

I read myself to sleep via the voices of the survivors in the required books. I told Sandy that I fantasied about strangling pedophiles, or shooting them, or beating their brains out with a baseball bat. Sandy suggested in her calm, matter-of-fact teacher voice, "We could tie ropes to their wrists and ankles and dangle them naked, penis down, over a water tank with great white sharks in it."

We received a letter from Ches:

"Dears, I don't know where to begin. Am shaking too much to write but need to put in my two cents worth, even though I'm eighty+ years old. Will admit to having rewritten this letter twice and should rewrite it again. After all, this is a family affair that affects all or us. From this time on, I'll try to stay out of it, but you—Sandy and Mike, Wendy and Bob, Hedy and Christopher, have many years ahead of you to seethe with anger and cry your eyes out.

There is no quick or long-time fix to such a delicate subject, but many a family has had to face it through the ages. We are human and do unspeakable things. Some people are messed up for life while others manage to take it in their stride along with other heavy baggage that life passes out.

I've been told via phone that Chris, our natural-born athlete, has possibly admitted to having 'fooled around' with Hedy 15 years ago. If so, that so-called fooling around may have scarred his life. How about his success at school, his inability to stay in jobs, his failed marriage to Amy? Could it account for what we view as mental illness? Regardless, we all agree that he needs professional help badly, just as he's needed his dad's backup all his life.

Since high school, our pretty songbird Hedy had been floundering, not knowing what to do or where. She seemed frustrated and unhappy. Any kind or degree of violation to her person at such a tender age has stayed in her memory, and in a sense, has blocked her ability to move on, in spite of having every advantage along the way. Too bad she didn't confide in her mommy and daddy sooner.

I'm aware of and have taken part in lovely memories that Christopher and Hedy have shared throughout the years, such as family gatherings and celebrations. Now, Sandy and Wendy, you have something 'real' to be hurt and angry about, things that have been building up over the last year or so.

I'd like to see Hedy and Christopher confront each other face to face in the company of professionals in a special setting. It seems only fair. Time can fade it all, provided how you deal with it. We could all use some good old-fashioned help sometimes.

Will add, too, that I harbor some bad memories that never completely go away. The young teenager involved with me grew into an exceptionally good man—certainly not a sexual pervert. Many children share dark secrets. Little girls are especially vulnerable, so in need of constant protection, and young guys need constant guidance, but of course, they can't be under surveillance 24 hours a day.

I haven't meant to preach and will try not to comment on the subject again. Will hope that Hedy and Christopher can come to grips with the problem and not allow it to haunt them for the rest of their lives. You, too, Sandy & Mike and Wendy & Bob. We surely don't want or need to spread a story that could hurt innocent family members or anyone else.

Love you all with all my heart, Mom, Gran'ma"

This letter was the closest Ches would ever come to acknowledging that Christopher may have committed rape. Grandma Ches, the letter writer, sounded different than the hysteric woman screaming at us on the phone a few days earlier. As for her staying out of it, or not commenting again on the subject, she did just the opposite and became a devoted, vocal defender for Christopher and Wendy; she became an attacker of Hedy. The PACT [Protecting/Abetting Christopher Tenaciously] wasn't about to fold; after this letter, their gloves came off. Wendy had greater influence over the elderly Ches and damaged Tim than we imagined. Ches was eighty-three and vulnerable. Tim with his head injury and his years of investing a lot of money in Christopher was also easy prey for Wendy and her campaign to combat the enemies in her private game: the world against her Christopher.

Tim and Ches listened to Rush Limbaugh on the radio fervently. Once when I called Limbaugh a pig, Tim gritted his teeth and left our house. So, Tim had already put me in the league with Satan before the family entered into this feud. Tim would want to take an opposite stance on anything I stood for. Our views were on opposite spectrums. But I also called Bill Clinton a pig, that he should have been impeached and tried for rape. Tim and I once had a heated argument about the Gulf of Tonkin.

I said McNamara admitted it was a lie to get us into war. Tim said I was crazy. The liars in our politics have a mantra: "control the narrative." They control the narrative when most of what the media wants you to believe as truth is false. That's where we were in our family. Sandy, Hedy, and I were on the side of "fair and balanced" and Wendy played the media—putting forth false narratives.

Who wouldn't be upset after finding out that their daughter had been raped and slandered and the perpetrator had fled the state? But Ches and Wendy were not even going to let us get to the point where we could sit down together and say, "Well, where do we go from here?" Grandma was screaming at us, "It never happened!" That was the only narrative we were supposed to embrace. That's how Ches was taught to handle her assault. "Little Chessy, you've got to do the right thing and say it never happened, or you'll ruin your cousin's life. You don't want your cousin to die a miserable death, do you? It will be your fault if he does. Don't be a rat, girl. You don't want to be the one to ruin anybody's life. Just think how you would feel if you ruined someone's life." Wendy and Ches had strapped themselves to the same harness. Together, the two women pulled the cart with the head-injured Tim and the obedient Bob tied on their leashes trailing behind.

In our camp, we were seeing a bigger picture—a picture that went back centuries where men made immoral laws to justify taking child brides, to take children to be their lawful wedded sperm rags. We felt that these win-win situations for the men and lose-lose for the women and girls and boys had no place in a progressive world.

Globally, there has been a rising up for justice for human rights and women's rights, trying to point the world in a safer and saner direction. We joined that fight, maybe at first on stubborn grounds, but then on moral grounds. There was no going back, turning back to medieval times. Wendy had been spitting in our faces for several years and we never knew why. Wendy was angry with us for a number of reasons: (1)for *not* knowing about the crime; (2)for knowing the crime; (3)for being married so long; (4)for not giving money recklessly to Christopher like Tim; (5)for having children who were upbeat and successful; (6)for Wendy being forced to share Ches's time with us; (7)for letting her run over us; (8)for not calling her out on the hate letter.

Hedy felt pressure to come out when she did because she had witnessed Wendy's recent hostilities, her loss of control, and Hedy may have heard mention that Christopher wanted to get a gun to shoot rats and if he went down, he was taking everyone with him. Hedy had seen and heard enough. Her own parents were not even protecting themselves from the traitorous and mendacious aunt Wendy.

Over the years, one of Wendy's mantras was "It is a man's world! Men have stacked the cards in their favor. Men have it all; men get away with everything." We never asked her what she meant by *everything*. Did that mean raping little children? If Ches happened to be in the room listening to Wendy's angst about the fate of the sisterhood, Ches would nod and nod and force a smile, and blink and blink. It was a nervous twitch, for sure, but that smile was the base of her partial agreement, which was: "You have lessons to learn, little one." All the while, Ches would be imagining clearly the dark walls of the fortress of the men-masters, walls that could not be penetrated nor scaled except by those willing to die. "Any woman who thinks she can change the world," as Ches puts it, "is looking to get herself into hot water." The fortress was centuries in the making and guarded by mean, snarling men, looking for excuses to be violent against women. That's part of a man's world: looking for excuses to attack. Someday, baby girl, you will be okay with it being a man's world, but for now, I'll tolerate your iconoclastic thoughts, for it is, after all, a good exercise in mental toughness. Ches was okay with a woman speaking her mind as long as you didn't act. Ches once told Wendy, "Girl, you don't want to be labeled a troublemaker. Women survive in this man's world by wits, charm, and manipulation, don't you know that? So keep protesting my pretty daughters. Can't you see I'm blinking my approval? Squawk but be cautious." Ches was born in January 1920, eight months before the women's suffrage movement won the century-long fight for the right to vote in America. The legislation was signed into law before Ches could walk.

Chesna Mae had five daughters. Sandy and Jolie were middle daughters. And as Sandy liked to point out: "I was the most invisible of the middle daughters." Wendy, the youngest, was a poster child for demanding, overbearing babies. Wendy learned early that by holding her breath, she could often get what she wanted. The other invisible daughter was Jolie, a year older than Sandy. Kitty and Sandy were the two most level headed. Tim was the oldest of the six. Patty, the oldest of the girls, was like a little mother to her four younger sisters when they were growing up. There were only seven and a half years age difference with the six children, between Tim and Wendy. Ches, in her old age, one day commented, "It was like a whirlwind had entered my life during those first eight years of our marriage!" From her wedding night in early 1946 until the birth of her last child in June 1954, exactly one hundred months had passed. She was pregnant for 54 months (6 times 9 months, if all were full term). In between, she barely had time to catch her breath, learn new mothering tricks, and get ready for the next birth. It was little wonder that she blinked. Ches did most of this child-rearing on her own, as Tom was a busy copper and uranium geologist who traipsed over the world and the beautiful countryside where he lived in jeeps and 4x4s. He dragged Ches and the kids to new cities, new jobs, and exploring new mountains because they were there. Later, he worked on his doctorate via the GI Bill at Columbia University in New York where Jolie was born in 1950. Tom was in the Navy during WWII, but Ches was the one who should have received the Purple Heart for what she endured in the years after the war. By the time Tom died from nicotine and yellowcake dust-induced lung cancer in 1979, he was recognized as one of the foremost geologists in the country and especially in the four-state area. But I heard Ches cry out when she was in her eighties: "Oh, why did we have so many babies? Tom and I were so happy. We were going to have just two children when we got married. But we had six. It happened so quickly. If I hadn't stopped it, we would have had more—more heartaches. We didn't need six children. For crying out loud, what were we thinking?" At such times, Sandy looked at her mother in wonder and awe, and even Wendy would stop talking for a moment to contemplate Ches, her astonishing, secretive mother.

(2003) Sandy came home from work one day that Spring to find a message on our phone. It was from Christopher. He said, "Sandy, I have something to tell you." Sandy called me at the cabinet shop and I stopped at radio shack that evening and bought a recording device for use with the phone and our tape recorder. Why was he calling us? What did he have to tell us?

CHAPTER 7

Sandy's sister, Patty, telephoned one evening during the next week and discussed the situation with Sandy. Patty said she believed that Hedy was telling the truth. Patty was upset about Ches and Tim attacking Hedy for speaking out. She heard them rattle on about it constantly. Sandy was able to get Patty to share more of her history; Patty's early years had been shrouded in secrecy. Patty had mental problems starting in her teens, being put on anti-depression medication in the mid-1960s when the use of these mind-bending drugs was still in experimental stages. I first met Patty when she was twenty-two. Sandy had wondered about the rumors that Patty was molested as a five-year-old. Patty told this story:

When Tom and Ches, in July 1953, left the hospital in Grand Junction, with newborn, Kitty, baby number five, they drove across the state directly to Ches's sister Neva's place in eastern Colorado to retrieve their oldest children, Tim and Patty. (Sandy and Jolie were staying in El Paso, Texas with Tom's mother, Mary.) Neva and Harry and their three children lived on a farm not far from where Ches was raised in western Kansas. When Ches and Tom arrived, Neva was in tears. Neva told them that her oldest son, Marvin, age fourteen, had done something to Patty in the barn. Neva said Harry had given Marvin "a good whacking." Patty said she didn't remember most of it. She remembered the boy showing his penis and having her touch it, hugging her, holding onto her, and laying on top of her. Patty didn't remember anything else happening. Aunt Neva was hysterical and crying and kept saying she was sorry. Ches and Tom had to soothe and calm Neva down. When Tom and Ches got home to Grand Junction, they took Patty to a doctor. Patty didn't think she was raped. Years later when Patty was nine, Marvin, who was just out of high school and who was a troubled young man, came to live with Ches and Tom and the children in Flagstaff, Arizona for one summer. Patty remembered feeling uncomfortable around Marvin—that he was always watching her. Inviting Marvin into their home was Ches's way of trying to mend the family, to help Marvin pass his test. Ches would sacrifice the feelings and safety of her children for her Hollywood ideas of family. To Ches, everything had to have the appearance of being under control, always. The encounter freaked out nine-year-old Patty who kept up her guard and distance from the tall male cousin. Neva, like cousin Allen, had sent "extra money" to Ches every Christmas for as long as anyone could remember.

Ches did not tell Patty that Hedy was raped, so Patty was awestruck by that revelation. "When Christopher was a little boy," she said, "I told everyone that he was out of control. Starting when he was six or seven, he wouldn't listen to anyone. He tried to bully me. Wendy yelled at me if I complained. We used to get into terrible fights over his behavior."

Sandy and I remembered the blowups that Patty and Wendy had when Christopher was small and before we had kids. Those blow-ups were still going on when Hedy and Peter were small. Christopher was obsessed with bugging Patty and no one could stop him. On the phone, Patty told Sandy, "Ches is distraught and isn't sleeping. You shouldn't blame her. After all, Christopher was her first grandchild. Her only one for many years."

Sandy responded, "Well, then she's got herself a problem, a huge problem." The next day, Sandy sent Patty a prepaid phone card.

When Sandy was a little girl, seven or eight, she remembers being awakened in the middle of the night by the screams of a hysterical woman, a voice she didn't recognize at first. It happened on more than one occasion. That woman was her mother Ches. When the screaming started, Sandy and Jolie who shared a room together would slip out of their room and congregate with brother John Timothy and Patty in the hall beside the door to their parents' bedroom. As they listened to Ches, Tim cracked open the door to see into the room. Their mother, Ches, was sitting upright on the twisted sheets and howling in distress. Ches was acting out in her sleep. She shouted, "Tom, there's a wolf under the bed! Tom, it's going to claw through this mattress! You've got to stop it. It's coming! Don't you hear it scratching? The wolf, Tom! Don't you hear him, Tom?" Tim was the oldest and tallest and had the high view through the crack in the door, while his sisters crowded under him to see and hear. They watched their mother's every move. They watched in awe of this mother of theirs with her eyes shut, her face flooded with worry and screaming of wolves. Ches sat on her folded legs in the middle of the bed in an effort to distance herself from the scratching underneath. The sisters knew that they couldn't help her; father had said to stay back. Father Tom gently tried to coax Ches awake. "Ches, it's okay. Dear, can you hear me? You're having a bad dream." "Tom, scare it away! Oh, chase it away!" He told the kids, "Everybody, go back to bed. The show's over, folks. Nothing to see here." But they didn't leave, they were glued to the drama. They knew Ches would not be comforted until she was awake. Tom coaxed her out of her nightmare. He held her. Then he'd say, "It's gone, Ches. It's going to be okay. The wolf is gone. No more wolves tonight, they're all gone." Ches would moan, "Tom, it was so real. It seemed so real." The wide-eyed children watched as Tom helped their mother to lie back under the covers. He whispered to the audience, "Show over. Now get back to bed, everyone." Sandy and her sisters scampered past brother Tim, down the hall to their bedrooms.

[Late February 2003] Sunday morning started bright and sunny but clouds soon appeared. Hedy was out of the house and gone to work at the New Frontiers Market where she'd gotten a few more hours since quitting her night job at the C-Stop store. Hedy started taking her safety seriously. The phone rang mid-morning and Sandy answered it. She told me to get on the other phone, "You're not going to believe this!" I ran to the other phone. The conversation that followed was animated and surreal. Ches was shouting: It never happened! It never happened!

Sandy: I'm not your daughter!
Ches: It never happened!
Sandy: I'm not your daughter!
Ches: It never happened!
Me: What do you mean, Ches?
Ches: Mike, it never happened!
Me: Christopher raped my daughter when she was six years old!
Ches: It never happened!
Sandy: I'm not your daughter!
Me: Christopher raped my daughter when she was six years old!
Ches: It never happened, Mike!
Sandy: I'm not your daughter!
Me: He's a rapist!
Ches: It never happened, Mike!
Me: He's a rapist!
Ches: He says he didn't do it. Why don't you believe him?
Me: He's lying.
Sandy: He's a liar!
Ches: What about your daughter? She's been away in another state for four years. No telling what kind of trouble she got into!
Me: It was for six months, not years, and she didn't get into trouble. Christopher has warrants out for him in multiple states. What's that? Is he raping his way through the west?
Ches: Shame on you, Mike. Your daughter has been running around, sleeping with men. She's running around with a single father. Your daughter is out of control! She's making this up! A six-year-old doesn't remember things!

Sandy: You said he admitted it last week that he did it.
Ches: He has recanted that.
Sandy: Now he's recanted? How convenient.
Ches: It was never true! He never did it!
Me: He raped my daughter when she was six years old!
Ches: She can't remember that. It's been sixteen years!
Me: He's a rapist!
Ches: Shame on you, Mike! Why doesn't Hedy confront him then?
Me: He's the one who fled Arizona. She's right here in town.
Ches: Why didn't she confront him?
Sandy: I'm not your daughter!
Me: He's a rapist!
Ches: Why doesn't she confront him?
Me: She will in her own time.
Ches: Sure, confront him now—now that he's mentally ill!
Me: He did it, Ches. Time you face up to it.
Ches: Where's the proof, Mike? Where's the proof?
Me: I held the bloody panties in my hand—there's the proof.
Ches: Where are they now? You have no proof. Where are they now?
Sandy: You're not my mother!
Me: He's a rapist!
Ches: Shame on you, Mike!
Sandy: You're not my mother!
Ches: If your mother could hear you, Mike, she'd be so ashamed of you.
Mike: On the contrary, she'd be proud of me. She'd want me to do what was right, to stand up for what was right. Stand up for truth. To stand up against evil.
Ches: Shame on you, Mike.
Sandy: You're not my mother!
Mike: He's a rapist. Someone should put a bullet in his head.
Ches: Someone should put a bullet in your head.

Sandy and I said goodbye in unison; we hung up. Ches called back but we didn't answer the phone. A family can pretend things never happened if they choose. Families can stay stuck if they want. Families can cling to the slippery sides of a deep, nasty well and breath in the fumes of the deadly fungus of deception. Families can chain themselves by the ankle in the neck-high water in the well of lies. Hedy could recant the filthy things she said about Chris and all would be forgiven. Wendy was waiting anxiously on the sidelines to offer forgiveness. But we knew they knew the truth. Their pretending gave us headaches. The pretending was push back to keep Christopher from having to add his name to the county child molester rosters. It was a distraction to keep us from focusing on what Wendy had done and what Ches had done all those years earlier to lead us astray.

Six days later, we drove three hundred miles to Nogales where Hedy filled out a police report about the rape—exactly sixteen years after the fact. She was in tears while she completed it. The young police officer at the police station recognized Sandy as his former music teacher at a school where Sandy taught for four years. Sandy remembered him and the classroom teachers he had. Hedy didn't remember him. He was two years ahead of her. The young officer asked Hedy why she wanted to fill out this report after so many years.

"Well," said Hedy, "if I can help some child from going through what I have gone through, what we are going through, then it will be worth it. I know I should have reported it when it happened, when I was six, but I didn't know what to do. But I'm here now, to stand against that kind of violence, to help in any way I can."

I was a bit taken aback by Hedy's declaration. She said it with her shoulders back and her head high.

We ate dinner on the American side of Nogales in a little restaurant tucked into a shopping strip. We used to frequent that place. We had learned about muchaca there years earlier. A Nogales favorite, it was a spicy meat dish somewhere between a Swiss steak and a green pepper soup. It was one of our favorite discoveries in that border town. We drove back the Prescott that night arriving about three o'clock in the morning, a six-hundred-mile round trip.

After work one day, we contacted the Prescott Police department to see if they had anything new. Detective Small said Christopher was still keeping ahead of them. His movements were from a Camp Verde motel, and to Kingman, and then into California. We speculated that a lot of what Detective Small said was made up to appease us. They'll cool soon and they'll forget about it. It wasn't a murder so life must go on. The police weren't living in a family tsunami the way we were.

At spring break, Peter came home from Northern Arizona University. We had waited to tell him face to face. He was a sophomore in engineering. He was standing by the entertainment center in the arched doorway between the living room and the den when we asked him if he remembered Christopher ever touching him inappropriately. Peter laughed and said Christopher may have flicked him in the head with a finger once, and it really hurt. When we told him of the rape, Peter's jaw dropped. He looked over at Hedy and she nodded. He said, "I'm sorry for you, Hedy." He bit his lip. We told him of the family's denial, of going to Nogales to fill out a police report, and that we were cutting ties with Wendy, Ches, and Tim. We showed him grandma's letter. We told him about the shouting matches on the phone we had with her.

Bush and Cheney launched Wall Street's Iraqi war that week. The lies that came out of Washington D.C. that winter and spring were on a new level of corruption. But after what we'd been through for the last six weeks with our own family, Washington politics seemed tame. We had lost our refuge from the meanness of the world: our sanctuary in the family. We counted on it to beckon us to some bright star, to light up a dark corner, to act as a protective bubble. We were already living in a raging war since living outside our bubble.

Ches called again that week and calmly asked Sandy to please consider that Christopher was innocent. Sandy said, "No, mother, let's not play games." Ches commented that the war in Iraq had started, and because of the turmoil that had been stirred up by Hedy's allegations, Ches wasn't able to relax enough to enjoy the media coverage. Sandy said later, "Mom sounded really put out with us for disrupting her war."

Ches sent a card: Hi. For the life of me, I don't understand how you can cut me out of your lives like this. What have I done to deserve such treatment? How long are you going to harbor such bad thoughts of me? I'm worried about you. Anger can become poisonous and if prolonged can affect your health. I love all my family & don't deserve this distain or whatever it is. Don't we already have too much sadness in our family? For such, I don't have all the answers. Do you? If so, please clue me in. Always love, Mom PS: There is a frightening war raging in the middle east. Somehow it doesn't affect me as much as what's happening to our family.

Luv u all.

A year earlier, at the end of spring break (2002), the four of us, Hedy, Peter, Sandy, and I had traveled out of town with the goal to take Peter back to his dorm in Flagstaff. We decided to make a loop around the state. We headed south to revisit Nogales which we hadn't seen for thirteen years. We drove by our house in our old neighborhood. We stopped at the end of the driveway where Hedy and Peter sold kittens out of a red wagon, tried to sell other items, like lemonade, and learn a little horse-trading. We found the restaurant across the border that we used to frequent. A mariachi band serenaded our table with "Sol Ami," which Hedy said was the most beautiful song she ever heard. To the east of Nogales, we drove to an area of old mines in the San Antonio Mountains we used to explore. Nogales is a beautiful place for children to grow up in. We kind of regretted leaving that border town. (Thirteen years of living with a toxic narcissist will make you see green pastures everywhere.) Leaving town, we drove past the Tumacacori mission built in the early 1700s where we used to take out-of-town visitors—our go-to place. We passed the majestic Santa Rita Mountains where we saw dust devils churning at the base of the mountains. Nearing Tucson, I pointed out the distant Santa Catalina Mountains where Sandy and I were married on a west slope on Mount Lemon at sunset. Lee Scott, a minister, who taught humanities at Pima College, married us under a darkening sky on St. Swithin's Day. In Tucson, we visited my sister, Sharon, and her son, Jeff. We had a fun evening with them. The next day, we sang and laughed our way through the desert valley before and aft of Phoenix. We stopped for treats and sang some more as the freeway climbed the Mogollon rim. There is something mystical and beautiful about gliding across a vast desert. The shadows in the distant mountains beckon: Come play, come touch our secrets. It was a fun junket into our past trails and we all had eaten free of the manna of hope and adventure. It was a time of sleepy innocence for our family, a time we felt in tune with the whole concept of family. We stopped that evening at a Chinese restaurant in Flagstaff, and Hedy became anxious as we were walking up to the building. We now know it was her PTSD flaring up. It was one of the first times we had seen her suffering from it and we really didn't know what she was dealing with. She took off down the sidewalk and disappeared into the night. It took us a couple of hours to find her. She laid in the backseat on the way back to Prescott, in a blue mood, the secret boiling inside her. She told us later that she wanted so much to tell us about the rape on that trip and was struggling with how to tell us.

CHAPTER 8

In late April, I read the last of our books on child abuse. Many families had it worse than our family. Some of the stories I couldn't read all the way through—they were so horrendous. Denial by the family members was common. A fierce backlash toward the victim was to be expected. *I Thought We'd Never Speak Again* by Laura Davis was especially timely. Its main message: forgiveness is nearly impossible if the perpetrator doesn't admit the wrong.

The next book on my reading list for the year was *Blood of the Prophets—Brigham Young and the Massacre at Mountain Meadows* by Will Bagley. The story and the mysteries surrounding it parallels the secrecy of our family crisis. An Arkansas wagon train bound for California in 1857 was targeted and destroyed by Brigham Young and his Mormon militia. One hundred and twenty people, most of them women and children, were murdered and their unburied bodies were left to lay on a plain in southern Utah for two years. Seventeen children under the age of six were spared because they were deemed too young to be able to give valid testimony against the guilty. Guilty adults even then preached that six-year-olds couldn't remember events.

During the massacre, the Mormon militia dressed like Indians and then blamed the Indians in the area for the slaughter. There were a few Indians among the murderers but most were young Indian men who had been "adopted" during the first decade of Mormon influence in Utah. The second half of the book tells of the denial and the cover-up of the massacre. One of the murderers, John D. Lee, acting his part as a scapegoat, was executed in 1877, twenty years after the murders. The second half of the book gave new insights into the pressured, overworked minds that deal with the lies and secrecy attached to heinous crimes. The corrupted, overworked mind of Wendy fit easily into the folds of this story of deception. The LDS church is still trying to bury the story of the massacre; any mention of the atrocity has been expunged worldwide from most reference books. It was also an embarrassment to the United States government who failed to procure justice for the families of those murdered. President Buchanan and Brigham Young were both culpable in igniting the Utah War that cost the members of the wagon train their lives. Jordan Peterson wrote once: The capacity of the rational mind to deceive, manipulate, scheme, trick, falsify, minimize, mislead, betray, prevaricate, deny, omit, rationalize, bias, exaggerate, and obscure is so endless, so remarkable, that centuries of pre-scientific thought, concentrating on clarifying the nature of moral endeavor, regarded it as positively demonic.

Years earlier, I had read a book on the Oregon Trail—a collection of journals kept by the emigrants. In a camp one morning, a fifteen-year-old boy raped a five-year-old girl as the wagons were being readied. The men held a meeting that led to the teenager being taken behind boulders and shot and buried in a shallow grave. The father of the boy shot his own son. The boy must have been unremorseful, showing signs of psychopathy for a father to agree to such a thing. The boy's history must have come into play. Frontier justice.

In May 2003, we received a letter from Martha Chase of the Santa Cruz County District Attorney's office informing us they were *not* going to pursue the matter of Hedy's rape/assault for lack of evidence, but it would remain on file. Chase never contacted us to ask if we had evidence. We no longer had physical evidence, but we had witnesses and receipts for doctor's visits and ex-rays and the perpetrator had fled into the night. DA Chase's justice was dying in a drawer.

Sandy's middle school choir performed for the 8th-grade graduation in early June. Wendy and Bob's son, Nicki, graduated that year. His parents and brother Patrick were in the audience. Sandy turned her back to them all evening.

Sandy also said she had a difficult time getting through the spring semester because making eye contact with any of the older middle school boys at her school, the seventh and eighth graders, was upsetting. What secrets were they hiding, what perversions? She said, "Innocence and goodness were lies."

We used to trust Christopher around our children unconditionally. We thought we knew everything we needed to know about him. We were so trusting of our family that we were negligent. We were blind to the many clues and shielded from many more. We trusted Wendy to raise a child by herself. She didn't want anybody helping her. She didn't want Christopher's creativity stifled. She didn't want anybody's advice. She failed miserably. Psychopaths are born the way they are many psychologists have said. Christopher was warped by his mother; Wendy should be blamed for the making of a psycho. If Chris was the way he was from birth, there was no curing him. From Ches's and Patty's experiences as children, Wendy learned to take solace in the fact that monsters were common.

In Boy Scout summer camps, like those I attended with Pete, they teach a lesson to children about families. The campers are asked to head to the woods to find two straight sticks about a foot long and about a half-inch thick. After the sticks are gathered and brought to the circle, the leader asks the children and adults to break one of their sticks. Everyone can easily break a stick. The remaining sticks are gathered together from each person and tied in a bundle. The campers are asked to come forward and try to break the bundle of sticks. No one can break it. The leader holds up a single stick and says, "This stick is you." He then holds up the bundle, "And this is your family." At one time, that was a profound lesson: stick with the family and you can't be broken. The lesson wasn't so profound anymore. Too many sticks in our family bundle had sharp, twisted, and malformed edges, with mold and disease, with crawly things slithering out.

June 2003 seemed unseasonably cool. Prescott is in the Bradshaw Mountains and there, the high desert flora gives way to the pine forests at 6,000 to 7,000 feet. Downtown Prescott is at 5,000 feet. One year in early June, we saw a few snowflakes fall high in the mountains. Usually by late June, you can feel the heat coming out of the valley. Prescott is eighteen degrees cooler on average than Phoenix; when Phoenix touts 118 degrees, Prescott may hit 100. But the old-timers in Prescott warned us not to plant tomatoes before June first. Maybe it was the loss of family insulation that made it seem so cold that summer. Family trust lay dead at our feet while the cold winds of chicanery chilled us to the bone.

Were we ready to say goodbye to all of that family history? Could it be salvaged? The answer to that depended on one person. That one person was Wendy who had caused most of the turmoil in the family by being such a grouch, by first conspiring with Ches in the cover-up, and then concocting the pantry scene to blackmail and derail Hedy. There seemed little hope of compromise and rescuing this family if we were relying on Wendy to confess her evil deeds. Wendy was either a psychopath or a sociopath with psychopathic tendencies.

A looming war in Iraq dominated the news that month, as did stories of priests and pastors molesting children, which are crimes covered up by all the churches. That news had been around for years but I usually tuned it out. That year, I tuned in and not only listened to stories that came along but I also pursued them. Nothing chills you like a good religious leader-child-molestation story. Sandy had dropped away from news viewing, as she was seeking out help at a spiritual center in town and they told her to block out the news. Sandy found a Buddhist store in downtown Prescott, right around the corner from Whiskey Row on Montezuma Street. She brought home a few things to set up an altar in our bedroom as she strove to get her good sleep patterns back.

In mid-June, Patty came by bus to Prescott for a church camp. I drove Sandy to the retreat and left her in the pines with her sister. Pat told Sandy she was under a lot of pressure from the PACT to stay away from us. Pat said the PACT was saying: "Sandy and Mike wouldn't divorce the family. You can't divorce your family. They will buckle under sooner or later." Sandy and Pat talked for three hours. Pat had the look of a beat-up warrior; thirty years of anti-depression medication can do that.

Pat was a talented classical pianist. She received a BA degree from the University of Arizona in Tucson at age forty-five after three decades of ups and downs, setbacks, and fighting through the little steps that it sometimes takes to move ahead. She played Rachmaninoff and gave me the chills with her great depth of feeling. Mention the word savant and it still brings me images of Pat at the piano. Pat taught us to say *Shos-ta-ko-vich* when we cussed: "It sounds like cussing but it's not vulgar at all," she said. She wasn't the worst joke teller: "What do you call a guy who hangs out with musicians? A drummer." Her good qualities aside, Pat was damaged, stuck in a prison of her mind. No one denied that Pat's piano talent was on a high level but her emotional level was in shambles all the years I knew her. Her struggles with mental illness might have been caused by any number of things. Ches said Pat's troubles started in junior high, a vulnerable age.

Over the years, we could be awakened by a phone call in the middle of the night to find Pat cursing at us or screaming uncontrollably on the other end of the line about a psychic boogeyman that was tormenting her. Sixty miles away or thirteen hundred miles away, she called when the notion struck her. We couldn't help her. There was no rhyme or reason to her lashing out. Sandy could usually calm her down. Pat spent stretches of time at the mental hospital in Phoenix. When Pat and Wendy had their battles, I stayed out of it, but often, Sandy supported Pat, something Wendy never forgot. Pat had a legitimate gripe about Wendy's child-rearing that no one else was brave enough to address.

In her twenties, Pat fought to keep herself off of medications. The doctors fought just as hard to keep her on them. Ches, like many in her generation, took pride in her ability to follow the direction of doctors, of authority figures. Ches listened to doctors and followed their directions never doubting their intentions and never questioning they might be wrong. Pat, being the artist she was, could think of plenty of reasons not to take those medications and intuitively rebelled against these potent pills. There was much uncertainty and experimentation in the 1960s and 1970s dealing with these drugs.

Ches denied that Pat's molestation at age five could have been responsible for Pat's mental ailments because to admit that, Ches felt she would be betraying her sister Neva, mother of the perpetrator. Ches had promised Neva that everything was fine. Harry and Neva were honest and forthcoming about the hurt their son had inflicted. Ches was determined to leave that incident in the past. Ches believed she could snap her fingers and make everyone move on. Ches's mother, Sylvia, embraced that same it-never-happened theory. Ches was not honest with Sandy and the other children about Pat's assault nor was she honest about her own rape. If Ches would have said one thing that she learned from experience, that some teenage boys cannot be trusted around children, she would have saved worlds.

Ches liked to tell the stories she'd heard from her mother about the American Doughboys in France in WWI charging the German machine guns again and again and getting mowed down KIA 500 per day and thousands wounded. For weeks, it went on. Eventually, the Doughboys pushed the Kaiser's forces back but not before a half-million were killed or wounded. "You do what you have to do—you go on," Ches would say. That story sounded like slaughter. It's what abandoning diplomacy looks like. It's what rape inside that family, Ches's family, looked like. What happened to little Patty was not a big deal to Ches, not something you should dwell on. Children get hurt and then you move on; that's the way life is. You pick yourself up, dust yourself off, and start all over again. Get back in the race, pauper, for crying out loud. A little before midnight, Sandy phoned for me to come get her.

Hedy was working a lot and trying to spend time with her band practicing. I heard them when they came out to practice at our garage in previous years, Hedy singing the lyrics in rapid-fire. Hedy wrote a few songs then; the drummer wrote some of their songs. I don't remember his name. He was a heavy guy with a crop of curly blond hair. I wish I had sat down outside of the garage and listened to them, listened to her sing. One of my regrets. We should've got rid of the pool table we had in a corner, let them have more space, put a wood heater in the center, and made it into a year-round hangout. Prescott was the most conservative city in Arizona, yet a number of rock bands bloomed there.

In June, I went to a stress test for my heart at the Mayo Clinic in Scottsdale. After postponing an open-heart operation for seven years, the time had come to do something. The good news was the doctors at the Mayo Clinic in Scottsdale thought a *repair* could be made on the mitral valve without resorting to a replacement.

Hedy broke up with her boyfriend Chuck and she wasn't seeing anybody else. Peter and Hedy avoided each other that summer. He went back to Flagstaff for summer school. He was on scholarships that paid for most of his college expenses. Hedy could have gotten any number of music departments to take her on scholarship for her viola-playing and voice but she didn't pursue that. She was pulled toward the sound of punk rock, not Uncle Bach.

Soon after Patty's visit, Sandy wrote a letter to her brother Tim. It was a plea to Tim to wake up to the truth and ask him to stop being such a tool for Wendy and to stop being so heartless toward Hedy. She told him that Christopher was not some long-lost prophet from the Bible and God wasn't going to knock Christopher off his horse, nor was God going to change his name. She told Tim that Ches was being unreasonable and Sandy hoped he would stand for the truth. Sandy told him we were in therapy, trying to cope. Tim sent this return letter:

Dear Sandy,

I'm glad you finally again wrote. Most of what you are saying is what the psychologists would say, but most of what they say is based on a religion called Humanism. Humanism is the worship of man. In this religion, man worships his own ideas. These ideas are things they think are their own. As he is worshipping his ideas, he comes up with the idea that he is God. He thinks he is God but doesn't even know that his ideas were put there by Satan. Like in Isaiah 14:14, Satan says, "I am like the most high. I will ascend to the throne of God." In other words, I will take over God's authority. Satan doesn't realize he is deceived, not giving thanks to God, who created him, and that he will never rule over the universe.

So, for the most part, the psychologist, being deceived, can only make money in the world by deceiving others as they print their untruths.

Only the ones who can discern truth are the ones that are not deceived. They are the ones who are on the track to begin to know God's word.

The unbelievers are in a state that they cannot analyze anything and their unregenerate readers cannot analyze according to the truth. You are judging others because you cannot see your own sin. You are forgetting the sinful relations of your youth and the sin of not receiving Christ 20 years ago. If you had received Him, you would have received the wisdom of God in how to protect your child to some degree. At this time, your children are old enough to know that they are also sinners and must receive Christ and so miss going to hell when they die. Repenting and turning to Christ is the only way to miss hell at death and start having real victory in your lives now.

Stating that others knew something of Christopher or others does not make you or others innocent. The only hope for you and for your family is Christ for real life as long as you live and forever. Justifying the continued judgment of others will only reap the judgment of God on you in which He allows demons to torment you and so speed up your death. Everybody will be judged "according to the things they have done" so that is up to God, not man's wisdom.

An example of the stupidity of man is to say that rape is a crime of power but not connecting the sin with the correct remedy. Boys would not have perverted themselves in the peak of rape if the producers of pornography had been cut out. Sure, the rapist should be punished, but the adult making money on porn should be stopped, to stop the plague. Congressmen have swallowed the lie, the half-truth, poured out by the psychologist and will not cut off the Internet porn, in the name of speech freedom.

I love you but I feel that it is the responsible thing to tell the eternal truth and not beat around the bush.

Love, Tim

I didn't know what a humanist was. I never heard of anybody who thought it was a religion. If it was a religion, it sounded good. Dear Mr. Brain Damaged, Mr. Judge Mental, Mr. Holier Dan, Dearest Jesus Dude, who is no longer part of my family, thanks for recommending humanism to me. I wrote a scathing letter that I never sent. I threw it away, and glad I did because it gave me time to cool off. I would have regretted sending it, knowing Tim would wear out that letter, pondering all of the names I called him and the harsh words I used to poke at his soul. He would continue to refer me of the devil's stock no matter what I did or said, but with such a letter, he would have a document to wave in people's faces, like Wendy's hate letter we were wearing out.

Sandy's sister, Kitty, had married a Mormon in the mid-seventies (his great grandfather was one of the murderers at the Mountain Meadows Massacre) and Sandy had married me, a former Catholic, and these were two of the three religions (along with Islam) that irked Tim's Christian sensibilities. Ches told her daughters that they could marry anyone they wanted to but please don't marry a Mormon or a Catholic. Be careful what you wish for. Sandy and Kitty married a Catholic and a Mormon respectively. The evil stock he mentions in his letter was referring to my upbringing in Catholicism. Tim had raised the ire of Kitty's husband a number of times denouncing the LDS church as being beyond evil, and he did it to Craig's face. Over the years, Sandy and I had gone a few times to Tim's church with him. I don't remember Tim's pastors preaching hate and malevolence against other churches and religions. Where Tim latched on to his beliefs, I don't know. Tim's reading sources were a few well-worn lay Christian books and the Bible. Like Ches, Tim was a selective listener. He expected us to unconditionally forgive Christopher. Our point: What was there to forgive if Christopher never admitted he did this crime? Christopher had recanted all that he confessed to. At least, Wendy told Ches he had. Like Laura Davis pointed out: Forgiveness without accountability has no teeth. An innocent man wants to prove his innocence.

CHAPTER 9

Sandy had her summers off and settled into activities to build up her strength, mentally and physically, for the grueling ten-month teaching schedule. Over the years, Wendy belittled Sandy's teaching job; she made comments like, "You've got it so easy being a teacher. I wish I could get off anytime I wanted. Teachers have the easiest job in the world. It's unfair." Wendy never experienced teaching. She had to have an idea how strenuous it can be, since her one student, Christopher, had worn her out. I was a teacher for four years and knew it was like having thirty-six kids in ill moods in the same small room at the same time. Wendy would have drunk a gallon of Kahlua per day. Wendy was a nurse and looked on other professions as beckoning green fields. In the late 1980's she proclaimed, "Nursing is the most stressful job in the entire universe! If I had my choice to do over, I'd be a teacher and have a cushy job, too." Most teachers are working 24/7 during those ten months they are under contract to teach, thinking about classes, taking notes, researching, rearranging, going, making things, preparing, always working, solving problems, mitigating, scouting, expanding, and improving. Teachers need the two-month break they get. Then, most of them spend time at the universities in the summer, advancing and researching for the year ahead and don't take much of a break at all. Arizona school districts over the previous decades moved back the starting dates for the school year to the first week in August and pushed the ending of the school year to June—a whole month eliminated from summer break. Sandy kept herself busy volunteering, cleaning the house and yard, practicing, playing music with the Old Time Fiddlers, having lunches with teacher buddies, and hiking in the mountains. My job at the cabinet shop was four ten-hour days and so, most of my Fridays were off, making it easier for us to take short road trips in the summer and for me to get maintenance projects completed.

Wendy and Bob did not contact us. Christopher never came back to town, at least not in the light of day. We didn't hear from Ches in May, June, or July.

I started reading a book that Sandy had just finished: *The Tibetan Book of the Living and Dying*. In it was the story of the warrior king, Gesar, celebrated in song and literature as one who "could never be put down." For years, starting from the time of Gesar's birth, an evil uncle, Trofung, tried to kill Gesar, but the child survived each encounter. The attacks made Gesar stronger. The lesson: If Trofung had not been so malicious and scheming, Gesar could have never risen so high. It was a lesson that Hedy embraced when we first told her the story. Hedy recalled Wendy making snide remarks over the years. Wendy did this when the two were alone together in a room. For instance, when Hedy graduated high school, she made the comment to Wendy, "I've made it through high school and I'm still a virgin." Wendy leaned close to Hedy and whispered, "I know you're not." Then she smirked at Hedy until Hedy got the point. Hedy said she felt she'd been stabbed in the face. Hedy got up and left the room, feeling the eyes of Wendy burning on her.

Our water well went dry in June. When we bought the place in 1992, the father-son team that came out to inspect the well said our well was the best well in Yavapai County. Ten years later, all the wells in the Williamson Valley area were dry or going dry. 2,500 of them had gone dry in and around Prescott. A golf course and a couple of sub-divisions drilled twelve-hundred feet deep wells a mile north of our place. Those wells undercut the higher aquifers on which everyone else depended. I was told that the water was glacier water and it didn't replace itself during the yearly monsoons. Our original well, drilled in the 1960s, was two hundred feet deep, the deepest at the time. With the new one, we had to go down to 420 feet, which was as deep as a six-inch bore could go. The well digger said the next well would cost triple that price as it would require an eight-inch bore. Another golf course was planned.

That June, my sister Madonna called and said that she was being treated for pancreatic cancer. Sandy, Pete and I drove over to Mission Viejo, south of Los Angeles, the next weekend. Two sisters, Marlys, from Iowa, and Arlene, who lived in Oceanside, met us at Newport Beach near Mission Viejo. Our trip to the beach was memorable partly because the seagulls dropped poop bombs on Donna and me. "Not a good omen," Donna said.

In the first days in August, the week before public school started, we drove over to Pasadena where Hedy tried out for "American Idol" at the Rose Bowl. The television show, hosted by Brian Seacrest, was one that Sandy and Hedy watched together during the first seasons. I tuned in for laughs when the bad singers were being weeded out. Hedy had been writing songs and singing with her band. In her senior year, her Prescott High classmates voted her as most musical female. She was determined to drive across the desert in her old vehicle to try out, but we offered to take a road trip with her. As we rolled across the desert, Hedy practiced her songs, "The Son of a Preacher Man" and "A Town with No Pity." She was in high form. When we got in line at two AM in Pasadena that Saturday morning, two thousand other hopefuls were ahead of us and fifteen thousand would follow by sunrise. We took turns in line under the lights, going back to the car to catch naps.

I had a conversation with a tall security guard who reminded me of both Christopher and his father, Richard Johnson. I had met Richard at Canyon del Oro high school when I was fourteen and he was thirteen. My parents retired from farming in Iowa in 1967, moving to Tucson in the middle of January. My sister Sharon was a junior; I was a freshman. My parents were in their forties when they had us. On my first day at the school, I got in the lunch line behind a group of ten boys who invited me to join them at their table. They were the Chess, Science, Math Club, guys with pencil holders, braces on their teeth, and slide rules at their belts like swords. After finding a table, we were surrounded by a group of eighth-grade bullies who reached into the plates to take what food they wanted. The nerds were okay with it. But when one reached into my plate, I twisted his arm and pushed him away; I stood up and threatened the gang; they backed away. Moments later, one of them hit me in the back of the head with an aluminum crutch. I chased the gang out of the cafeteria, down the stairs, and out onto a soccer field. They were having a hoot. They taunted me as I stood with my foot in the door, daring me to chase them; they would have beaten me to a pulp. An aggressive blonde-haired boy squawked like a chicken, daring me to chase him. That boy was Richard, Christopher's father. Christopher grew up to look like his father, only taller. It's hard to comprehend that that blonde boy, who yelled hateful obscenities at me from within the safety of his gang of bullies, would one day marry my wife's sister, and they would have a son and that son, when he was a fourteen-year-old teenager, would rape my six-year-old daughter, and when my daughter came forward with the truth about the rape, the thirty-year-old son of that bully would flee town in the dead of night and the jezebel mother of the rapist would preach false witness against my daughter.

  When Richard married Wendy in 1972, Wendy had just turned eighteen and Richard was nineteen. Three months before the wedding, Wendy graduated from high school and took a job at Yellowstone Park in Wyoming. After she lost her job, she said that she slept in the meadows and survived on twigs and leaves. She came back to Tucson in mid-August and startled everyone when she announced that she and Richard were getting married. She looked skinnier than normal, but at the same time under her flowered green, wedding dress, her belly protruded slightly. She said the bump was caused by malnutrition from her twig-eating and the near-starvation she endured through the summer. And no one questioned her. For the honeymoon, they drove up to the White Mountains where Christopher was born three days later in the hospital in Show Low. He was two months premature. Tom and Ches, dismayed but happy about having a grandchild, came over to our apartment to tell us the news. Tom and Ches wanted everyone they knew to be as stunned and happy as they were. We, too, delighted in the story of Wendy's miraculous motherhood. We got to hold baby Christopher a few days later. He was a thirty-week preemie. Researchers have found that the brains of babies thirty weeks or less have a higher percentage of brain damage than those thirty-one weeks to full term at thirty-nine weeks. 1972 was five decades ago; the medical improvements for the care of premature babies have advanced exponentially. Christopher, in the hospital for two days, was not treated any different than full-term babies. He had learning difficulties in school his entire life. His father Richard tried to get Christopher into special education classes but Wendy would not let that happen. She was thinking about herself and Christopher's creativity.

Soon after the honeymoon, Wendy told the story of her tryst with Richard to Ches who relayed it to us years later: A few nights a week during the previous winter, Wendy, a high school senior, would sneak out of her bedroom window a couple of nights a week and ride her bicycle to Richard's house just off Orange Grove Road. There, Richard waited at his bedroom window with his long blonde hair for his highway girl. They spent a few hours entwined before she rode home again. Quite a senior paper she could have written. The consequence of that year of secrecy was Christopher.

Sandy and I lived in Tucson for the first two years when Christopher was growing up, so we saw him and Wendy often, especially after Wendy and Richard split up. Christopher was one determined baby boy. He was walking at ten months, talking and running towards the street at one year old. He was in love with the world and the wonder of it all. He seemed to be a happy boy, though spoiled by his family, and stubborn as a mule.

A few months after we were married, I commuted forty-five miles to work at the Magma Copper Company underground mine at San Manuel. The mine had a schedule of seven days on and one day off which lasted for six weeks followed by a four-day weekend. Sandy worked as a receptionist at a printing company. We saved money while Wendy struggled to pay rent and feed herself and her little boy as Richard paid no child support for years. Wendy and Christopher lived with her parents or her boyfriends. Sandy and I lived in a small apartment at the back of a house on Balboa Street. We could see Miracle Mile cemetery from our yard. The apartment had a kitchen, a bedroom, and a bathroom but was not big enough for an extra adult with a child or Wendy would have gladly moved in. My sister Sharon and Wendy tried once to share an apartment when their boys were two years old, but that experiment lasted only a few weeks because of the disputes caused mostly by a grouchy Wendy demanding she her way and holding her breath a lot. It was Sharon's apartment and Sharon took it back.

(Pasadena 2003) The American Idol line started moving at nine o'clock in the morning. We were seated in the middle looking down on the stage. The MC, Mr. Seacrest, gave a pep talk that lasted about twenty minutes. Then, he roamed far and wide with his microphone. As we burnt in the sun, he talked about what fun we were all having. He'd give a whoop, "Ain't this fun!" "Yes!" everyone was supposed to yell; quite a few did. He stopped near us. We could have touched him. Hedy got a big, broad smile on her face and as she leaned toward us, she sighed and held her breath. Seacrest kept moving through the crowd. Then, it was time for Hedy to line up for the auditions at the tables under the judges' awnings with the judges located around the front of the stadium. Most of the judges were younger than Hedy. The oldest a contestant could be was twenty-eight years old, and the youngest sixteen; Hedy was twenty-two. A judge listened to Hedy for thirty seconds and said, "Thank you for coming. Goodbye." And that was it. If you were bad enough, a really horrid singer, producing laughs for the show, you had a better chance than someone who could really sing. Just bellow loudly like an off-key goat and you'd get a spot on the show in January. Then, you could stun the judges with your real voice and have at least a chance to show what you had in the second round. We didn't think of that approach until we were walking out. Hedy had a four-octave range, a one in ten thousand voice and it was a shame they missed it. At that coliseum, what we witnessed was the softening of vices. It was a time when the deadly sins of gluttony, greed, vanity, and pride were being turned into virtues in our new culture. After a century of change, the deadly sins have become virtuous. Lust, envy, anger, covetousness, and sloth have become virtuous or sources of entertainment in our society. The virtues of platonic philosophy, justice, prudence, temperance, fortitude, and those virtues added later by the early Christian moralists, faith, hope, charity, and love are often held in contempt by our modern spin-doctors. Corporations are doing this to us. Music as an art form is struggling to stay alive. Much of our music is created as a disposable product designed to sell to mass consumers. Corporations and lawyers who use brainwashing techniques to sell their cold music products have manipulated musical tastes. I guess that goes on throughout the world.

 Oh, oops, do I sound like a bitter, protective father? Well, so be it. Call me Pappy Schmo, a father who didn't protect his children. Even if they get hurt through no fault of his own, say like, through a rape and a conspiracy by a wicked aunt and her psychotic son, Pappy stilled failed to protect them. It is still under Pappy's watch that the injury occurred. I found a list of a father's duties: teach, defend, protect, provide for, encourage, and empower. I failed to protect Hedy.

 Pasadena is sixty miles from the beach and we didn't feel like fighting the traffic to go there so we headed back across the desert in the cool of the night. Fifty miles west of Barstow, just after midnight, we came across an accident where a small car had rolled and flipped onto the guardrail. The emergency vehicles were just coming on the scene. Hedy was asleep in the backseat. It made me think of another trip: When Hedy and Peter were small, we drove one summer from Nogales to Kino Bay on the coast of the Sea of Cortez. They used to call that stretch of a two-lane, ditchless highway between Nogales and Hermosillo the Highway of Death. On the way back, we were behind a semi-truck and I was looking for a safe place to pass when we came upon an accident scene. A van and a pickup truck had collided head-on; bodies were being carried from the vehicles and laid on the ground. The semi ahead of us plowed right between the two wrecked vehicles and shoved them aside. We had Hedy and Peter hide their eyes and I drove slowly past the two steaming cars. Citizen flagmen waved bright shirts to move us through. Five miles down the road, a pair of cars from an earlier collision sat off the road like twisted headstones.

Another trip that I already mentioned, we took in January 2002. Hedy called from the high desert city of Bend, Oregon, after spending six months there. She was living in her Shadow in the mountains outside Bend. "Is it alright if I come back to Prescott?" Sandy told her, "Oh, honey, you don't have to ask." Near Sacramento, Hedy's red Shadow caught on fire. With the help of duct tape, she made it to Burbank. While idling at a drive-through at a Taco Bell, the engine caught fire again. Some homeless people in the alley, just settling down for a long winter's nap, ran to Hedy's rescue. Sandy and I got a call about ten o'clock that night from the Western Union in Burbank. On the other end of the line was the young man who said he had rescued Hedy by breaking her windshield with a fire extinguisher and he had helped push the car into the alley. He said, "You need to send money for your daughter. She needs cash, lots of cash. Five hundred would fit right now."

"Well," I said, "Thank you for your help and your concern. I'd like to speak to my daughter, Hedy."

"He wants to speak to his daughter," he said. Background laughter.

Hedy said, "Yeah, the Shadow caught on fire. I don't know if it can be fixed. I'm out of money. But I've made some new friends. They helped me put out the fire and they brought me over here. We're in this small lobby and it's really crowded." More laughter. She sounded like she was high. I realize now that it was her PTSD talking. One of them spoke over Hedy's shoulder to me, "Sir, you don't want your daughter to become homeless. Believe me, it's a downhill spiral, man. She can't live in the Shadow; it's pretty messed up. She needs your help, tonight. Right now. This is your daughter, man. Send it now!" More laughter.

"Hedy, we're coming out there," I said. "Stay by your car." Sandy and I left Prescott before midnight. We arrived at the Burbank Taco Bell mid-morning. Down the alley a half-block, we found the Shadow on the edge of an empty lot. In the front seat, Hedy lay wrapped in a blanket, sleeping. The alley people were gone. We tapped on her window. She had only been gone for six months and she had lost a lot of weight. She was in a good mood. She wanted to save her car if possible. Under the hood, we could see death of a car. The cost of parts and labor would be twice as much as the car was worth. Towing it was no option either. "You look hungry, Hedy. Let's go eat," I said.

At a Harry's Café, Hedy could not focus on the menu. She said she hadn't had a good meal in weeks. "I'm trying," she said. "I just can't make up my mind." She kept getting distracted, looking around the café. We finally called the waitress over to the table; after ten minutes of Hedy shaking her head and rolling her neck from side to side, she eventually ordered three meals. I ordered orange juice and Sandy ordered coffee. Hedy shared the leftovers. Her hesitation in making any decision was what I understood to be depression: someone who had become so dysfunctional, so confused that they are incapable of making simple decisions. Hedy had turned twenty-one years old just the month before. It was twelve months before she would tell us about the rape. But that day, sitting in the booth at that Harry's, I watched Hedy's green eyes light up as the waitress set out the plates of food. I was reminded of a little three-year-old with those same beautiful eyes riding in our van in Tucson when we stopped at a red light and a brisk, desert breeze was flipping the pages of a book lying by the curb. Hedy peeked out the van window, "Look, everyone, the wind is reading that book."

(2003) Hedy had been scheduled to work at the movie theatre Saturday night and when we left town on Friday, she had called in. The message never made it to management. Hedy was fired from the theatre. She was down to the one job—at New Frontiers store. That week, her cousin Nicki came by the store after school and saw Hedy working there. The following Sunday evening, Ches and Tim showed up on our porch.

CHAPTER 10

We started keeping the doors locked after Hedy came forward. In late August, Ches and Tim made a visit to Prescott. They figured they could walk right in like they had done before. Wendy had been the biggest offender, banging our doors open, barging in, usually angry with Sandy, who had the nerve to contradict Wendy every so often. For ten years, we let angry-girl Wendy barge into our house without consequence. We just smiled, as if we were helping an injured bird.

Mother-Dear and Holier Dan seemed stunned to find our doors locked. They yelled on the porch. They rattled the front door. Woody barked from the side yard. Booger went running up the live oak in the front yard. Ches addressed us through the front door with a stern voice, "Let us in! We want to speak to Hedy." Underlying Ches's we-mean-business tone was this message: Hedy has broken generations of the protocol by ratting out the family rapist of the generation. Don't you know you have to live with what the Lord had dished out? I opened the kitchen window an inch or two and said, "Hedy doesn't want to speak to you."

Ches said, "We want to speak to Hedy. We're not here to speak to you. You won't speak to us, Mike. You've made that clear."

"Let me check then." I paused for a moment and said, "Oh, yeah, that's right, now I remember. She doesn't want to speak to you." More seriously, I said, "You need to leave our property. Now, you've been asked nicely, so you need to go away. In two minutes, I'm calling the police."

"We need to end this now!" Ches said. "It has gone on long enough."

"What? Three, four generations of molesting children, raping children. Yeah, I think it has gone on long enough."

"You know what I mean, Mike."

"Goodbye, Ches." I closed the window. They rattled the doors a few times and left. We didn't have a back door. Woody continued to bark until their car disappeared. Hedy came out of her bedroom and asked, "Are they gone?" Sandy and Hedy hugged each other in the hallway.

The next morning at 11:20, Hedy called me at the cabinet shop and said Ches and Tim had shown up at her work, at New Frontiers. She was calling from the back room of the store. Hedy said, "Please don't make a scene." Our shop on Sun Dog Ranch Road on the Yavapai Indian Reservation was only a couple of miles from downtown. I arrived at the store a few minutes later.

I found Ches and Tim in the deli, seated at a table for two. I asked, "What at you doing here?"

"Oh, hi, Mike," said Ches in the sweetest voice she could muster. "Want us to get you a drink?" Tim laughed. He turned his head and would not look at me. Ches said, "We're here to talk to Hedy."

I crouched down to be at eye level with her and said, "Hedy doesn't want to talk to you. She doesn't *have* to talk to you."

"Oh?" said Ches.

"The sooner you admit it, Ches, the better off you'll be. Christopher did this. Please stop playing this game. You can stop it now."

Her voice became even more patronizing. "And what did he do, Mike?"

"You know he raped my daughter when she was six years old."

She lost the sweetness and answered sharply, "That's not true! That's a lie! You have no proof!"

"I held the bloody panties in my hand. That's proof."

"Well, why didn't she say something then?"

"She was trying to protect the family."

"She waited sixteen years! Mike, I don't believe that."

"Well, believe it. The panties were bloody and they were found."

She exhaled and said through her clenched teeth. "Why didn't you do something then?"

"We did. We took her to the doctors all over southern Arizona. You were there. You met us the many times we came to Tucson. You were always there to meet us after those appointments. Remember? I remember."

"Why didn't you confront Christopher then? Why didn't you blame him then? We could have given him a whack then!"

"We never put two and two together."

"You should have!"

"We trusted the family back then. Who would suspect a boy you've known all his life to do such a thing? Christopher never crossed our minds. We didn't know someone had hurt her. He was there the weekend before we found the bloody panties and he never crossed our minds. That's how trusting we were. How stupid we were. We never suspected him."

"You should have suspected him. You should have done something then!"

I looked at this eighty-three-year-old woman; her face had paled like a raw fillet of sole and her eyes were wild. I was surer than I ever had been that she had known of the rape since the day it had happened. She had a reason for insisting to come to meet us in Tucson every time Hedy saw the doctors. She only would meet us in restaurants; she never came to the hospitals with us. In fact, she stayed as far away from Hedy as she could. She was always there to assure us: I started bleeding at age six and look, I turned out to be okay.

I said, "You know what the doctors said: that little girls sometimes hurt themselves on bicycles and trampolines. We never suspected Christopher."

"You should have!" she snarled with a shaky voice. She was saying: *I knew! You should have known!*

I said, "You knew, didn't you? Why didn't you tell us?"

She yelled at me, "I never knew. I never knew that, Mike."

I said, "We think you did. You told Tim before he met with us that you knew something bad had happened. Before we said anything." She didn't answer me. I said, "Hedy doesn't want to talk to you. She doesn't have to talk to you."

She made an attempt at being pleasant again. "Oh?" She paused and spoke again with sweetness. "Mike, you don't realize how much this is hurting Christopher. As you know, he has mental problems; he's really down about this. He's depressed. You're killing him with these accusations. He's suffering so."

I said, "Well, why doesn't he step forward and come talk to us?"

"He's afraid we're going to try to kill him!" she blurted.

"We want him to talk to us. That would be the best therapy for him—to confess what he did. And be contrite."

"He didn't do it! It's all lies!" she shouted.

I said, "In fifteen seconds, I'm calling the police and you'll be removed."

She showed her fangs and shouted, "Go ahead and call the police."

I put my hands in the air and went back to find Hedy. A girl named Tiffany escorted me to the back. The store's manager and his assistant were there also. "They won't leave," I told Hedy. The managers departed in a hurry for the front of the store. Hedy held me back for five minutes.

Hedy was in anguish. "Oh, don't make a scene, please, Dad."

"I'm trying not to. Grandma's hysterical."

"God, what does she want from me?"

"She wants you to recant."

"Christopher confessed. Why won't she believe me?"

"They say that he's recanted everything he said. Grandma knows the truth. She just doesn't want to say it or hear it. It's too hard for her."

"Please, don't make a scene."

I headed to the front of the store. Ches and Tim, along with the manager, were standing just outside the front doors. A policeman was approaching from his patrol car parked at the curb. The manager said something to the officer and came back inside just as I stepped out.

"Hello," I said to the officer, "my daughter works at this store and she is being harassed by these two people."

Ches said, "She's my granddaughter. I just want to talk to her."

"This is my mother-in-law and my brother-in-law; they won't leave my daughter alone. You see, my daughter was raped when she was six years old by a cousin and grandma wants my daughter to believe it never happened."

"It's all lies! It's all a story they made up."

"It's documented," I said. "We filed a police report with the Nogales Police department. It happened in Nogales sixteen years ago. You can check it out."

"Sixteen years ago and it's all lies!" Ches shouted.

"My daughter doesn't want to talk to them," I said.

"Because she's been brainwashed by her parents!"

"She's free to talk to anyone she wants," I said.

The officer spoke, "Ma'am, listen to me—"

"She's ruining our lovely little family. She's torn the family apart. I can't write. This man sends my letters back. I can't call. I went to their house last night and they wouldn't let me talk to her. They chased us away. I just want to see my granddaughter who I love."

I said, "But who you won't support." Ches gasped. The policeman frowned at me and I made the gesture of zipping the mouth.

"She's tearing the family apart. I just want to talk to my granddaughter."

"Okay, listen, Ma'am, stop talking," said the officer.

"But I just want to—"

"Ma'am, listen! I'm going to go in and talk to your granddaughter and hear what she has to say. I'll be back in a few minutes. Stay calm." He went inside.

Ches scolded me, "You and Hedy are killing Sandy."

"Sandy is as strong as ever."

"You and Hedy are killing Sandy."

"Sandy has found some spiritual help and it's made her stronger. Sandy's going to be alright."

"She doesn't look alright. She looks fifteen years older than she did the last time I saw her. She looks haggard."

"Of course, this is stressful, but she's stronger than you can imagine." Then I asked her, "Ches, something like this happened to you when you were six, didn't it?"

"Yes," she said, "but it wasn't near as bad as this."

"Could you tell me the name of the cousin who molested you?"

"It's none of your business!"

"It is my business. It's my family, too. Was it Harrison or Merle or Mac? Or was it cousin Elvin? Elvin was our first guess."

She was taken aback that I knew the names of her cousins. She said, "You don't need to know! It's none of your business!"

Tim spoke for the first time. "Mike, what church are you going to? I mean, I maybe could believe some of this if I knew what church you and Sandy were going to."

I thought: What planet are you from? But I said, "It's none of your business, Tim!" I pointed a finger at Ches. "You're hurting Sandy and Hedy for not supporting them. For not even considering their feelings. You've closed your ears, your eyes, and your heart."

Ches said, "Daddy had to come to the rescue! She's twenty-two years old and daddy had to come to the rescue!"

In 1926, when Ches was molested or raped or roughed up or held down or used as a sperm rag, her family came to the rescue all right. They came to the rescue of the reputation of the boy who hurt Ches and damn that little girl. They made sure the incident was swept under the rug. For family's sake, for Christ's sake. They may have told Ches: "Things like this happen all the time in the lives of children, especially in this family. You, Ches, are not unique, so forget it and let's all move on." The man who molested Ches had to be a blood relative to Ches's mother, Sylvia, because by then, the Dillinger family was out of the picture. After William Dillinger left, Sylvia stayed in close proximity with her family. This comment about daddy coming to the rescue was something that had haunted Ches her whole life. Ches never had a father to rescue her. Was she perturbed that Hedy had a father? William Dillinger left his family when Ches was only five months old. Sylvia struggled in poverty to raise the four children and depended on her family for every kind of support. She couldn't break from the family over this. "Suck it up and get over this setback or go it alone and perish." It was the classic lesson of the one stick and the bundle of sticks and Sylvia didn't want to become a lone stick with four little sticks depending on her. That was the bond that Wendy, Ches, and Christopher shared. For years, Wendy was a struggling single mother like Ches' beloved Sylvia. Christopher never had a real father, just a string of one-night-stand fathers. Christopher had rejected Bob as his father from day one.

The policeman came out of the store and addressed Ches, "It's like this, Ma'am: Your granddaughter is over eighteen. She doesn't have to talk to you; I'm going to—"

"This so-called father has brainwashed her against me!"

"Ma'am, I'm going to have to ask you to—"

"I just want to talk to my granddaughter."

"Ma'am, I'm going to—"

"This so-called man who calls himself her father."

"Ma'am. Will you be quiet and let me talk? Ma'am, I'm asking you to leave these premises. This is a warning. You are not allowed back in this store. If you come back, you will be arrested for criminal trespassing. Do you understand?"

"It's not right. She's tearing the family apart."

In the back of the store, I said goodbye to Hedy. The manager was breathing heavily and pacing around in circles behind us like he was ready to punch a fifty-pound bag of something. Hedy received hugs from the female employees who came back to offer their support. When I got to the front of the store, a second patrol car pulled up, blocking my vehicle. The two officers were standing by their cars when I approached. I mentioned to them the name of the Prescott detective who knew our case and told them I had to get back to work. I had to wait for them to move. In the Burger King parking lot, I saw Tim helping his mother back to their car. Their grey heads moved above the sea of cars like old soccer balls adrift in the waves. They looked small and weak and wounded. I felt sick.

CHAPTER 11

In late September, we went to Tucson. From the moment Hedy told us of the rape, we were certain that Wendy knew about it the morning after it happened. Ches knew from the beginning as well. Ches and Wendy had their first chance to talk face to face about twelve hours after it happened when Bob and Wendy stopped in Tucson. We had not pressured Ches about her role in the cover-up and Sandy wanted to do that.

When we first arrived at their house in northwest Tucson, we shared a few moments of civility with Ches and Tim. We talked about the violence in Iraq spiraling out of control, about Phoenix hitting 110 degrees that week, about fires throughout the west. When I mentioned to Ches that Hedy lost her job at New Frontiers because of the scene they made, Ches and Tim cheered. "I'm glad she lost her job!" Ches snapped with clenched teeth. That marked the end of our civilized chat. Ches added with a smirk, "You know, it puzzles me why you two are making such a big deal out of something you say happened so many years ago. Sooner or later, Hedy would have had to learn about sex anyway." Tim laughed.

"What? Six years old, mother. She was six years old. That's just sick. Are you kidding? You're a sick woman." Ches was smiling. Sandy hesitated, then said, "You *knew* back in 1987 that Chris raped Hedy, didn't you, Mom? Right after it happened. Wendy told you back then. She told you that day. She took you aside when she came to visit you in Tucson, didn't she? So Bob and Tim couldn't hear you."

Ches said, "I didn't know about any rape."

"But you knew she was attacked. That she was molested."

"I don't know anything about any rape."

"You knew about the blood we found." Sandy took a piece of paper from her pocket and unfolded it. She read from a list we'd compiled, innuendos, and loaded remarks Ches had said over the years. "You told me when we were moving to Prescott that we would be making a big mistake. You said and I quote: 'You might open a can of worms if you go up there.' What did you mean by that?"

"Auk, I didn't say that."

"Yes, you did, mother. Why would you say that? Last year, when I told you I was going to counseling with Wendy, you said, 'Oh, be careful. You might open Pandora's box!' Mother, what other secrets are in Pandora's box?"

Ches said, "I don't remember saying those things."

"And, Mom, you said, and I quote you again: 'You're not going to like living so close to Wendy, I guarantee it.' Why did you say that?"

"Auk, I don't remember saying those things," Ches said. "I didn't say those things. You're putting words into my mouth."

"We had Christmas at Patty's apartment one year and Patty said, 'I bet if Christopher were here, he'd molest Hedy and Peter.' And you quickly escorted Patty out of the room, told her to stop staying things against Christopher. What was that about? No one would ever explain that to us. It didn't concern us, you said. It was six months after he raped Hedy! You hid things from us. Didn't it concern the parents of little children that a pedophile was loose in the family? We were mushrooms to you and you fed us shit."

"Stop this, Sandy!"

"Why did Wendy lock herself in her bedroom for two weeks in Prescott? You knew what was happening. Bob said he called you. It had something to do with Christopher. He had just come back from Utah then—what was that all about? He was gone for months. Did he rape somebody in Utah? In Idaho?"

"Auk, I don't remember that. You're making things up. I didn't know anything about anything sixteen years ago. Why are you asking me these questions?"

"The truth is important to us. It should be important to you. You hid everything from us. You knew about it from the start. Those times, you were spying on us for Wendy—when we brought Hedy to the doctors in Tucson. For weeks, you and Wendy called us after we discovered the bloody panties. The two of you called us like clockwork, like teamwork. Do you remember that? And we thought you were concerned for us, for Hedy. But no. You knew something sinister had happened, didn't you, mother? You and Wendy conspired against us."

"I don't believe that. I'll never believe that Wendy knew this happened."

"Are you kidding me? It's out, we know. We know both of you worked together. You can stop lying to us. Or are you afraid you'll go to jail for aiding and abetting a rapist and his criminal mother? It was just a big act, a big production, every time we got together. You and Wendy putting on the show!"

"Sandy, you're being absurd."

"Hedy is telling the truth and you can't change the truth."

"No, it's not the truth, she's lying. You won't consider that Christopher is telling the truth. I won't believe that he did this."

"It was rape, mother, not just molestation. There was no fooling around. She was six years old, for Christ's sake. He was out of control. A monster."

Sandy stood up, looked around the house, and said, "You know, these pictures I gave you of our family, I'm taking them back. I don't want you to have them." She swept across the living room gathering up the many family portraits we'd given Ches over the years.

Ches stayed seated but shouted, "Those are my pictures, you gave them to me! You can't take those."

"I've changed my mind. I don't want you to have them. You don't care one iota about our family. I'm an invisible daughter. You don't give a crap about my family." Tim rose up and tried to stop Sandy but by then, she had cleaned the shelves. "My whole family is invisible to you! Hedy is invisible! Pete is invisible! You can't think of Hedy without getting angry with her for telling the truth! All you see is poor Christopher. Poor baby Wendy. What hard lives they've had. Everybody has tough times. What kind of a mother are you? You're a sick mother, that's what you are. You hid this crime. You made Hedy suffer alone all those years. I don't want you to be my mother anymore. Who are you? Where am I from?"

"Sandy, don't be like this. You know I care for you."

"Well, I don't believe you. You sure don't show it. You're a dangerous, angry, old woman. I don't want my family to be around you. You're poison. Stay away from my family. Don't come to our house. Don't call me. Stay away from our work. Stay out of our lives. Stay here and wallow in your hate."

We opened the door to leave and Tim said, "In Isaiah 4:24, it says respect your parents for they are the true gift from high."

"Shut up, Timmy," Sandy said.

We drove away from their house determined not to talk about it all. But we only made it to Ina Road. We had been obsessed for seven months, thinking and discussing it, reading about, and constantly looking for clues, trying to pry open the heaviness of the cover-up. It was like working on a fifty-thousand-piece jig-saw puzzle and family members had swiped handfuls of the pieces and pitched them down a rat and cockroach-infested mineshaft. There was no way the puzzle was ever going to be complete.

Once the daughter of a geologist, always the daughter of a geologist. Tom worked as a mucker in a Texan mine in 1939, before the war. After the war, he rode the GI Bill to get his career started and became one of the top rock hounds in the Southwest. After walking in his shadow for years, Ches knew where all the old mineshafts were. She's been to the brink of them all. She'd drunk the air at the rim of the precipice. The puzzle would always have pieces missing.

Johnny Cash passed away from complications from diabetes that fall, four months after his wife, June Carter, passed away from the complications from heart surgery. Because our insurance company vetoed our plans to use the Mayo Clinic in Scottsdale, I was forced to go bargain shopping for a heart surgery package. Finally, we found a heart surgeon, Dr. Tibi, an associate with Good Samaritan Hospital in Phoenix. The surgery was set for mid-December.

In his 1987 book *Assault on Truth*, Jeffery Masson told a story about how a young Sigmund Freud in the late 1800s was asked by wealthy families in Germany "to help cure" certain female family members who suffered from panic attacks, depression, and other maladies. Freud had achieved some success with an approach he called cognitive psychoanalysis where he encouraged his patients to talk openly about their problems. When these women came to see him and sat down to talk, Freud was not prepared for what he discovered. Neither were the families of these women. In case after case, the women in their twenties, thirties, forties, and fifties told story after story of being molested as young children and teenagers by the men in their lives: uncles, fathers, brothers, grandfathers, cousins, family friends. The simple act of telling their stories to caring and trustworthy listeners was helping these women. Freud concluded that the suppression of the truth had caused harm to these women's psyches. These ailments then morphed into physical complaints. Getting their stories out was of great value to these women and they began to regain their health right before his eyes. At first, Freud was excited about the implications. The women were also sparked. If telling one person made them feel so good, then telling many should make them feel even better. That's what they did. They formed groups and talked to each other. The perpetrators, the men, the wealthy men, ascended on Freud to set him straight, to shut down all this talking for crying out loud. Freud, because he liked being funded by those wealthy donors, capitulated. To the shock of the women, he announced to the world that the stories being told by these women were illusions, mere fictional fantasies created by aroused imaginations because of some minor slights in their past.

Critics of Masson's book were many and brutal in scope. The critics accused Masson of sensationalizing and leading his readers toward lynch mob outrage at Freud's betrayal. These critics appeared to be too schooled, too organized in their defense of Freud to *not* be a conspiracy to protect him. When you're a prophet, no one has the right to criticize you, so say the disciples who stand sword-ready to defend their champion decades after he's passed. Maybe these critics were bought off, maybe not, but the truth remains: rape and molestation are betrayals on one level but the cover-up and spin that Freud did were in many ways worse than the original attacks. Those women trusted him and he let them down. But they were women and women carry on, however they must, usually by helping each other through each ordeal. Freud's patients could continue without his help because he gave them the tools to do so. These were tools, simple in scope, talking, that the women could utilize in far-reaching ways. I'm sure they thought warmly of Dr. Freud with each step forward they took. *Assault on Truth* was on the best-seller list in March of 1987, the week Hedy was attacked by Christopher.

That fall, Sandy read *Blood of the Prophets* and pointed out more insights. "The murderers spent a lot of time and energy running and hiding from the law not unlike Christopher, Wendy, and Ches." Also, she noted that the murderers in the meadow in 1857 had formed a pact on the killing field as the sun was setting on that first bloody 9/11. Each murderer swore to kill any man present who revealed the truth to anyone about that day, even to their wives. I'm sure Wendy would have silenced Hedy by any means if and when she felt she could get away with it. Christopher wanted that gun to silence the rats.

Sandy received a birthday card in the mail and returned it to Ches unopened. In early October, Sandy sent this letter to Ches:

How can a mom disown a child? When I have that thought about you, I end up forgiving you because knowing that you were told to forgive the cousin that abused you at age six and then you were told to deny the hurt. But, I also know how weak and vulnerable you are as an elderly woman and that you let your baby daughter's charisma hook you on her side. And you have taken sides. Tim also has taken Wendy's side against the truth. This is very typical of most incest cases. Family members take the side of the perpetrator because the truth is too difficult to face.

I am breaking the cycle of denial. When you were a child, sexual abuse was swept under the rug. Rape is a crime against the state, and the state prosecutes it often now. Wendy knew the law would have to be involved and Christopher would be put in prison or at least teenager prison. Not in your generation. Human rights have come a long way since then, baby.

I am a middle child. I can hear your distain and sarcastic thoughts of these analytical statements of mine, but I am writing them to you anyway. Invisibility is a trait of middle children. Stupid me. I should've known that the next step would naturally be abandonment. The one reason this crime happened—the invisible child's child got hurt by the spoiled baby's child. Mom, you trained me well in understanding and helping vulnerable people: Patty, Jolie. I only wish someone would have warned us about Christopher's problems, a 14-year-old that was into pornography. Family secrets. We had two little children and no one told us of Christopher's involvement in porn. Tim knew. You did. Why did no one tell me and Mike? We had two little children at those family gatherings. Was Wendy's embarrassment more important than protecting my kids? The stage was perfectly set for Christopher to do his thing.

I feel I have no foundation of a family. I love both my children so much but have the innate sense to know not to pit one against the other, as you have done. But then again, I never went through sexual abuse as you did and then told to hide the hurt, so I do forgive you.

Why can't you love me and my children as much as Wendy's? What did I do to make you deny me and my children? My heart sometimes feels like it will explode with tears, but I tell myself to be strong. I know that my morals are not crooked like yours. I love you, Mom, but I love myself more. I have to, not just for the children, but for myself. This world is a beautiful place. I've done nothing wrong and I feel I'm making this world a better place. Not just for today, but for all the tomorrows. We all come into this world alone and leave alone. The way we treat people on this earth, in this lifetime, will affect us and the rest of the world, now and forever. Do you think I'm stronger than Wendy? Is that another reason why you took her side? Mom, we never really knew each other. I'm sorry for that. It is too late to get to know you now because I cannot be with you and your cruelty. I love you and forgive you most days, but also know I cannot ever be with you or anyone else who denies the truth of what Christopher did to Hedy. That is so cruel. For you to even think that I could be with you is cruelty on your part. You are an elderly woman who may not realize how cruel you really are being to one of your daughters. Tim is being cruel when he comes to visit and talks about forgiveness. He's not thinking straight because of his head injury and the bible cult he has submitted himself to. Living under the same roof of a head-injured Jesus freak doesn't help you, Mom. Also listening to a half-mentally ill daughter, whose son raped his six-year-old cousin, and who begs you for pity, does not help you either. I understand what you are going through.

I see all three of you floating in your little polluted protective bubbles. Mom, you're hiding from hurt from when you were abused, and you think Hedy should buckle up and do the same thing. I know you loved your mother. You can still love your mother and disagree with her. You can be angry at the things she said to you, such as, "Oh, little Chessy, what happened to you was nothing. You'll get over it. But you can't ruin that boy's life. So just forget and go on. He won't do it again." She probably said something like that to you. Just because you had to bury all the hurt for 80 years, doesn't mean your granddaughter will. No way. Look what it got you—hiding toxic family secrets. And what really happened to Patty? Why didn't you ever tell me about what happened to you and her? It could've set off warning signals to me at all those family gatherings. Was hiding this personal secret so important to you, to let a little granddaughter be sacrificed for your sake? And Wendy and Christopher's sake? For the sake of family secrets? Were we really that invisible to you? You and Tim and Patty knew that Christopher was sick in the head in middle school. Why were we not told?

Tim is hiding in his own little polluted bubble, surviving with quotes from the bible, being fed perverted thoughts from you and Wendy. There's no telling what Wendy is going through. If she hasn't had a nervous breakdown yet, it proves she has no conscience, unless it has to do with eliciting pity for her suffering son. She doesn't give a crap about anybody or anything besides *her* or *hers*. What happened to Wendy to make her so power-hungry? (Rape is a crime of power and control, not sex.) She never could get enough attention for herself or her own children. Maybe it's a trait of being the baby of the family. Maybe that's why you took her side—you have that birth order in common. I doubt if she has a conscience. Anyway, at least all three of you have each other to protect Christopher from the "bad Wallriches." It's always good to have a support group. All I can say is good luck in death. Death happens to all of us. I cannot live people's lives for them. Each individual has to be strong with herself, and you three have chosen strength in hiding the truth. I'm sorry for you all. I'm also sorry for myself—for not getting to know my own mother. She is now probably senile, living with her vulnerable, head-injured, bible-toting son who listens to the perverted thoughts of his church-going sister who is a hateful schemer. It's all so sad.

Yes, I'm in judgment. Yes, I caught myself in an angry moment. I'm writing this letter to make sure you know that although the world's a beautiful place, I also know there is perversion. I would have never thought it would be in my own family. It always happens to someone else. This has torn the family apart. I will never be part of "We've got to stick together!" and "Put it in God's hands." I will put myself in God's hands, outside of this crooked so-called family unit. Jesus said you have to be ready to forsake your family if they forsake the truth.

What is so hard about saying: "I know Christopher did this, please tell us if there is something we can do to help." Instead, you scream, "Prove it!" You are just feeding a sexual predator's dream. That's your choice. We all make choices. Please don't let anyone make up your mind, heart, or soul—especially a crying, pitiful daughter who denies, denies. Of course, Wendy doesn't want to confirm it. Christopher hasn't told us he is innocent. What rapist wouldn't deny it if others gave him the chance? If everyone around him is fighting his battle for him, insulating him from justice and accountability. Well, you have all given him a golden chance. Is he gone crazy yet? Has he found a hiding place in the bible?

I'd like to say: "Ride with the criminals, hang with the criminals," but I think God has taken pity on all of you. I have taken pity on you. I see you as a group of hyenas, nipping at our ankles. I will just pat you on the head and walk away. Please do not attempt to visit any of us. This is another reason for this letter: I'm saying everything that needs to be said. Mom, I know your mantra has not changed: "Prove it!" And Tim, your mantra still is: "You've got to forgive." Mom, we don't have to prove anything to you. We know the truth and you do, too. Besides, I would never even think about putting my daughter through torture anymore, especially for you. And as far as forgiveness, like I keep telling you, "If there is no crime, forgiveness need not happen." But I do forgive you all. I know what weak creatures you all are. God is watching.

Love, Sandy

They never responded to this letter.

The baseball playoffs were on that week; I was pulling for the Cubs, who hadn't won the series since 1908. But the Cubs spent all week blaming a fan—who had touched a foul ball—for the reason they lost three games in a row. I stopped watching. How trivial professional sports seemed at that time. I felt like Ches and her war interrupted. Bill Cooper said that the whole reason for professional sports is to distract the citizenry, so the masters can steal and plunder unquestioned.

Two years earlier, shortly after Peter graduated from Prescott High School in 2001, I remembered patting myself on the back, thinking we had kept both of our children away from pedophiles. Hedy graduated two years earlier in 1999. Protect and provide—I had done my job. Pedophile Catholic priests were in the news, like every year. The bishops would protect the priests and the cardinals would protect the bishops and the pope would go about saying, "Can't we all just get along?" I quit the Catholic Church the summer after high school because they obviously were not serious about removing pedophiles from the priesthood. Since then, I have been inside Catholic churches on only rare occasions, like family funerals.

CHAPTER 12

By late October, my sister, Donna, was losing the battle against cancer. She suffered extreme weight loss. Her son, Randy, learned to score marijuana to help boost her appetite and it worked; she felt better; she ate better. I asked her on the phone in late October if there was anything I could get for her. "A new body," she said. When I got off the phone, I put a picture of Donna's face on the shoulders of a young model in a sheik dress. I sent it to her and she sent a note back with a smiley face. She passed away in November on our father's birthday. Donna knew how devastating deception inside the family could be. In 1975, when she discovered her husband was having an affair, she said it was like a sucker punch. Her boys were still young, ten and eight. Donna said she had for years ignored her intuition that was shouting at her that things weren't right. She told me it was as if her husband was trying to get caught and she kept looking the other way. He went to live with the other woman, but it didn't last. Then he was ready to come back and be a good husband and a good father but Donna didn't want him back—she didn't trust him. Family is a place of sanctuary from a hard and cold world. Donna never married again. She had a lot of friends from her work at the hospital. They helped her build a new life.

On a Monday afternoon in mid-December, Sandy and I drove to Phoenix and checked into the guest lodging at the Good Samaritan

Hospital. My surgery was scheduled for the next morning. Sandy's principal at the elementary school, Kelton Aker, had heart surgery that Monday morning. We saw his wife that evening in the lobby and she said Kelton was awake and doing well. That was welcome news.

The next morning, they knocked me out: surgery a success. Sharon came up from Tucson the next day. I stopped taking opiates on day three. Sandy, restless between reading her book *Awakening the Buddha Within* and listening to my complaints, returned to Prescott for a couple of days. Christmas by then was just days away. She was afraid that Ches and Tim might come up that week, harass Hedy, and continue with their demands for our surrender.

Sunday dawned—another walk around the path, another college volleyball game on the tube, another changing of someone's colostomy bag to run from.

My roommate was Bill Spry from Payson, twenty years my senior. He asked if I was a college professor; he said I looked like a southern gentleman. He was born in Georgia. I did not tell him that my great grandfather fought on the Union side. He told me he was ending his marriage; he was tired of being around someone who didn't care about him. Before his wife Ellen came to get him that evening, Bill said he had reconsidered and didn't want a divorce. I said, "That's good to hear, Bill. Because I think she loves you."

"How can you tell?" he asked

"I know these things, Bill. I'm a professor."

"You ain't no damn professor."

After Ellen arrived, he told her he thought he'd keep her. And when they cried and hugged each other, I found myself crying with them. I had more tears in my eyes in the last few days than I had over the last two decades. Maybe it shouldn't have been a surprise— they do call it "open-heart" surgery. I read to Bill and Ellen from a newspaper clipping that my sister Donna had sent me: *Things You Don't Want to Hear During Surgery*. My favorite thing from the list was: "Max! Max! Come back with that! Bad dog!" It was Donna's humor and it was more touching knowing it was one of the last things she sent me.

Christmas eve came; Ches and her family miraculously left us alone. Peter came home from school. Hedy had moved out of the house while I was in the hospital. We went to Granite Lake trail for a hike. We watched *The Fellowship of the Ring* and *The Twin Towers* in anticipation of going out to see the last of the trilogy on the big screen. I cried through all three movies.

The day after Christmas, Woody our spaniel had a stroke. He was eleven years old. The left side of his face and body drooped including his left ear. His rear legs gave out. The vet said to be patient that he might regain his strength over time.

The holidays felt different: they were calm and peaceful. Because no one was angry and spitting into our faces, it didn't seem like Christmas at all.

I wasn't supposed to drive or lift anything over twenty pounds for two months. One evening, when Sandy and Pete went to the middle school, their car was trapped in the parking lot by a custodian who locked the gate. They called me to get them in our Volvo. I felt normal enough when I left our driveway, but I was soon disoriented and dizzy and barely made it to the school.

The next week, Sandy and Hedy left on a road trip. They wanted to check out other parts of Oregon that Hedy kept talking up. Sandy, too, was determined to move somewhere, far away from her so-called sister. Woody and I waved goodbye to them early one morning.

Prescott had a gloomy wet January that year. Our root cellar had a few inches of water in it. We had fifty bottles of wine in the cellar that I had made over the years. The doctor suggested I should not consume alcohol for a few months. A door in the laundry room led down a few stone stairs to the cellar's dirt floor. During the first two years we lived at the Bridle Path house, a large salamander lived in the cellar. Mr. Hewitt had planted the salamander to eat the termites and spiders. The second winter we lived at that house, Wendy's boy, Nicki, at age five, killed our salamander by stomping it with his boot. The two boys had gone into the cellar by themselves to see the famous salamander. Nicki was five and Patrick was three and a half. When we asked them about the demise of the salamander, Nicki said it was dead when they got there. Brother Patrick's eyes got big with fear when Nicki said that. We knew Nicki was lying. But we let it drop so as to not upset Wendy who offered that one of us had stepped on it ourselves. Then again, *she* might have killed it, and Nicki was covering for her. What do they say about young boys who kill small animals? That incident with the salamander took place two months before the pantry scene. When Nicki was growing up and came to visit periodically he seemed to always have mean thinks to say to Hedy and Peter. And these mean things seemed to come right out of the mind of his jezebel mother.

Sandy and Hedy called from California to say they were lost in Lodi. They had stopped for lunch there and they couldn't find their way back to the freeway. They thought it would be funny to tell me they were stuck in Lodi since I was a John Fogarty fan. On that trip, Sandy and Hedy had a lot of good times together, a lot of laughs, and saw a lot of beautiful country, wonderful sunsets, and giant redwoods next to the ocean. But Sandy said Hedy showed signs of the PTSD from her ordeal—the rape, the secret, the accusation. Aunt Wendy, Grandma, and Uncle Tim were people that Hedy once loved with all her heart and soul; they were angry with her for telling the truth. Hedy and Sandy came back from their weeklong road trip excited about Oregon. Sandy was determined to get counseling help for Hedy and her PTSD. The trip had scared Sandy awake as to Hedy's condition.

At the end of January, Hedy called from the county jail. She had been picked up for a DUI and was going to have to spend the night in jail. Her car was impounded and her fines were steep. Much of the money she had been saving for two years was about to go down the reparations hole. We could see her if we got to the lobby before five o'clock. Sandy and I raced over there in time to see Hedy marching in a procession of ten people linked together and wearing orange jumpsuits. She didn't look at us as she headed toward lockdown.

A week later, a tall, blonde young man named James came over one evening to take Hedy on a date. (She was staying with us again.) He looked like a stoner. Talking with James confirmed my suspicions; I noticed he had the worse teeth. Crystal meth caused twisted teeth. We told Hedy we were concerned; she needed to take care of herself.

A few days later, Hedy got a flat tire on the Volvo up in the Bradshaws on a forest dirt road where she was dog-sitting. I drove up there in Sandy's Taurus. We switched cars and I stayed and fixed the flat that was in shreds. When I returned to town, Hedy called to say she had hit a curb and took out a front tire on the Taurus. She had hit the curb hard enough to ruin the rim.

I asked, "What the hell is going on?"

Hedy said, "It won't happen again, I swear." We hoped her experiment with "under the influence" was over. Hope, that thing with feathers.

In March, I played on my wood lathe and insulated the inside of the garage. A doctor Fleck asked me to work at her house for a few weeks, refinishing and building a few cabinets and lining her sauna with cedar siding. I had told a few people that I was planning to work for myself out of my garage and not return to the shop. About that time, Kinney, who replaced me at the shop, cut his hand on the table saw and would be out for weeks. Then Chaff, the foreman, wearing a cast on one hand after an operation for carpal tunnel, cut his free hand. Against my better judgment, I went back to work at the shop.

On the radio, I heard that local police were looking for a fugitive named Lee Sonny Johnson, which sounded close to Christopher Sonny Johnson, so I went to the police station after work and asked the detective if it might be my nephew. The detective showed me a stranger's mug. We discussed our case; he said, "Pedophiles get bolder as they get older."

One evening at ten o'clock, Hedy, Sandy, and I were in the living room watching the end of the detective show *Without a Trace* when an ad for Red Lobster appeared. No one muted it and at the end of the commercial, a voice said, "I'm George W. Bush and I approve this message." We all laughed. "What was that about?" I said. Then an ad for Home Depot came on, followed by, "I'm George W. Bush and I approve this message." That tickled us again. Sandy switched the channel and we heard a newsman saying, "Some parishioners at an Indiana church are not happy about a play that was performed at their church this week." Film footage showed a grownup dressed in a bunny suit being chased by children swinging dowel rods and plastic bats. "The play was put on by the youth group and was called The Passion of the Easter Bunny." (We had just seen the Mel Gibson movie: *The Passion of Christ*.) The kids on the news soon had the big bunny on the ground and were beating him up. The newscaster said, "The play was aimed at young children of the church, to get them to stop believing in the Easter Bunny. But parents were upset by the extent of the violence in the play." By then, Hedy and Sandy and I were laughing and couldn't stop. I rolled on the floor, hurting—my eyes were wet with tears. Sandy flipped the channel and we all took a breather, only to hear: "I'm George W. Bush and I approve this message." I thought I was going to laugh my heart out of my chest. Hedy and Sandy choked with laughter. No four minutes had ever been so funny. That laughter, that best of medicines.

In early May, we received news that Patty had died. Age fifty-six. When Sandy called down to Tucson, Tim said that Patty had stopped her medication abruptly, that the shock to her system caused her death. He also said at the end she was talking craziness and acting crazy and had worked herself up with anger "over stupid stuff." He wouldn't give more details. We've always wondered what that stupid stuff was. Patty had said that Ches and Tim never stopped talking about the family crisis. Patty had made it clear to them that she sympathized with Hedy, which of course was crazy and stupid.

Sandy didn't go to Patty's funeral because Wendy would be there. We could foresee how such a meeting was going to play out. With respect to Patty, and to not cause that scene, we couldn't go.

When Sandy's sister, Kitty, died from cancer in 1983, Sandy didn't get to Kitty's funeral either and she always felt bad about that. Wendy and Ches went to Kitty's funeral and never stopped voicing their disappointment with Sandy for not being there. At the time of Kitty's death, Sandy and I were living on the Hopi reservation where I was teaching. Hedy was two and Peter was seven months old. Our van was broken down in the driveway; we were a hundred miles from a car rental office. Sandy struggled with making that decision.

In mid-May, Paul Manz, the middle school band teacher, and Sandy took middle school students to regionals at the high school in Camp Verde. After a day of competition, Sandy supervised the students who went swimming that evening at the hotel. Bob's youngest son, Patrick, who was thirteen, was the last to leave the pool. Sandy told Patrick that she was sorry about what was happening and that she loved him. He was in good spirits and said he was sorry about it, too. She didn't share any information with him. We speculated that Patrick and Nicki heard the accusations against his older brother, but it's just as likely that Wendy and Bob kept it secret; never told Patrick and Nicki the truth. If Bob still hoped it could be a learning experience for his boys, he would have to fight Wendy to play teacher. More likely, it had turned into a learning experience for Bob—to do what he was told.

In June, the weekend after school was out, Ches and Tim showed up at our Bridal Path sanitarium where the healing laughter of all was progressing nicely. I was at work, and Hedy was working. Sandy sensed there would be conflict, so, in her car, she led the way with them following in their car. They drove to the parking lot below Thumb Butte, Prescott's most predominant landmark. Tim left his car in a lot and Sandy drove them up to a day-use area closer to the Butte. Beneath the beautiful ponderosa pines, with the fresh cool air of the lovely Bradshaw Mountains turning back the summer heat, they sat together at a bucolic picnic table and shouted at each other. Ches was mad with Sandy over missing Patty's funeral. "An unforgivable act!" she said.

Sandy said, "I wasn't coming if back-stabbing weasel Wendy was there."

Ches said, "Shame on you! Sandy, you are being cold-hearted."

Sandy said, "Mom, you need to look at yourself in the mirror."

Tim pulled out his Bible and began to read. Sandy stopped him. Tim said, "Why can't you acknowledge Christopher is innocent?"

"I can't do that, because it's not the truth. He did it. He's a liar. Satan is deceiving you, Tim."

They were only at the table for ten minutes, but they were hoarse when they left. When Sandy drove them back to their car, Ches laid in the back seat of Sandy's Accord, kicking the back of Sandy's seat and shouting over and over, "Tim, don't let Sandy come to my funeral!" When Ches got into Tim's car, she was scowling and talking to herself in a low voice. Her hair was a mess and her eyes wild—she was a giant six-year-old sliding into her seat.

The next week, a sniper terrorized Phoenix. That meant another reason not to go to Phoenix. But traveling to Tucson from Prescott can get complicated if you have to avoid Phoenix and the millions of people who live there. March through November, temperatures in Phoenix will surpass 100 degrees 100 times every year. Forty of those hot days will surpass 110 degrees. A few days in July will hit 120 degrees or more. What could possibly make people want to shoot each other?

In June, Sandy and I took a road trip to Clear Lake, California and then drove up the coast into Oregon following the same route she and Hedy had followed. She talked to school administrators in Brookings, Coos Bay and Roseburg. She was hoping her Arizona retirement might carry over to another state but it wouldn't. She was four years away from Arizona retirement and locked in.

Heading south and east across Nevada, we came into southwest Utah to visit the site of the Mountain Meadows Massacre and a monument built there in 2000. Our family hadn't been bludgeoned to death or had our throats slit and left to rot on the meadow. It just felt like it. Well, stabbed in the back, we did have that. We thought we understood the audacity of criminals. In July of 1999, workers digging at the MMM site unearthed a mass grave with the skeletal remains of thirty individuals and the Antiquity Law of 1906 required an investigation. The Governor of Utah, a descendant of the murderers, was able to rush the story out of the news and out of sight. As author Bagley stated: "Mountain Meadows was a crime of true believers." That a leader, like Brigham Young, could order his followers to commit mass murder is unimaginable to many, but Sandy and I have no doubt that he ordered the atrocity and then ordered his followers to cover it up.

As we drove into the community of Colorado City on the border where a large polygamist population still lives, we saw women and children dressed in clothes right out of the 1850s. Women and girls were playing volleyball in bonnets and long dresses near the street. That summer in 2004, polygamist leader Warren Jeff, husband to seventy-nine wives, was forced to flee Utah and Arizona. While on the lam, Jeff was sentenced to multiple life sentences in Texas for filling his harem with teenage wives, some as young as twelve. It was surreal being in Colorado City, all those throwbacks from the past, looking at us in a shiny, new rental car like we were the odd, crazy ones. How could they judge us like that?

Years earlier, when I taught in northern Arizona, Sandy and I had visited another massacre site, this one located in the Hopi reservation. Hedy and Peter were small then, three and two. The village of Awatovi on Antelope Mesa was part of the Pope' rebellion of 1680 when the mesa pueblos across New Mexico and Arizona rose up on the same day in early August against the Spanish after a century of slavery, torture, murder, and the punitive religious dogma of the Catholic Church. The missionaries returned to Awatovi twelve years later and attempted to rebuild the mission, but the village was abandoned in 1700 after a bloody confrontation where traditional Hopi from the neighboring mesas slaughtered hundreds of Christianized Hopi men leaving their bodies in the ceremonial kiva and strewn throughout the site. Most of the women and children were spared and dispersed among the families on other mesas.

A dirt road that begins off Arizona highway 264 between Polocca and Keams Canyon winds its way up the side of Antelope Mesa. Non-Hopis are allowed access to that area only with written permission from the Hopi tribe and only when accompanied by tribal police. One of my students acted as our guide and our van followed a police officer's SUV on a race to the top of the mesa. On that dusty road, we wound past boulders and twisted cedars near Talahogan wash and then up an expanse known as Wind Swept Terrace. The officer drove so fast I could barely stay with him. Coming onto the top of the mesa, you could see in every direction scores of eroded piles of russet-colored rubble. Many buildings had been razed at the time of the second massacre; the rest had fallen since. Scrub cedars had grown out of the mounds of debris for the last three centuries.

"There's the old church," said the officer. Only one corner of the church, about five feet tall, was standing. He said, "The morning of the massacre, they first killed all the priests." As he spoke, chattering sparrows and finches surrounded us and darted between the gnarly cedars. As the officer walked us through the site, he pointed out where the kiva was buried and where roundhouses and pueblos used to stand. The south and east side of the mesa was a sheer cliff. "Don't touch anything," the officer repeated often. The middle of the church was a forest of twisted cedars. Pottery shards and tiny sun-whitened bones were everywhere. The officer scooped up a handful of dirt and pointed out the tiny bones. "Do you know what these are?" He let Hedy and Peter see what was in his hand. "These little bones are the bones from fingers and toes of the people who died here." Hedy looked worried and said, "Oh," and Peter echoed her. The officer smiled broadly. On the highway below, tiny vehicles reflected daggers of sunlight. To the east, you could see the cliffs at Steamboat lit up yellow by the sun.

CHAPTER 13

Throughout the west that summer, we noticed the film *Fahrenheit 911* by Michael Moore was showing and when we returned to Prescott, we went to see it. In early 2002, just months after the buildings fell, Ralf, a friend of ours from the Arizona Old Time Fiddler's, turned his barn loft into a research center for exposing the truth about 9/11. Ralf, an engineer and an architect, was born in 1940 Nazi Germany—it was in his DNA to question authority. Ralf immigrated to America in 1958 at age eighteen; he played guitar in the folk music scene in New York, rubbing shoulders with Bob Dylan, Joan Baez, Hedy West, Judy Collins, David Van Runk, and others before working his way through college. I was hesitant to embrace Ralf's accusations, but when I visited his loft, I was won over by what he had to show me. His architect friends across the world, and many in New York, believed as he did, that the government was lying about why and how those buildings fell. At the top of the stairs into his loft, Ralf had a large poster of George W. Bush with a Hitler mustache. Ralf and the other engineers shared their discoveries freely. As Danish philosopher Soren Kierkegaard said, "There are two ways to be fooled: One way is to believe what isn't true; the other is refuse to believe what is true."

In early July, we heard the news that a pastor in Prescott was arrested for molesting teenage girls. He turned out to be the new pastor at the church we once shared with Wendy and Bob. We assumed Wendy was still singing in the choir there and keeping out of the discussions on the rape of children.

Hedy worked at the cinema again and took classes at Yavapai College. She took art classes this time instead of music. And Sandy sent back a birthday card unopened to Ches for the second year. I got a state teaching certification and planned on substituting. Peter was into his last year at NAU.

We went out for Sandy's birthday and after watching the movie *Mystic River*, Sandy had a revelation when Jimmy's wife tells him it is okay that he murdered his boyhood buddy—he did it to save their family. "Jimmy, you're a king," the wife said. "No one has the power to take that away." Sandy saw Wendy's Bob, like the wife, that he had embraced that save-the-family mantra: "Hedy's family can be sacrificed to save our family. It's them or us." Sandy said, "Sometime after Hedy came out, Wendy either told Bob the truth or with more lies convinced him that he must protect his young sons from the angst of the truth." We always hoped Bob would step up to act as a voice of reason, to stand up for justice. But we could see clearly Bob's balls were gone and he was not getting them back.

Sandy was hoping I could get back into teaching. Over the previous twenty years, Arizona eliminated most of the shop and home economics classes in the public schools. Prescott high had one woodshop class and Prescott Valley and Chino Valley had drafting and auto mechanics. "All those real jobs are gone," I said, "replaced by computer labs."

"Then you need to find something else, something with a future."

"You want to move," I said, "to get far away from Wendy. So where is that going to leave my new job? It's going to be hard to move to Timbuktu."

"You'll have to figure that out."

A few days later, she gave me an ultimatum: "Get a real job, with a real future, with a real pension, with a real salary, with real security, or I want a separation. I'm tired of your drifting. And don't you dare think you're going to work for yourself out of the garage. I won't stand for it." For decades, the city of Prescott had a brochure welcoming visitors to the city: "Come and shop and dine and enjoy the sites and sounds of Prescott and the hiking. But don't plan on moving here unless you have a job lined up."

One of the new employees at the shop was a young man named Monte who worked with us a few years earlier whom Lowell had fired for bending the chop-saw blade while making pipes for smoking dope.

At lunchtime one day, Monte told Chaff and I a story that was hard to forget. When Monte was in his early twenties, living in Oakland, he found out that two men had raped his fifteen-year-old sister. Monte and his friends enticed the two rapists to a warehouse on the bay where Monte and his team tied them up, beat, and tortured them to death, and then dumped the bodies in San Francisco Bay. Monte was proud of that—proud of the protector aspect. "Yeah, it was the right thing to do. Woo-wee! I didn't like being on that water in that old boat on a cold winter's night, but we did what we had to do. We almost capsized, woo-wee. But we did it. We dumped them suckers and they sank fast." As Monte walked away, I asked Chaff, "Why did he tell us that?" Chaff said, "He was obviously making it up."

The heaviness of the murders that Monte described hung on my mind for a while. "Sank just like that." It's smug to think you could end a life, whack somebody who has done you harm, do it efficiently and easily, but it's another thing to see the consequences of that reality. You say that you can't believe someone could do a heinous crime like murder but when you say that, you're talking to yourself and you're trying to be seen as a saint. You could not commit that atrocity, so you say. The criminals in the world, those monsters, know they *could* commit that crime. They *will* commit those crimes. They *do* commit atrocities. Murderers get away with crimes partly because people say, "Come on, people wouldn't do that—they couldn't kill their own people. They wouldn't do something so evil." Hitmen for the mob are soulless monsters. Some days, I think murderous thoughts against people who have harmed us. Sadly, I think I'm capable of it. Nietzsche said, "Be careful when you go to fight monsters, that you don't become one. When you stare into the abyss, the abyss stares back into you." Gandhi said, "An eye for an eye makes the whole world blind." Monte left California either because he ran out of "strikes" or he was on a hit list; those rapists had families, too. As an old saying goes: When you seek revenge, dig two graves; one for your victim and one for yourself.

Sandy went to a lawyer to get coached for our separation. She wanted a document to stick on the refrigerator, next to the kid's old kindergarten artwork, to verify her seriousness: You need to land a real job. What could I do to change her mind? Superman Christopher Reed had just died that fall—and what could I, a mere mortal, do to stop this separation?

That winter marked the 34th anniversary since Sandy and I first met in American Indian History class at Pima College in Tucson in January 1971. The teacher was from Acoma, New Mexico, a pueblo town implicit in the Pope' Rebellion. Sandy and I were the first to arrive at class that day; we started talking and within a week, we were spending hours on the phone with each other. She was taking an array of classes, finance, history, dance, art, and geology. I was taking design, acting, writing, history, weaving, and painting. I housesat for a literature teacher that summer and Sandy came to stay with me for a week at Los Lomas, a community of stone cottages west of Tucson, built in the 1930s for the Old Tucson actors. She stayed there with me but we didn't sleep together. We danced naked in the rain, hitchhiked with her sitting on my shoulders, slept in the same bed, danced and played like big kids, and hiked the mountain trails. It took a year before we went from being friends to falling in love. We didn't care that the world wanted to think we were shagging each other; we were having too much fun to care about trivial things like sex. At the beginning of my last semester at Pima College, a year after we met, I moved into a tent in a ravine a mile to the west of the campus between Speedway and Anklam. I could walk to classes and take showers on campus. I camouflaged my tent and spent three months in the beautiful desert, hiking or biking to classes. Sandy came by frequently and helped feed potato cubes to a peccary mother and her two offspring. Sandy was considering moving out with me, but her grandmother Mary, visiting from El Paso, talked her out of it. When Sandy got sick and spent a week in bed, her grandma said it was an omen. I turned twenty that week. The professor for whom I housesat the summer before lured me to her place "to watch *The Seven Samurai* with her friends." When I realized I was the only friend coming, she called it "a private viewing." When she disappeared into her bedroom and returned wearing a see-through teddy, I fled on my bicycle. After grandma went back to El Paso, Sandy came out to the campsite one afternoon, planning to leave before dark. We talked and joked about my near seduction and cooked a meal over the campfire. One thing led to another and we spent the night in each other's arms. I had a cold the next week. Great memories. But . . . wake up, fool! She's kicking you out. The one-woman man and the I-don't-need-a-man woman were splitting. I moved into the extra bedroom.

One night, I went down the hall to the bathroom and to get a drink of water in the kitchen. I had just settled back into bed when Hedy pounded on my door.

"You woke me up! Are you doing that on purpose? Are you trying to torture me like Wendy? I need to work in the morning, why did you wake me?"

"I didn't mean to," I said.

She screamed, "Aaa! I won't get back to sleep. I hate you. If you are waking me on purpose, God is going to make you suffer."

"I'll keep water in the room from now on. I'm sorry."

"I won't be disrespected."

For a long time, I thought I understood why Hedy didn't tell about Christopher. He threatened her, but that wasn't enough. She had always doubted her ability to stop her tall cousin if he came looking for her. He towered over her for ten years. Maybe she could stop him by being silent, that he had got what he wanted and wouldn't try again.

In a scientific journal, I came across the two concepts of kin selection and group selection that may have played a major role in why she didn't tell. Humans survived over the millennia because they worked together in groups. A lone human was soon a dead human. It's something that is instinctive in our genes. It's no coincidence that people who are sociable are healthier than loners. They say the best thing a person entering old age can do is to keep active and stay connected to people. After the rape, Hedy's first instinct was to think of the safety of the group, even over herself. Like a wounded deer who would sacrifice himself to a pack of wolves or hyenas so the group can escape, Hedy had been drawn to keep quiet. She may not have realized why she was doing what she was. Many of our soldiers, who are in fierce combat, and experienced life and death situations, have a hard time adjusting to a normal life once they have returned from war. Sebastian Yunger interviewed a number of these vets and thinks he's found an answer. These men had reached a point during the trials of battle where they were completely willing to die to save their group. It was like they had reached that point, the noblest of notions, a willingness to die for others. After reaching such an intense experience level, their mundane lives seemed just that, mundane. They had reached their highest calling when in combat. They were not just imbued with the label of a protector, they had *become* the ultimate protector, one willing to sacrifice their life for the survival of a group. Hedy said that she didn't understand why she didn't tell. Maybe her DNA was making that decision for her. Was she willing to die for the group and not even know it?

Before Christmas, the shop collected food for Kinney because he was broke. On opening the box, he squealed with delight in his raspy Irish voice. That afternoon, Lowell and Chaff held their yearly Chinese gift exchange, an event I had skipped the previous years. CEO Cheryl was present for the first time. She tried to understand my reasons for opting out of the game. As the rest of the shop partied,

I worked on a pair of duck decoys that I had started over a year earlier. Cheryl made a big deal out of my not participating in their game. Two weeks later, I resigned and started substituting in area school districts.

I went to Sandy's lawyer to sign the separation papers they had put together. Sandy said she needed it. She had divorced her family and now she was cleaning up the ragged edges that made up the unfilled parts of her life. She tried other churches in Prescott but never felt connected. She was searching for some truth she could latch on to. She needed to find herself. "Wendy and Ches caused PTSD in all of us," she said. "It was my family that did this to us."

"It's my family, too," I said.

"Not blood—this was my blood!"

"My blood family has flaws, too."

"Oh, that makes me feel so much better—the whole world gone to crap."

Numerous times, I had told her the story about my brother Tony coming home drunk in the wee hours of his senior year in high school and peeing on my five-year-old body as I lay sleeping in the room we shared. I yelled for help. My mother came and yelled at Tony. Earlier, from ages three to five, I shared a double bed in the attic of our old house with Tony when he was fifteen, sixteen, and seventeen years old. When I was four, I remember waking up in the attic and screaming for help. My mother came up the stairs and scolded Tony: "Don't do that to your little brother! Not your little brother!" I can't remember what he did. After Hedy came forward, my sister Sharon told me that when she was six and Tony was sixteen, he showed her his penis and tried to drag her into the barn. She escaped him and ran to mother who went after Tony with a willow switch and gave him "a good whacking." Sharon was one of the lucky ones. "That incident was the reason I never wrote or went to visit him," she said. "I never got over what he did; he betrayed my trust."

Sandy returned to Arizona Old Time Fiddlers' Friday night jams that were held at Mason's Barn just to the north of us on

Williamson Valley Road. We stopped going to the jams the week Hedy came forward. Sandy played the fiddle; I played backup on guitar. Sandy especially loved fiddling with old Ray Gardener who had played fiddle for over eighty years starting at age three. Sandy didn't want me coming with her to the jams. Ray was so sweet, so I couldn't get jealous.

Fridays after work, Sandy met with a group of her teacher friends at a cafe on Willow Creek Road. Anita and Polly B. and Jane and Karen knew all about why Sandy divorced her family; they became Sandy's new family, her rock. Sandy wanted her memories of her family to be buried. These buddies rallied to Sandy's aid. They told Sandy they had gotten worried when Sandy came to work looking like an escapee of an insane asylum in early 2003. Sandy's principal Mr. Aker at Lincoln was concerned about her also and he called her into his office. She told him she was going through some hard times and he didn't pry. Her teacher buddies turned out to be the best therapists.

Sandy wasn't going to listen anymore to me complain about my work. We had worked out our biggest marital problem when I had landed steady work when we came to Prescott. We had paid off the mortgage when the millennia arrived. The cars were paid off. But she said she was tired of the whole thing—the scrimping, the constant problems around every corner, heating with wood, the new well, forest fires, life in general. Our sex life was on hold; it was nonexistent.

On weekends that spring, I made improvements on the property. Peter and I repainted the interior of the house. A new leach line to the septic tank was in. I cleaned up the place and hauled loads to the dump.

Sandy wanted to sell the house and move into town to make it easier to leave Prescott as soon as she retired. I said okay. Then she made it clearer: "I want to be in *my* own townhouse for a few years." Living in the same town as Wendy was intolerable to both of us. Her teacher buddies said it was the time to sell if she was thinking about it, as the market was hot.

I said, "Okay. Whatever you want, whatever makes you happy. But what will make you happy? Have you figured that out?"

She said, "I don't want to be here when the new well goes dry."

"We could be a decade before that happens."

"Yeah, but it will happen. Maybe next year. What else is going to go wrong around this place?"

"Well, everything that could go wrong has gone wrong. Fixed and ready for sale, if that's what you want."

"That's what I need," she said.

I couldn't make much of a case to keep the place. Every time we turned a corner or went into a store, there could be a confrontation waiting to happen. I willingly helped in the loss of my job, my dog, my cat, my marriage, and my home. I was qualified then to write country-western songs.

CHAPTER 14

Winter morphed into spring. Hedy found a second part-time job at a dry cleaner and was back to living in town with her friends. Once she came by when I was having a yard sale. I took a break and sat with her at the picnic table.

Hedy said, "I saw Wendy driving her car. She looked really unhappy."

I said, "She's always like that, we just didn't notice it. They haven't bothered us in almost a year now."

Hedy said, "She got what she wanted: she wanted Ches all to herself and now she has that. Tim and Bob support her. She's doing great, I imagine."

I said, "Never saw Christopher again."

Hedy said, "Crazy Christopher. He is. If you don't see it, then there is something wrong with you, Dad. He's dangerous. Ches and Tim are keeping the focus on he-said, she-said, me-said, you-said, and that lets Wendy keep the heat off her lies and his craziness." A noisy car passed by out on the highway about a quarter-mile away, and we glanced at it. "Dad, I wrote a play. Actually, I wrote it a while back. I just found it again and have been rewriting it. It's pretty good."

"What's it about?"

"It's about a hundred pages long," she laughed. "More of a screenplay. It's kind of a Romeo and Juliet. I didn't know what I was doing. But I think I can make it work. It's set in Nazi Germany."

"It should make a good horror story then."

"It is scary. I can make it even scarier. They try to escape Germany after the boy is drafted into the army. The girl is the daughter of a Jewish farmer—you know the first people the Nazis went after."

"Will you let me read it?"

"Not right now. It needs a lot of work. Hey, I have a new friend—Kim, she works at the dry cleaners. We are going down to Phoenix this weekend. It's going to be hot. Well, actually Sunday. But we're going to the water park, it just opened. I'm so excited. I haven't been there in a long time."

I said, "Oh, yeah. When Peter turned twelve, remember, we went? It was one hundred and twenty-one degrees that day and I'll never forget it."

"I've been once since. Heat doesn't bother me if I have water to splash in."

"Don't burn your feet, bring your sandals." She rolled her eyes. The car pulled into the yard. Hedy drove away while I was attending to customers.

Realty signs for our house were up and down Williamson Valley Road—a good time to be a seller. Investors from California drove up the prices and they tended to skip over the Phoenix market in favor of the outlying areas. If old-timers thought we were insane for paying such high prices in 1992; those old folks would have their heads explode in 2005. I substituted in Prescott, Chino Valley and Prescott Valley and as far away as Mayer and Spring Valley and saw for sale signs everywhere.

Sandy thought she had it figured out: build a new identity and family based on her teacher buddies, change her name, and she had her little Buddhist prayer altar. She said, "You know, I moved right out of my father's house at age twenty and got married and moved in with you. I've never really been by myself or able to be myself or to find myself—to let the wind blow through my hair. I've been perpetually controlled by a man, my fate tied to the fate of a man, and these men, always on the move and dragging me around with them." Her father Tom and I had complicated her life and she was out to get it back. Sandy's buddies helped her search for herself and search for a townhouse. These gals were savvy at three things: finding the center of the universe, the art of dumping men, and how to hunt for real estate bargains.

After my fifteen years of ten-hour workdays, a seven-hour substitute day was like a vacation. From the beginning, Prescott placed me in the kindergarten classrooms. If he can sub kindergarten, he can sub anywhere. Those kinder teachers were sick a lot. I stopped wondering one day why that was after I found a booger the size of a quarter stuck to my forearm after "Reading Time on the Rug." The area schools kept me busy watching out for boogers. Our cat Booger passed away that spring from a gum infection.

In May, we got an offer on our place we couldn't turn down. Then Sandy bought her townhouse. It was around the corner from the new Walmart and close to the Safeway off Iron Springs. In late June, Sandy brought home a black tuxedo kitten that seemed to like Celtic fiddle tunes. She named him Brian.

A year and a half after his stroke, Woody passed away in May. I had a last garage sale this time without Woody helping me, as he had a relapse, and we buried him in the garden. I sold a woodshop of tools along with a lot of other stuff. One thing I should not have put out for sale: a bottle of tequila. Sandy had bought the tequila years earlier to be mixed with herbs, for a cure-all her friends told her about. The seal on the bottle was never broken so I put it in the sale at half price. It was a windy Friday and Sandy was at work. The wind gusted through and knocked things over from time to time. Three teenaged boys came by, spotted the tequila, and offered to buy it. I laughed and said sorry. But after they left, I noticed the bottle was gone from the table. I flipped out, imagining the worst: "Inebriated Boys Die in

Head-on Collision on Williamson Valley Road." A woman, who had just pulled into the yard, saw me frantically rummaging through the stuff and asked me why. I told her and she spotted the bottle under a table. The wind had blown it off. "Oh, thank you," I said, picking the bottle up. "I think this is going off the market." I ran it into the garage and stashed it out of sight. When I returned, the woman was cooing over a dollhouse I had built when Hedy turned six. The woman tried all the doors, the oven, the fridge, kitchen cabinets, and the flush handle on the commode and the sink's little faucets. "This is so beautiful. Why are you selling this?"

"My little girl's all grown up. She doesn't want it anymore. We're moving or we might try to keep it, for grandkids."

"I'd love to have it but I don't know where I'd put it." Later that day, our neighbor, Cathy, bought the dollhouse.

Dennis, who lived down the road, showed up in his '47 Chevy hardtop coop that his father used to own; he gave Sandy and I a ride around the area. The car smelled like oldness leathered over. When we offered him first dibs on the garage sale leftovers, he loaded up his backseat.

In May, we went to Flagstaff for Peter's graduation. He looked so handsome marching down the aisle. The ceremony was held inside the dome at Northern Arizona University. Sandy actually let me sit by her. She said, "I don't want to hear anything you have to say." She cut me off the moment I opened my mouth.

"Now isn't this fun," I whispered.

"I'm not listening to anything you say ever again," she said. "Don't ever give me any advice." We were in month three of the Big Cold Shoulder. I was not known for being a talkative person so I didn't get what she meant. I stared at the intricate ceiling of the NAU dome, trying to understand how it was that some things that seem to be impossible stay up as long as they do.

Peter moved home. He had one wing out the door that summer. He sent out many applications and responded to job offers in California. We finally had a computer that worked for a whole year and he was able to speed up his process. All his life, Peter displayed a sharp intuition; our family came to trust his advice. He saved our buns on more than one occasion. He could be stubborn, especially when we did not heed his warnings. When he was ten and we were hiking in the desert in the 100 plus degree heat near Bagdad, Arizona, he warned us at a certain point that we should stop and head back; when we didn't listen, he sat down on the trail and wouldn't budge. "You go right ahead and go up that trail, I'm not going one step further." Who did this little squirt think he was? But we all turned back. We hadn't realized we had hiked so far, and we were out of water and exhausted by the time we got back to the car. We thanked him for his stubbornness. In Yellowstone, on the trails overlooking the falls, he coached us to take every step as if it were our last. We listened. He was nine. If he didn't feel right about it, he wasn't going to do it.

When we moved, we left our collection of large rocks along a path that ran from the house to the wash. This included large petrified wood specimens and six large metates that Mr. Hewitt had left for us, some rocks with veins of raw copper, and peacock iron pyrite I'd brought out of the underground mine thirty years earlier. Old Hewitt had hauled the metates out of the hills all over Arizona and New Mexico before the reformed Antiquities Act became law. We had planned to live at that home until we joined the ancients pushing up sagebrush under the shadows of Granite Mountain and I joked once that those metates could be used to grind our bones into powder. As a member of Junk Collectors Anonymous, I had a lot of junk to get rid of. It seemed the spirit of Mr. Hewitt, pothunter and collector, haunted our place, and his germ had somehow gotten into me. He passed away in Prescott Valley shortly after selling his house to us, but I believe his spirit came back to roost in our trees above his metates and junk iron buried nearby.

We would most miss Byron Carlson, our neighbor of fourteen years. We watched over each other's houses and animals when either of us left for a day or more. Byron had a pair of old Springer spaniels,

Star and Doodlebugs, that would come into our yard at exactly five o'clock because Byron had told them before he left where and when they could find their dinner. It was uncanny.

The rustic picnic table was too big and had to stay. Once, when Hedy and Peter were teenagers, a bothersome fly buzzed around us as we ate at that table. We shooed the fly away but it kept coming back. Hedy at the time was eating her meal with chopsticks. As the fly flew by her, she plucked out of the air with her chopsticks. I couldn't remember if the fly survived but years later, Hedy swore she didn't hurt the fly but let it buzz away. I do remember watching in disbelief as Hedy nonchalantly walked to the kitchen to rinse off her chopsticks.

We moved Sandy into her new townhouse the weekend of the Fourth of July. Dennis came by that day and we gave him a few more things.

I heard about a job opening in Stayton, Oregon, one of the few Industrial Arts openings that were posted at the time. Positions labeled "technology" were really computer labs and not real hands-on shop classrooms. Home Economics and shop programs had been cut out of the curriculum in most schools, nationwide by 2005.

Manuel arts used to be an important part of education in the early development of our public schools in the early twentieth century. I decided to become a shop teacher because I was in love with the thrill that came with completing a project with my own hands. What a thrilling career: to help young people to experience that thrill. The early educators thought that way, too. Learning to use a handsaw or a chisel and a drill, all the wonderful tools developed over the centuries of mankind's progress, helped children improve dexterity and to develop good organizational habits and work habits. The whole person was addressed. Taking pride in a project you completed was a foundational building block to install into a young person. After experiencing all the stages of the project coming together, they could see that they could create order out of chaos. They could accomplish anything they set their minds to. I thought it would be the perfect career for me. But the times were changing. I talked myself into getting back into teaching after twenty years—to turn the youngsters around Stayton and Sublimity onto the thrill of creation. Sandy said she was leaving Prescott the moment she was eligible for retirement, three years away. I was young enough to still land some kind of a pension. I would go to the job and stay there until I died. That was my plan. That had always been my plan after college: to land a job and stay at it for thirty, forty years. But things don't always go as planned.

 I was heading to Oregon and Sandy of the Winding Path was settling into her new townhouse for three more years of tea parties with her teaching buddies and playing old-time fiddle with Ray Gardner. We signed the closing papers and that same day, we went hiking together on the ridges above Cayuse day camp off the road leading to Granite Mountain Lake for old time's sake. After we parted, I camped out in Williamson Valley on a dead-end dirt road with a straight view of Granite Mountain. Mining companies over the years tried to get permits to plunder the riches of that mountain, for its gold and other minerals, but they were repelled by thousands of Granite Mountain lovers from the area and around the world. In the pioneer days, the mountain was called Old Stony and it was a beacon for sturdy souls coming into the area. I don't know what the ancients called it. One of the old fiddlers we played with was Holmes Stoneman from Pennsylvania, who went by the nickname Stony. We used to play with him at Mason's Barn where he gave history lessons about Old Stony, the mountain. He was especially adept at playing "The Arizona Waltz" and "Chinese Breakdown."

CHAPTER 15

I left Yavapai County northbound pulling a small trailer behind my Dakota. I stopped at Drake and climbed on the train trestle overlooking Hell's Canyon where we had hiked when the kids were teenagers. Near Seligman, I connected with Route 66 toward Peach Springs. I planned to visit Grand Canyon Caverns, but when I pulled into the parking lot, my urge disappeared. Sandy was the one who was in love with caves, not me. It's not that special anyway to share memories with yourself. I returned to the highway.

    I pulled over again when I got the idea to drive the fifty miles on a free-range gravel road to the trailhead on the Havasupai Indian Reservation that led down to the village of Supai. It was high on Sandy's Bucket List. Sandy and I had been a team for years, weighing things out before we made decisions. I studied the mountain peak in the distance; on the map, it was called the Tower of Babylon. The voices that sprouted in my head did indeed babble on. The scar on my chest itched. I rubbed it with a fist as I turned away and drove on toward Hoover dam via Route 66.

    I made it to the outskirts of Las Vegas by chowtime and was tempted to stop. Sandy and I had only been to Las Vegas two times; we spent a total of $3 gambling; we'd spent money on shows instead. As the exits to Las Vegas whizzed by, I decided to skip the city and camped in the desert.

Sandy and I had helped each other weather temptations. Sandy, even at age twenty, scolded me when I drank too much. By age twenty-two, I swore off getting drunk. I made that vow on my knees, worshipping a porcelain god. I never got drunk again. I challenged Sandy to stop smoking; she did. Gambling intrigued me but for Sandy, the thought of losing hard-earned money was appalling. Our cabinet company remodeled the casino in Prescott in 2000. We were at the job site at six in the morning, in time to see the gamblers of all ages who had been drinking all night stumble out to their cars. Early bird gamblers soon took up the vacated seats at the machines and ordered their free drinks. It was disgusting to watch: a local business turning fellow citizens into alcoholics, vagrants, and homeless.

I passed Reno and Susanville, skirted around the base of Mount Shasta, and crossed into Oregon. In Stayton, I found a room to rent by the week in an old three-story building in the middle of town. I filled out an application for the teaching position at the middle school in Stayton. I also found an opening for a cabinetmaker in Independence (on the other side of Salem) and by my second afternoon there, Medallion Cabinets hired me to start on Saturday.

My room in Stayton was on the second floor of a men-only dormitory-type building with shared bathrooms and showers. Everybody in the building smoked. You could see smoke rising from under each door. On that first night, when I was trying to sleep with the stench rising around me, I wondered if I had died and gone to hell. I finally dozed off and awoke to see smoke fumes in the dim light crawling under my door. I stuffed towels and clothes against the bottom. It was a decade after municipalities across the country began banning cigarette smoking in public places; I thought Oregon was supposed to be enlightened.

The second night in non-smoker's hell, I didn't sleep well either. I went to complain to the managers Dave and Betty, an older couple who lived in the little house behind my building; a newly planted lawn grew in their front yard. Through a screen door, I heard Dave and Betty practicing karaoke. When I tapped on the door, the crooning and the music stopped. I told Dave the smoke was getting to me. He said, "We told you there were smokers living here, didn't we?" I noticed the cigarette pack in his shirt pocket.

"Yes, you did, Dave," I said, "but I didn't realize they were going to be smoking non-stop, every minute, out of every orifice. I haven't slept; instead of sleep, I'm getting headaches. I know now why I haven't seen any bugs in this building—it gets fumigated every night." In the dark living room, I saw the dark silhouette of his girlfriend Betty as she lit up a cigarette.

"Well, what do you want me to do about it? These men have permission to smoke. I can't police how much a person smokes. I'm nobody's watcher. What you need to do is seal up all the cracks. Get you a roll of duct tape."

"I tried that—I believe it's coming through the walls. I'm starting a new job tomorrow and I need my sleep."

"You got a job already?" he asked. I told him about it.

He said, "Try to hang in there; you'll get used to the smoke. It won't bother you once you get used to it." He took the pack out of his pocket; he tapped out a cigarette and pulled it out with his lips. He did not light it. "You know most of those guys are homeless vets. They all smoke and they all have emotional problems. They're just trying to get by. Some of them are barely getting by. No one wants to hire a whacked-out vet." He took his light out of his pocket. "Would you like to come with us to Smittie's bar tonight to see the show we're in? It's a karaoke show. Me and Betty are singing tonight." He lit his cigarette.

"Maybe some other time," I said and left abruptly.

I sealed up the cracks as best as I could and that night, I finally slept, only getting up once to pee in the kitchen sink. No way was I about to open the hall door.

The Medallion plant put me in specialty cabinets. At lunch break, I walked into the lunchroom and bilge of cigarette smoke drove me out. It was still light outside, so I ate on a picnic table with other smoke refugees. A parade of pickup trucks came driving through the parking lot; people in the back held signs: Support Union Cabinet Shops; Support Living Wages; Globalize Somewhere Else. Security guards asked them to leave.

    The principal at the middle school called early the next week—the board had voted on someone else for the position. I was relieved. The thought of going back to a classroom was causing panic attacks. I taught for four years and had left teaching with my own case of PTSD. Sandy never forgave me for quitting teaching but she didn't live through the hell I experienced. I taught successfully for three years on the Navajo Indian Reservation in Arizona and I was ready to stay with teaching as a career when we found a job closer to Sandy's family in Tucson. Actually, Ches had found the job opening for me. It was in Oracle, a community north of Tucson and near the Magma Copper mine I used to work at. Most of the population of Oracle was made up of miners and their families. Because the town sat high in the foothills of the Catalina Mountains, the poisonous fumes from the smelter smokestacks in San Manuel seldom drifted into town. Sandy and I celebrated finding such a place. But something was wrong with that school district. The district superintendent, Mr. Hartles, had driven the teacher's union out of his district before I came to work there. There were twenty teacher positions at the junior high and ten of us were new. The daughter of the superintendent was in one of my eighth-grade shop classes. They had no place else to put her after getting kicked out of her other options. After a run-in with her, I went to Mr. Hartles with my concern for her behavior. He kept his office dark. The little man was barely visible behind his heavy desk and its dark backdrop. He said, "I'm well aware of her spirit." That's how a toxic parent describes bad behavior. He said, "Ha-ha, she's been that way ever since second grade when her mother started law school. I told her mother not to start back to work so soon, but you know how that goes. And so, Sherry's been leading her classmates, ha, into trouble, ha-ha, ever since. She's quite the leader, quite the gal, I tell you. So, what else do you want to tell me?"

    I said, "She's out of control."

"She's not out of control. She knows what she's doing."

"Well, you should talk to her teachers. I'm not the only one who's concerned." Sherry spent 40 days in school suspension that year.

"I don't need to talk to anyone. She's doing fine."

Sherry's boyfriend, Skip, a fifteen-year-old seventh-grader, a foot taller than his classmates, was sexually active. He had been held back twice in elementary schools, not because he was a dullard but because he was uncooperative and stubborn. Skip had a twenty-two-year-old brother who had just gotten out after three years in prison for raping a waitress at a café three years earlier. During the first semester, Skip threw boiling water on a classmate in Home Economics class and was suspended for three weeks. Skip's brother came by during parent/teacher night and threatened to hurt the Home Economics teacher, Ms. Spitzer. The teacher locked up her room and hid out in my classroom the rest of the open house. Before Christmas, I got a letter from principal Williams praising my "high standards and diligence." It was his first year as a principal, a black man in an openly racist community and the year was testing him in ways his time in Vietnam never had. During the second semester, Skip and two boys attacked a girl in my wood room. They held her down and groped her. Skip was suspended again. I was not offered a contract for the next year because of that incident. Both the shop and the Home Economics programs were eliminated to make way for a computer lab in the fall, something that Mr. Hartles had planned before he hired us. During the last week of school, the teachers voted on whether to let Skip advance to eighth grade or if he should be held back for the third time. I voted to get him out of there, but the other teachers voted to hold him back. One teacher explained it to me: "He's going to turn sixteen this summer—he won't come back. Guaranteed." Or so they prayed.

After leaving Oracle, I took a job at Nogales High School, hoping that my lack of speaking Spanish wouldn't be a problem. It really wasn't the problem—I was the problem. I was still reeling from my year of hell at Oracle. I couldn't sleep; thus, I couldn't focus; students picked up on that, which put me at odds with them. Also, a gang war was going on between the Arizona students and those from the Mexico side. Fights in the halls and behind buildings broke out constantly.

The previous year, an incident in Nogales high school occurred that made national news. Boys on a bus returning from a baseball game in Tucson circulated a porn magazine. Some of the aroused younger freshmen were held down by older boys and forcibly ejaculated. Parents of the victimized boys sued the school district. It was still in the courts and all of the coaches who were on that bus were still praying for mercy. I didn't share my Oracle experiences with anyone. Lack of sleep had left me on wire's edge and I resigned and left after the first semester to work for a homebuilder in Nogales.

Sandy and I heard all these stories dealing with the twisted minds of teenage boys, at least two years before nephew Christopher had joined the ranks of the twisted. We heard about and saw the crap those boys pulled but never thought it could touch us. Nobody warned us. Our family was above such filthy thoughts. Did we think we were safe from that just because we went to church most Sundays? Oh, yeah, the preacher at the church in Nogales was Mr. Hyde, a deacon, who was filling in until a full-time pastor could be found. The previous pastor was fired for molesting the children in the downtown nondenominational church.

CHAPTER 16

I went with Dave and Betty to karaoke night. My wedding anniversary was that week, number thirty-three, and I wanted to raise a toast. I was up for a night with music and dancing, to sit and watch people being happy.

We shared a tall table near the stage. As I ordered a whole meal, Dave and Betty eyed me suspiciously. On stage, a heavy set gal belted out "What Part of No Don't You Understand." Betty was short and wiry and reminded me of a little dog I once knew that liked to nip at people's heels. Betty told me she and Dave had been together ten years. "I never wanted to have children and I never did," Betty said. "Do you want to know why?" Before I could answer, she said. "When I was little, my father and my older brothers molested me and my sisters and my little brothers. It drove me crazy. All of us suffered craziness. Because of them, I had seven different personalities to deal with before I got well." I looked over at Dave; he was staring straight ahead, bobbing his head like he had heard her story a thousand times and it had turned into some kind of music.

"I had twelve brothers and five sisters, you see, eighteen of us in all."

Why was she telling me this? What had I done to invite this? Betty, I hardly knew you. I tried to change the conversation. I pointed to Betty's hands, to her fingers covered in rings. I asked her, "Why so many rings?"

"Fifty rings tonight!" she said. "I'm going all out. I usually just wear thirty-five rings when I go out. Do you like them?"

"They're beautiful," I said. "You look like a gypsy fortune teller."

She smiled proudly, stuck her hands out better for me to see. But she was anxious to get back to her therapy session. "Anyway, father was convicted of molesting us and also for molesting some neighborhood children and so he was sent to prison. But they let him out after two years because he had found Christ. He had been saved, they said. See, they believed the bullshit he fed them. His lies. As soon as he got home, he raped us again. They sent him back to prison and he wasn't there a month when all of a sudden he died." She made a click! with her tongue. "He died! Good riddance!" She leaned in, "See, the cooks poisoned him; they poisoned that damn bastard." I glanced at Dave. He tolerated her broadcasting of her horrific story because he didn't have to be the therapist for that evening. He could enjoy the music instead. Dave glanced over from time to time, I guess, to watch my face change shape and lose color. But he never spoke once.

"Want to hear something funny?" Betty asked. Yes, I was ready for funny—tell me something funny, Betty, lift me to new heights. Oh, yeah, tell me that one, about a rope that walks into a bar. But she whispered, "Do you want to know why my father wanted so many kids?" I had no clue. She leaned in: "Because he made a bet with his childhood buddy, Harlan, to see who could have the most kids! Ha! What do you think of that? How about that? I was part of a frigging bet."

"That's kind of sick," I said.

"Kind of? If that's not the goddamn sickest thing that ever was, then I'm a farting Patti Page. Old Harlan had twenty-four kids, so dad lost the frigging bet. Harlan never collected—dad stiffed him. Dad became a stiff and stiffed him!" She laughed and winked at me, which made me feel a bit stained.

Betty sneered triumphantly and said, "I hated my father. I hated that bastard. I wish I could have been the one to kill him. Want to know how he met my mother?" I braced myself; I bit my lip. She leaned in again, "He bought her for ten dollars. She was ten years old and he was nineteen. He bought my mama from her mother who was trying to get rid of some kids because she couldn't feed the ones she had. For ten dollars! You look shocked but that sort of thing went on in Arkansas in the 1920s. They were damn Baptists. Dirt poor. I hated my mother. She didn't protect us. She said I asked for it because I sat on his lap. Christ, a child doesn't ask for that. A child wants to be loved, not raped. Rape, a joke on her, ha, ha. My mother joined the Mormon Church before she died. She said it was all cleared for her and for dad to get into heaven because of all the kids they had. All those so many blessings, all of us kids paved the way. I don't want to go to heaven if those two piles of shit are there."

As I sat recuperating from that story, Dave and Betty broke away to take their turns on the stage. This ought to be interesting, I thought. Dave sang "Crying My Heart Over You" and Betty sang "I Know a Heartache When I See One" and she kept looking at me, and winking. I guess my color was coming back. In round two, she sang "Hey, Good Looking" and Dave sang "Amos Moses." "Just hit 'em in the head with a stump, oomph." After I regained my appetite, I forced myself to count the chews between each bite. Betty and Dave were on top of the world when they were on that stage, prancing around and singing their pain out to the world—trying to push back the darkness one song at a time.

Pema Chadron wrote, "When the world is filled with evil, how do you transform unwanted situations into the path of awakening?" It was something I was wrestling with. She suggested by starting to connect with your soft spot, "Not only the stuff we like but also through the messy stuff." That seemed impossible if that meant communicating with the enemy heart to heart. The word diabolic comes to mind when I think of what Wendy and her son did to Hedy, to us. Christopher raped my six-year-old child and Wendy went after my daughter, to destroy her, to keep her son's atrocity secret, and to drink from the jealousy pool. Diabolic, fiendish, outrageously wicked. It is hard to grasp that a member of my own family would plot and scheme like she did. Wendy was the Cain from the Bible story, jealous and envious of Sandy, the Abel. Sandy and I worked hard to raise two blooming and prospering children while Wendy was seething with jealousy and hatred because Christopher was crashing and burning his way through life, addicted to drugs, addicted to sex, bouncing off the tracks at every turn. The time Wendy locked herself in her room for two weeks, something broke inside of her. Jezebel from the Bible was not a prostitute, but she was an evil, lying schemer who held false witness against many people, causing many to be executed.

Hedy had been meeting with counselors over the years. The counselors suggested helpful strategies to help her, but Hedy said they all rolled their eyes when she tried to explain the pantry scene to them—the lies and the false witness blackmail. These trained professionals couldn't believe that someone like Wendy existed, that someone could be so calculating and cold.

From Stayton, I called my brother Tony to wish him a happy birthday and to tell him I was in Oregon. The last time I had talked to Tony was in the spring when Sandy and I were getting ready to sell our house. Tony still lived in the home place where he moved with Kathy and his children when father moved us to Tucson in 1967. Tony worked on that farm all his life. When the farm was sold in 1998, he and Kathy bought the seven acres with the house and farm buildings. When Kathy died at age 57 in 1999 from lung cancer, Sandy and I drove out to Iowa for the funeral. Hedy and Pete threw a party for ten of their friends and one hundred and fifty young people showed up. Three police cars joined the party.

On the phone, Tony seemed aloof, not understanding a word I was saying. He had worries on his mind. He said, "A car pulled into the yard and Kathy got in it. When I ran out to the car, it backed away and raced up the driveway. She's leaving me. Do you know why

Kathy is leaving me? There's some young guy she's been seeing. If I get a hold of that son-of-a-bitch, I'll fix him."

"Sounds like you were dreaming, Tony."

He said, "What is she doing? Why did she leave me? She's running off with a young guy. If a catch that son of a bitch—"

I changed the subject. "How are Pam and her family?"

"I don't know where Kathy went. She took all her clothes and she left."

"Oh, she'll be back," I said.

"You think so? I don't know why she left me for that young bastard."

"Are you having a cake for your birthday?"

"Kathy never made one, she ran off."

I called my sister Marlys in Hospers, Iowa. She said Tony was in the early stages of Alzheimer's, the disease that had taken our father down. Marlys thought I knew; Tony had been diagnosed for months. Dad had Alzheimer's for four years before succumbing to pneumonia.

Tony's predicament unnerved me. Seems I had run off, too, and didn't know where I was. I resigned at the Medallion plant, moved to Coos Bay on the coast, and camped at an RV park right on the beach. My spot was by a trail that led through a tangle of wind-ravaged trees to water. Surfers came in the afternoons when the fierce winds had ratcheted up the dangers. It was a noisy camping spot; waves crashed on the beach; the wind howled through the nights. "Sandy no like this place at all. She no like the wind," I said in my best Sean Connery to the trees. I caught a glimpse of my ragged self in a mirror. Sean spoke again. "Where is Sandy? She ran off with an old guy. If I catch that son of a bitch, I'll fix him."

I couldn't make decisions. I was slipping on the slope. I had the idea then that I should end it all. "Doctor Kevorkian where are you?" I walked on the stretch of beach at dusk. A mist had rolled in and brought the ceiling of the sky to just out of reach—no sunset that evening. The mist swirled above me and also danced on the water.

The waves churned and I knew it wouldn't be an easy task to wade out to reach the sharks. I focused on the mist overhead; a pelican darted out of the fog above me and then disappeared again. The mist was a broken cloud with ragged edges like the swirls that twisted in my mind. I couldn't decide.

That's when I smelled it. Something dead. I never had a good sense of smell after growing up on a pig farm, but this pierced my nose hard. Up the rise of sand near the base of one of the large trees was a large dead sea lion. He was stretched out on his back. I walked over holding my nose and a swarm of flies buzzed their annoyance. The fellow was about my height, from the heel of his hind flippers to the top of his head. His head was cocked and his mouth ajar. A grey tongue stuck out a corner of his mouth with long whiskers still tense in their sockets. His arms had come together on his chest. At his ankles, the flipper pads were crossed one over the other. I strolled around him, taking in every angle. A cut above an eye was the only wound on him. He was no youngster; he was an old fart like me. I didn't miss the implications that this three-hundred-pound-old man from the sea represented. If I were to continue with my death wish, the high tide might swap me out with him and I would be the stinking one that curious schoolboys circled around, poking with their sticks.

The next morning, I packed the trailer and headed south on the coastal highway toward Prescott.

CHAPTER 17

I hugged the coast south to Eureka, then headed toward Interstate 5. The next day, I plowed down the middle of the state, and two days later, I was in Prescott.

Sandy greeted me: "You look like hell." She wasn't happy to see me. It was the end of August and she had been back to work for three weeks. "Why didn't you stay up there? That was your plan."

"I can't focus on anything," I said. "I'm going crazy. I can't go into a grocery store and decide on a can of beans. Everything is a blur. Now I know what Hedy's going through when she struggles."

"Oh, God, why did you come back? You can't stay here. You're not going to bring me down. I'm doing fine. I'm doing what I'm supposed to. I didn't quit my teaching job—I stuck it out. You're not going to bring me down. I won't have it. You can't stay here, not even one night. You have to go away. What happened? Why didn't you stay there?" I put my hands up and walked out.

I drove out on Williamson Valley Road and turned onto Bridle Path, drove by our old place, our old asylum, which I needed desperately at that moment. I slept that night in the trailhead parking lot where people with horse trailers congregate at the trailheads leading into the wilderness.

Why had I come back? Good question. Had I gone north to just hear Betty's life story? If so, I had accomplished that task and I was back. Was I to feel better about my own life, knowing that Betty's story couldn't be beat?

The next day, I rented a storage unit and unloaded my stuff. Sandy found a psychiatrist in town; he wanted me to call him immediately. I headed to the shrink that afternoon. I had been to a shrink two times in my life—the first time after college when I was freaking out at the thought of being a teacher and the second time after being a teacher for a few years. The Greeks said if the gods wished to punish a man, they would make him a schoolmaster.

Dr. Penny and his receptionist stayed late just for me.

"So, what brings you?" asked Dr. Penny.

"I'm a little confused with life right now," I said. I summed up for him the last two years or so. "I feel like I'm raveling."

"So, you've lost your cat and your dog and your house and your church and your job and your friends and your wife all in the last few months? That's quite a hit. It's a wonder you're doing as well as you are."

"I'm trying to hold it together," I said. "If I was working that would help."

"That might," he said. "Any thoughts of suicide?"

"Nope."

"None? Are you sure?"

"Well, I was standing at the ocean a few days ago and had the thought to walk out into the waves until I saw myself lying in the sand beside me. I came across this old sea lion rotting on the beach and that changed my mind. I wasn't ready to have people holding their noses on my account." He laughed.

We talked about my children: Hedy's rape, her secret, her coming forward, and the family's pushback; Wendy's evil. I mentioned Pete taking a job in California. We talked about the big boulder of chaos that was about to roll off the mountain and take me out. Doctor Penny wrote me a prescription for anxiety.

WOLF UNDER BED

I pulled my truck into Dennis's driveway as it turned dark. A young German Shepard barked from the deck. Dennis stuck his head out the door, "Who's there?"

I called, "Lucky doesn't remember me."

He said, "It's okay, Lucky. It's Mike. Lucky, you know Mike. Come on up, Mike, and say hello to Lucky."

The aroma of pinesap from lumber filled the air. He caught me gawking at the raised boardwalk that led out from the porch to four mini-cottages he had built recently. Dennis had a mini-sawmill and had hauled logs out of the forest all summer. The bark beetle devastated the forests surrounding Prescott that year. Dennis had been busy on his project of bringing the Mekong Delta to Arizona.

"It's coming along, isn't it?" Dennis said. "Let me show you the lights; I just got them up today." He flipped a switch and a stringer of lights came on. "Three apartments are done. I'm about to finish number four. Some of my buddies are coming up this weekend. I can't wait to see how they like it." Lucky growled in a whisper as he followed us from shack to shack. Starting at age seventeen, Dennis spent three years in Vietnam as a long-distance reconnaissance patrol specialist or LRRP. His Vietnam buddies from the Phoenix area would be coming to escape the heat and soothe their PTSD. I could not argue with what Dennis believed—that the vets from Vietnam had gotten the short end. Defense Secretary McNamara by then had admitted that the Gulf of Tonkin incident was a lie to push us into war, but Dennis didn't want to believe that and it was futile to argue with him. He had a selective memory like Tim and Ches. He wouldn't let you make your point because he knew he couldn't stop himself from exploding in anger. Dennis said, "Contrary to popular beliefs, vets don't have an easy time getting help from the VA." Dennis gestured to his pump shed. "The well went dry last week and Lucky and me have been hauling water." I worked out a deal with Dennis to rent an extra bedroom in his trailer and paid a month in advance.

The next day, I met Hedy at my storage shed to give her some sketchpads for the classes she was taking that fall semester at Yavapai College. Sandy and I had set aside some money from the sale of the house to help her finish college. Hedy was in high spirits and feeling good about life. I told her I was getting rid of most of my books and offered her a big book about the magic of birthdays. She said, "Sure." I said, "Catch" as I dropped it from the second story railing into her arms. She was always a good fielder. Hedy played soccer, basketball, and softball for ten years starting at about age seven. She was a pitcher in fast-pitch softball and I played catcher when she practiced her pitching at home. Fast-pitch pitchers with a good sinker make their fathers sing soprano. Her summer softball team finished in second place four years in a row to a team from Bagdad, Arizona. When Bagdad opted out of the tournament that last year, Hedy's team finally won their trophy.

Hedy displayed many talents when she was growing up, but she was first of all a gifted musician. She played viola in first grade and picked it up again in seventh grade; something clicked and she became a sensation. She won scholarships for three consecutive summer music camps in Flagstaff. She dropped out of sports to concentrate on her music; she played with the orchestra and danced and sang with the show choir.

During her graduation, Hedy led off the singing of "O Sifuni Mungu" a song that had the three hundred and fifty graduates singing along and grooving in place. During that performance at graduation, we sat next to Wendy's family. When Hedy started singing, Wendy started talking and wouldn't stop. Sandy got after Wendy to shush it but Wendy only talked louder. It was only after the song ended that Wendy stopped talking. Again, when the grads were walking up to get their diplomas, Wendy started talking loudly. Looking back, we can see that Wendy was trying to distract and disrupt us from witnessing Hedy receiving her diploma and cheering on our girl. It was a blatant act of aggression. Wendy must have been seething inside, mainly because Christopher never graduated. We just thought it was just Wendy being Miss Me-Me-Me. We never watched movies with her because she just wouldn't stop talking during them. So, it seemed reasonable that she was just being herself. Two years later, she pulled that stunt again, talking nonstop, trying to distract us when Peter was in line about to receive his diploma. Grandma Ches never came to Hedy or Peter's graduations, because Wendy talked Ches out of coming. Wendy's birthday was in mid-June, which Ches never missed.

(2005) After Hedy drove away from the storage unit, I found the screenplay she had been writing; she left it on the seat of my truck. I sat in my truck and read it. A Romeo and Juliet love story set in Nazi Germany about a Jewish farm girl and a Christian boy. More like a synopsis. It was thrilling piece and captured the terror of the time.

In the Safeway store, I couldn't make a decision in the soup aisle and left the store in frustration. These new meds were not helping at all. I was worse. I was also losing emotional juices from a wound in my heart, not a physical wound. My heart had been beating to the rhythm of Sandy's heart for so many years it didn't know how to beat on its own. It was hopping around like a rabbit in a cage. The raveling cord coming straight out of my gut had attached itself to a cliff in the clouds and was lowering me deeper and deeper into the mist.

I gave Dennis a box of my old stuff, which included vinyl LPs and videos. He was delighted. Dennis was addicted to television while I had a hard time concentrating on it. I couldn't read either, so I wandered his property under the watchful eye of Lucky. Dennis and Floyd had built a two-car machine shop that Dennis had planned to make into a business. It was filled with junk. The neighborhood needed a good mechanic, he said.

That evening, Hurricane Katrina plowed into New Orleans. Like an old couple, Dennis and I watched television as the drama escalated. I was on edge more than usual because Dennis kept switching back and forth between a dozen different shows, two of them the weather channel and Dawg, the Hawaiian Detective. The meds in my system were affecting me and I couldn't sit still. My standing behind Dennis was driving him batty. "Leave or sit down!" he yelled. I left. Through the next day, the massive storm continued into Mississippi causing extensive damage. The levees along Lake Pontchartrain above New Orleans broke open causing massive flooding in the city. Thousands of people scampered to the sports dome in the city hoping to find refuge and be rescued.

I was splitting wood the next morning when Dennis came out and declared he needed to clean up the site of his old trailer house that he had been dismantling. We built a bonfire and tossed in the unsalvageable. I had given Dennis a few of my paintings and he got the idea we should burn them. So, we did. They were drip and smear portraits in the combined styles of Jackson Pollack and Salvador Dali—the smoke trail they left was quite stunning.

That evening while watching the Katrina devastation unfolding, Dennis said, "There you go, Mike. Why don't you go to Louisiana and help those people? Do something useful. Go out and help those people." That wasn't a bad idea and I was just messed up enough to do that. But luckily, I couldn't decide.

We watched as a news helicopter hovered over the dome refugees who had been without food and water for days. Many people in the crowd cheered the helicopter; many were angry that no one was coming to help. A camera crew got into the superdome to see how desperate the situation was. A group chanted help, help, help; a woman spoke to the camera, "Someone needs to come now! We need help for the hundreds of old people trapped here—many of whom were dying nightly." Another said, "It's not about rich people, poor people, it's about people." One black lady pleaded, "We need help, sir, we're dying in here, and babies are dying." Another woman, "No one's helping us; they locked us in here and said we couldn't leave. We're in hell. President Bush should be ashamed of himself."

That's when Dennis lost it—he jumped off the sofa. He screamed. He grabbed ahold of the TV and shook it. When he took a step back, I thought he was going to kick it. "Son of a bitch, that damn bitch." He flung his arms. "How do they get off? Ungrateful people! They're dry! They haven't drowned. They should be thankful! Don't blame Bush!" Dennis gave me sideways glance.

I said, "No water or food for four days. I think we'd be yelling, too."

"Well, go there and whine with them!"

"Not today, Buddy."

"Get out of my house!" I left and walked the area.

A week later, I went hiking with Sandy on the trails at Granite Lake. We started out of the Cayuse parking lot. As we walked, she filled me in on what I missed that week. Pete bought a car and moved to California for a job with Raytheon. Hedy was into her classes at Yavapai College and working part-time at the theatre. Sandy said she got a birthday card from Ches, which she opened.

"You're looking better," she said.

I said, "My gut is on its way to recovery, thank you."

She asked, "Your new meds are treating you better then?"

"Yes," I said. I didn't tell her I wasn't taking them. She knew of Dennis's water problem and invited me to come over and shower. Which I did.

Dennis threw another fit. "You sick bastard. You think she's going to take you back? She doesn't want anything to do with you. She's the reason you're all fucked up. She just wants to make sure you don't spend money on yourself. Let me tell you about women. All they want is to take, take, take. My ex still wants me to throw money at her. They're never satisfied. Women have made me pay through the nose, let me tell you. Women only care about themselves and the money."

Sandy called one evening and told Dennis she wanted to speak to me. Dennis told her to leave me alone and never call his place again. She called the police and officer came out to check on me. Dennis threw a fit after the officer left. "Who in the hell does she think she is? Don't go near her, Mike. She's trying to screw you up."

I started lifting weights in the machine shed. Early in the morning, I would drive over to the Granite Mountain trailheads. Years earlier, Pete and his friends had found the top of a split boulder covered in petroglyphs; they said no one else knew about it. They took photos of the site and Pete teased that I would never find it. Sandy and I had found it once but I forgot where it was. I set out on every hike trying to find it. I knew the general location. I wandered deeper and deeper into the wilderness area.

One night at dusk, Dennis drove his '49 Chevy across the street to the Deacon's place. I was in the living room when I heard Dennis shouting from the street. I smelt skunk in the air. I was on the porch when Dennis called, "Lucky! Mike, open the gate and let Lucky out!" Lucky burst down the driveway, his hind legs churning and to the Deacon's place he ran. Dennis shouted, "Get 'em, Lucky! Get 'em!" Lucky disappeared behind their house. I heard a yelp and a squeal, then a shriek. Lucky ran past Dennis, and down the road and into our yard with Dennis running behind him. Lucky smelled like skunk. The dog circled around me; he had what looked like a rag in his mouth. Lucky ran back to Dennis, then around him, stopping at his feet. Dennis jerked the trophy from Lucky's mouth. It was the tail of a skunk. Lucky had taken a full dose in his face and his chest. Dennis didn't seem to notice that the air had become toxic; he was so proud of his skunk dog. He ran back to the Deacon's house waving the prize with Lucky jumping at his side. It was that time of year when smoke from wildfires makes the sunset red.

Dennis and Lucky left early one morning in the Chevy pickup pulling a car trailer loaded with the sawmill. They came back later that afternoon with a huge Ditch-Witch riding high on the trailer. One of the wheels of the heavy trenching machine had broken through the floor. The machine, bigger than a backhoe, was about to topple off. Dennis eased it off the trailer. He said, "I rented it for laying pipe. The neighborhood needs someone with a Ditch-Witch." He was renting it for a week or two with options to buy it. He raced his new tractor over to the Deacons to show them. He was over there for quite a while. When he returned, he dug on a trench for an hour as it turned dark.

That evening as we watched television, Dennis leaned toward me and said, "I can buy that Ditch-Witch for five thousand dollars—that's a deal. It's going to be my new business. I took the sawmill back; they wanted too much for it, but this I really want to keep. Do you think you can lend me the five thousand dollars?"

"I'll have to think about that. That's a lot of money. I'm not in any condition to make decisions right now. I'm not really thinking straight."

"I need to know soon. I've got to fix that trailer. I need to know tonight."

"Well, then I have to say no, Dennis. I need some time. It doesn't feel right, like I said, to be lending money now when my head is in a fog."

"I need this. You know I'm good for it."

"Well, I don't know that. You've lied to me before. You and your dad both lied to me." I was referring to a Chevy pick-up I bought from Dennis and Floyd. The title had been doctored and read 87,000 miles as the odometer reading. We visited Floyd in the rest home and he swore the number was correct. The new title the DMV sent me showed 187,000 miles.

"My dad didn't lie," said Dennis.

I said, "He lied right to my face. I saw you signaling him behind my back but I let it slide, hoping the truck would last. It didn't. No, I don't want to lend you any money." I left the room.

The next day, Sandy and I went out to eat. I was using her computer when Dennis called. "What are you doing over there?" he said. "Didn't I tell you to stay the hell away from her? Hey, I need you to help me to lay some pipe."

"I thought you weren't doing that until tomorrow," I said.

"Well, I need you to come here right now before it gets dark."

"It's dark already."

"Well, you can hold the flashlight. Just get here as fast as you can."

When I got to Dennis's place, I pulled up to a pile of my clothes and things that he had thrown in the dirt driveway. He said, "Take your shit and get the hell out of my life." He was packing a gun on his hip. He smelled of alcohol.

I drove over to the corral by the trailhead and camped. I had to clear off my bed before I could crawl in. Dennis had kept a lot of my junk. Good riddance. I turned on the classic rock station KSLX out of Phoenix. "The Logical Song" by Super Tramp came on and it soothed my aching head. It was followed by the news. The Phoenix sniper had struck again. That evening, they were holding an open line discussion about the evil deviant in the desert; they were trying to gather tips about the crazy guy with a gun.

CHAPTER 18

The next morning, I hiked into the Granite Mountain wilderness area. Half an hour into Mint trail, a group of boulders rose up out of the wash. It was in the general area where the lost petroglyphs should have been. I climbed to the top of a high boulder. I didn't see any petroglyphs but stayed up there a while. Sitting Indian style, I took off my shirt and let the sun wash over me. I closed my eyes and practiced being in the moment, blocking out the white noise, all the voices, all the past. Just listen and be. I was far enough behind the mountain that I couldn't hear any traffic. Meditation is being in the moment, living in the present, stopping the swirling in your head, the voices, and the chatter. Breathe in, breathe out. Heat created, heat dispersed.

An abundance of noisy Arizona songbirds darted around me while Granite Mountain spoke the language of the Great Mysterious. Old Stony pointed straight into the universe. How old were these trails beside the mountain? They talked to the mountain since ancient man beat footpaths out of Mint Wash. Old Hewitt found some of his best pots and metates in the folds of this mountain.

I saw vultures floating in the heights. Flickers, finches, and tit-mouses peeped around me. As the big birds sailed on the high wind, I thought of Dennis. His High Desert Retreat was like a raptor rescue site. When Dennis flung me toward the wilderness, he knew

I was ready to fly. It takes about five weeks for injured wings to heal and that was how long Dennis tolerated me and nursed me with his toughness. He needed help as much as I did. His was selective healing. The sun was low in the west as I headed back on the trail. Near the crossroads leading back to the parking lot, a boulder caught my eye. I decided to climb it. When I reached the top, I was looking down on a giant boulder split perfectly in half, the flat surface slanted at about 30 degrees. On the slab were the lost petroglyphs. Dozens of figures danced in the sunlight as they did for Peter and his friends. There was a whole novel there on the gray rock's surface if I could break the code and unlock the suspense. Fleeing deer, hunters in the corners, every sort of animal was rendered in their stylistic pajamas. Every shape of plant and tree gave shade from the three suns and five moons on the border. There were ummingbirds as big as eagles. Wolves, with heads erect, eyed the children of man.

    I drove to Chino Valley to use a phone. I was able to reach J. Allen Woodman, the head of the English department at Northern Arizona University in Flagstaff and made an appointment to see him the next day. I camped on an old mining road below Bill Williams Mountain near the town Williams, named after the old mountain man. At NAU, Professor Woodman said he could get me in the MA program for the spring semester if I sent all the papers ASAP. He wanted samples of my writing, transcripts from colleges, and the hind teat of an owl.

    I came back to Prescott, made contacts, picked up some things, and headed toward Tucson to spend a month with Sharon and her son, Jeff. I drove through Phoenix, dodging the sniper, and via Superior, headed south toward the San Manuel mine. I drove through Mammoth that was fast becoming a ghost town. To the south was the town of San Manuel where the smelter used to be. (The giant stacks were gone, toppled in 2002. YouTube has a site that shows them fall.) The five shafts at the entrance into the mine were gone and a tall fence surrounded the property. I drove around Oracle looking for the house we stayed in when the kids were small, but I couldn't remember the street name. Sandy took Hedy and Peter horned toad hunting every day on those dirt streets. Not far from the town of Catalina, I recognized the road that headed into the foothills where the movie *CC Rider* was filmed when I was in high school. For a week, my friend David and I ditched school to watch Joe Namath and Ann Margaret make the worst movie ever made. I made it to Sharon's place after sunset. Jeff greeted me in his wheelchair with Sharon following close behind.

The Tucson library let me use their computers where I edited short stories and a handful of poems and songs. Wise men believed those who don't follow their hearts got ailments of the heart. Finally, the envelope, with my hopes enclosed, was mailed to NAU and Dr. Jellin'.

Sharon and Jeff's street was one of many loaded with little brick houses and desert landscapes built in the fifties to entice snowbirds from the Midwest. Many of those little houses started out with grass lawns until the desert-look became the norm. Tucson, at around 2200 feet elevation, is about six degrees cooler than Phoenix. At the end of Sharon's street was a house that she pointed out often. "There's your roundhouse, Michael." She referred to the time Sandy and I had built a geodesic dome in the woods of Arkansas in the 1970s during our back-to-the-land days and Sharon liked to tease me about it. Jeff had been confined to a wheelchair since about age 20. He was born with a deformed hand and a pair of legs that didn't match up. His maladies were associated with Sharon's rare blood type, AB negative. Sharon had worked at the University Hospital since 1980.

When Sandy and I were first married, we would go to the Swap meet near Tucson's Greyhound Park that opened every autumn. The tables were set up under the big cottonwoods that ran beside a wash. One day as we browsed past the tables, we came across two ladies who were having a fun time telling stories and hooting with laughter; they set a mood for the whole site. They were two sisters, probably in their early sixties, there to meet and greet people. We bought two porcelain plates with flower prints from them. They teased us and asked us when we were getting married. When we told them we had just gotten married, they laughed with glee. "You all look like babies! I don't believe it!" Sandy showed them her cheap ring of white-gold and mother of pearl. We told them we were getting a nicer ring soon, and one said, "You better, if you want to keep this girl." As we departed, the taller gal said, "You guys take care. Don't let them bed bugs bite." They laughed and hooted. That summer of 2005, I hauled those two plates around, up to Oregon and back. I told Sharon about the magic they held. Jeff asked if their magic would make Sharon's cooking edible. Sharon said, "See if I cook for you again, Mister Fussy Mouth."

In 1972, as newlyweds, Sandy and I frequented Fourth Avenue. We helped start The Food Conspiracy Co-op and volunteered there often. For months, we asked Sandy's folks, Tom and Ches, to go out to eat with us at Caruso's near The Conspiracy. But Ches refused to go. She said, "The hippies will stick heroin needles in my arm." She was serious. Tom finally talked her into meeting us at the restaurant where Sandy turned Tom onto anchovy spaghetti. Ches didn't trust me or Tom to protect her. She had spent her lifetime in distrust mode.

Sandy called me to say Hedy's friend Kim had been killed in a car accident near Prescott Valley. The two girls had bonded as friends the moment they met in the spring. Hedy was twenty-four and Kim was twenty-two. Their birthdays were in the same week in December. Kim was four months younger than Pete. Hedy and Kim had found in each other the sister they each always wanted to have. They were exploring the area's sights and sounds together and loving life. Kim's death devastated Hedy. She was taking art classes that fall semester but pulled back from everything for a few weeks. The driver of the other car was a woman on medications who had fallen asleep at the wheel.

Sharon, Jeff, and I went to the Fourth Avenue fair that fall. In a shop window, we spied a black-and-white photo of a man on horseback. "Who does that look like?" Sharon asked. "Kind of looks like Robert, huh?" Robert Dolan was Jeff's dad. Jeff looked a lot like Robert.

Sharon said, "Don't you recognize him? Think Mexican bandito."

"Oh, I remember! My sister married Pancho Villa! Jeff, rollover here by this picture and let me get your picture with Pancho."

Later, Sharon asked, "That old Jack Frost, how's he doing?"

"I haven't seen him for a couple of years. He's might be dead by now."

I met Jack Frost in 1999 at the Valley National Bank in Prescott. Right out of the blue he told me history. Jack's father was shot in Pancho Villa's raid on Columbus, New Mexico in 1916. Alvin Frost, died years later of lead poisoning caused by the dum-dum bullet fragments embedded in his chest and arm. Pancho Villa was assassinated the week Jack was born in 1923. Jack became a mountain man at age seventeen. He was drafted into the Navy during WWII when he was prospecting in the mountains of New Mexico. When I met Jack, he had two pairs of glasses hanging on strings tied around his neck and a third pair in his shirt pocket. He said his nickname in the navy was Hawkeye and he spent most of his time perched high on the ships. It turned out that Jack knew Thomas Mitcham, Sandy's father. They met in the mountains near Socorro when Tom was searching for uranium and so was Jack.

I asked Sharon if she ever ran into Ches or Tim around Tucson. She had not seen them for years.

In January, I moved to Flagstaff. I stayed at Gabaldon Hall and I shared the room with Varian, a young Navajo man in his mid-twenties. Flagstaff is a cold place in the winter. Ten below zero was the reading during the first week of classes, and when it warmed a little, it snowed. I spent much time indoors and redeemed myself with jumping jacks and push-ups. I signed up to sub in the Flagstaff school district and was soon buried in work. My professors were four ladies and Jim Simmerman who taught 20th Century American Poets. The Gospel of Judas was in the news then. Everyone had a different take on the traitor of Jesus. An article I read argued that Judas wasn't a traitor but a co-conspirator with Jesus in Jesus' own death. Since before I could read, I was taught by the nuns that the man named Judas was to be hated with all your might, and all your being, for he was the ultimate miscreant. But what if he really was a hero?

One day, I subbed for a woodshop class at one of the high schools in Flagstaff. The teacher had turned the class into a study hall. The machines were in disuse and rusting. Only a few hand tools were still in the cabinets and those were beaten up. There was no wood in the wood room, no sandpaper, no finishes. I couldn't believe what I was seeing.

During my years of teaching, I ran a great shop class and kept my charges busy at all times. When I was cabinet-making in Prescott, I used to take loads of scrap wood from Lowell's shop to the high school woodshop where a busy Mr. Bockman greeted me with open arms. But there in Flagstaff, I was seeing the end of a hundred-year-old manual arts program. Some would argue that shop and Home Economics programs were obsolete, created a century ago at the direction of manufacturers who wanted trained and obedient workers, and we should welcome the change. Since the corporations had left America for the greener pastures and slave-wages overseas, manufacturing jobs had been disappearing. And those jobs weren't coming back any time soon. America created new technologies but where were the jobs? In 1978, there were 23 million manufacturing jobs in the United States and the population has tripled since then, but there are only 11 million manufacturing jobs as of 2021. Our "debt and death economy" that today is being run by the corrupt elite and the military fanatics will collapse in the future and when that happens, people will have to rely on each other to survive. Do we have to create caveman survival classes in our schools? Ever wonder why a show like Naked and Afraid came into being?

That day, when I asked the handful of students in that study hall what they usually did in class, they said they sat around and talked. No lessons, no plans, no direction. I asked them if they would like to write poems. They were game. So that's what we did for the next week. Every class. They wrote about machines, about passions, about problems and dreams, about the latest rapper, the latest diva. What are you? Who are you? What would you die for? What would you live for? They were psyched. "My grandma is so ghetto," was one of the first lines of a poem by a Navajo boy and it ignited the class and the classes that followed. They wanted to keep their poems, show their friends, show their folks, get something posted on the front of their parents' refrigerator again. They made something special that day in the woodshop.

Sandy called near the end of February. Hedy had packed her things in her Volvo, left town. She dropped out of her classes at the college. Hedy didn't say where she was going but left a note saying she would keep us posted. I suspected she was heading for Oregon again, a place that excited her.

I wrote a few songs that semester. A song that came to me one evening while I was on the computer: "A letter from Iraq" was one I planned to use as the anchor for a website I created for a computer class. A graduate student from Sweden, Johanna, sang the song for me in Swedish; Varian sang it in Navajo; I had a Spanish singer lined up and a student from Pakistan to sing it in Urdu before I ran out of time. I ended up changing the project theme to a website on information on Ethical Wills but left a link open for the song to be heard.

The semester flew by and Sandy drove over to see *The Taming of the Shrew* that the drama department was putting on. We went out to dinner and afterward, she spent the night in my room; Varian had gone to the Rez to save his marriage and/or take a second wife. I told Sandy that sneaking a girl into the dorm room could get me into a lot of trouble. "We'll see," she said. We made love for the first time in two years. As we lay in bed the next morning with the window open to the screen, we heard strange sounds coming from a window on the floor above. "What's that?" Sandy asked. I knew right away it was the sound of a young woman moaning, about to come to orgasm, but as a tease, I said, "That's a bird cooing, a rare bird that's only found in the Flagstaff. Listen." Sandy caught on to the tease, and we giggled and put our hands to our mouths, like kids eavesdropping, before we slid the window shut.

The semester ended. I took summer classes and camped in the woods outside of Flagstaff. I took two graduate classes at the same time that almost killed me; in Shakespeare, we read seven plays in five weeks, wrote about them, and watched the film versions of each play. In Children's Literature, we read thirty books, discussed, and wrote about them. But I found some lucky feathers near my campsite, brought them to class, and let the other zombies touch and feel the magic that radiated from them. "With a feather," I announced, "you can read one hundred pages an hour." And everyone who took one was grateful.

I returned to Prescott as the summer term ended. That week, Sandy dreamed that Ches and Wendy showed up at the townhouse. In her dream, Sandy walked out of her bedroom and down the stairs and turned toward the living room where she saw her mother and sister sitting together on the sofa. They were smiling and then not smiling, drilling her with their eyes. Sandy said it was a terrifying dream but couldn't remember the rest of it. We were about to discover the rest of it.

CHAPTER 19

That weekend, my niece Pam called to say my brother Tony was in the hospital with pneumonia and he had suffered a debilitating stroke. His Alzheimer's was wearing him down. He was on his last days at age sixty-six. I checked with the airlines about flights to Sioux Falls. It was 120 degrees in Phoenix that week and over a hundred in Prescott. The police had added the baseline rapist to the Most Wanted posters. And the Phoenix sniper was still at large.

That same evening as I scanned through the NAU English department web pages, I came across a note: English professor, Jean Zucowski, had passed away. Another item told that Val Avery, a history professor, was also being laid to rest. I had not met either one. The Arts and Letters site had a picture of Jim Simmerman, my professor from the spring semester. He had died the evening of June 29, 2006. I called a classmate and he said Sim had committed suicide because of a terminal illness. It was Sim who had created my graduate program. I had a conference with him on the final paper that I wrote on war poetry at the end of May where he said my writing would improve if I stopped trying to be funny, that every point didn't need a punch line. Advice I would try to follow. Sim was born in early March 1952, two weeks after my birthday. So as his elder, I should've been the one giving *him* advice. Years earlier, I had stumbled across a Supreme Court case argued in February and

March 1952: Alder vs. the New York City Board of Education. That case affirmed the right of school districts to fire teachers considered subversive. McCarthyism was just coming on the scene. The teacher, James Alder, lost his case. So, what is poetry but a subversive act? A questioning? I should have demanded a conference with Sim, on my terms, assigning him to read Norman Cousin's humor collection, and write "Do Not Go Gentle Into That Good Night" two hundred times on a whiteboard.

Monday before noon, a knock came at the front door of the townhouse. Sandy was upstairs in the shower. I opened the front door and standing on the stoop was Ches and Wendy. I hadn't seen Wendy since late 2002 when she was mad at us for ruining her Christmas. I hadn't seen Ches since Sandy plucked the portraits from her shelves. Ches still looked like the fragile old Bonsai gardener I remembered her as, except that day she had dark glasses and wore a scarf tight on her head. Wendy had gained fifty pounds. The two seemed taken aback that I was there. Alas, instead of telling them to go away, I asked, "What do you want?"

Wendy said, "Mom was in the hospital twice in the last few months." Ches nodded. Wendy said, "Mom needs to see Sandy." Ches nodded again. Ches was 86 then. I opened the door wider. I gestured for them to sit on the sofa that was facing the stairs. I had forgotten about Sandy's dream.

I ran up the stairs to tell Sandy. She said, "Why did you let them in?"

"I'll tell them to go away," I said. "Maybe Christopher confessed. Maybe they want to make peace with the truth."

"I'll be down in a moment. Don't talk to them."

As I was coming down the stairs, I remembered that we had recently received in the mail a book, a memoir, from Tom's sister, Aunt Betty. I thought that Ches and Wendy might want the book if they didn't already have it. I said, "Oh, I've got something in here for you." When I came out with the book, Wendy was standing with a look of terror on her face. She put her hands up in front of her face and squawked, "Ah!" She thought I was going to shoot her in the face.

Ches shouted, "What's he got? Is it a gun?"

I showed them the book, "It's a book from Aunt Betty. Do you want it?" Ches took off her sunglasses to see better.

Wendy was angry, "No! We don't want it!"

I asked, "Do you have it?"

"We don't want it!"

I tossed the book on the counter and sat on one of the bar stools. There was an awkward silence until Ches said, "Has it been hot here?"

"Plenty hot," I said.

"It's a hundred and twenty in Phoenix today," she said.

"Too hot," I said.

"Do you have a yard?"

"Just that little square by the front door."

"What is your cat's name?"

"Brian."

"How old is he?"

"He's a year old." I heard Sandy coming down the stairs. She turned the corner and frowned when she saw the two women sitting on the sofa. It was a re-enactment of the dream, except I was with them and we weren't smiling. Sandy said, "Why are you here? Why have you come?" She pulled a chair from the dining table and set it in front of her mother, turning her body and the chair away from Wendy. Sandy sat down. "What do you want, mom?"

Ches said, "I wanted to see you, Sandy. How are you?"

"I'm doing fine."

Wendy scolded, "Mom's had two bad spells, she's been in the hospital, both times she was in a coma."

"Oh, I'm sorry to hear that," Sandy said.

"You didn't even know about that," Wendy said. "We thought we'd lost her. You told us to stay away from you, so we didn't call you."

"How was I supposed to know then?" asked Sandy.

"You didn't know at all."

"You could have gotten on the phone for something that important. But you didn't even try, did you? Why didn't Tim call?"

Ches said, "Sandy, I'm really worried about you."

Wendy scolded, "No one ever hurt you, Sandy."

Sandy said, "We've all been through bad things."

Wendy scolded again, "No one ever hurt you, Sandy." Sandy put her hands to block out Wendy who had leaned into Sandy's space. Sandy said, "I'm not talking to you. Stay back!"

Ches said, "Sandy, I'm really worried about you."

Sandy rose and said, "This is over. You need to leave now."

I said, "You better leave."

Wendy said again, "No one ever hurt you, Sandy."

"Stop it, Wendy!" Then Sandy leaned in closer to Wendy, "How does it feel to be the mother of a rapist?"

I yelled into the side of Wendy's face, "Your son raped our daughter when she was six years old!" I went to the door and held it open. "Now get out. Time to leave." They stayed seated on the sofa and I said, "We're calling the police in five seconds. Five, four, three . . ." They rose.

Sandy herded them to the door. "Get out. Get out of here now."

Ches said, "Sandy, I'm worried about you."

I said again, "Your son raped my daughter when she was six years old!"

Wendy stopped on the threshold, hooked her arm around the jamb, and wouldn't let us close the door. I pried her hand loose and escorted her a few feet down the sidewalk with my hand on her back and said, "Goodbye."

I stepped into the townhouse, but before Sandy could close the door, Wendy stuck her leg in and pushed the door open more. Wendy snarled with gritted teeth, "Nicki and Patrick don't hold it against Hedy and Peter when they molested my boys!"

"Yeah, because it never happened!" Sandy said.

"Get out of here," I said. Again, I put my hand on Wendy's back again to guide her down the sidewalk. Two young men were approaching the front of the townhouse. Wendy threw herself to the ground and yelled, "Assault, assault!" she spoke to the two men. "Did you see that? That was assault! Did you see that?"

One of the boys said, "Nope, we didn't see a thing." They kept walking.

Ches shouted, "Oh, no! Wendy just had knee surgery! Look what you've done!" Sandy spit in her mother's face and shouted, "Grandma rapist!"

Wendy, still on the ground, said to me, "Why did you lose your teaching job in Oracle? I bet you molested your students, didn't you?"

I slapped her across the mouth. "Stay away from us. You're poison." Sandy and I stepped inside and closed the door.

The visit only lasted ten minutes but it showed volumes of the resentment that we held for each other. We missed an opportunity to confront the PACT for their secret dealings. But at least, Wendy would have those words in her head: "How does it feel to be the mother of a rapist?" Something no one put in her ear before.

That night, my brother Tony passed away. I couldn't leave Sandy alone; I called his daughter Pam and told her I wouldn't be able to come to the funeral. Pam was disappointed but she said understood.

During my high school years, I left Tucson two summers in a row, went to Iowa to work on Tony's farm, and stayed with Tony and Kathy and their five children. My sister Marlys and her family lived thirty miles away on a farm near Hospers; I spent time with them, too. Marlys' husband, Marv, a Korean veteran, got me thinking at age nine toward joining the military after high school. I didn't need persuading. From the time I could read, I was in love with George Armstrong Custer. When I was ten, Tony disrupted my hero-worship by telling me Custer was an evil man and the history books didn't tell me the truth. By age fifteen, I had narrowed down the vehicle of escape from my parent's home to the Navy. But by early 1969, the veterans coming back from Vietnam were protesting the war and throwing their medals into bonfires; their speeches helped turn me away from any military service. At the same time, sister Sharon ran to Height Ashbury in San Francisco in search of meaning, and my parents were freaking out over her path in life and my anti-war rhetoric.

(July 2006) Two days after the pact's visit, a Yavapai county deputy sheriff knocked on the door with restraining orders against us. Wendy and Ches's claims of assault forced us to lawyer up. We went with DeRienzo in Prescott Valley. I admitted slapping Wendy across the mouth but not pushing her to the ground. DeRienzo asked me to demonstrate how I escorted Wendy toward the curb. I showed him. He said, "Because you put your hand on her back, you set yourself up. She might have gone to your home with that intent, to cause a scene, and you gave her the opportunity. All she had to do was hit the ground and cry assault. We'll never prove otherwise." A mediation hearing would be arranged.

On Sunday, we drove to Tucson and visited with Ches; Tim was at church. Sandy apologized to Ches, "I'm sorry I spit on you but in the heat of moment, I felt you were defending the rapist of my little girl. Little girls are like butterflies and Chris and Wendy ripped off my little girl's wings. How will she fly now?"

Ches said she accepted Sandy's apology. Ches said she was feeling tired and went to lay down on her bed. Sandy followed into her room and laid on the bed with her and the two of them held each other for a while until Ches fell asleep.

Over the years, Ches and Tim listened to the Rush Limbaugh show where they gathered twisted facts and tried to hug them into truths. During the Clinton years, Ches would get so mad at the thought of Bill Clinton being her president that she trembled like a late-stage alcoholic. I agreed with her that Clinton should have been impeached for lying to Congress and when women were accusing him of assault and rape. I became an independent because of Clinton. When I told Tim and Ches we had four presidents in a row who lied constantly, Ches and Tim got mad; they could not believe that anyone could believe that Reagan and the two Bushes were just as bad as Clinton. They wouldn't tolerate me saying that George W. and Dick Cheney were evil liars, and they should be in prison for lying us into wars. Ches said, "Bush and Cheney never did bad things; they just wouldn't." Tim said, "President Bush goes to church; the Bushes are good people."

An innocent act, the sneaking of sesame seeds, was twisted and spun by the guilt-ridden mother of a rapist. The unenviable task that Wendy faced was to answer this: How do you explain to the world that your bright-eyed son morphed into a rapist on your watch? How could you bear false witness against your innocent niece? Her answer: You do whatever it takes to keep the world from finding out, plus you deny, deny, deny. Then you start scapegoating everybody near you. Pretty soon, though, the crowds gather in the streets below the window and Fagan climbs on the roof. Somebody throws water on the witch.

That week, detectives in Phoenix arrested the two snipers who had terrorized the Phoenix area for fifteen months. Polygamist Warren Jeffs, was captured in Nevada disguised as a woman.

CHAPTER 20

In early September, Wendy was granted a third delay for the mediation hearing. She kept moving the date back. She said she needed Ches and Tim and Bob to be at The Festival for the Burning of Family Heretics. Sandy and I were breaking with family tradition, a tradition that sanctioned the raping of small children. Tradition! What audacity had we to call out a generational ritual? Tradition! Sandy and I were the guilty parties in need of public humiliation.

This was the first letter Wendy wrote to the judge:

TO THE PRESCOTT JUSTICE COURT

> I am writing this letter in response to the defendants, the Wallriches' request for mediation. At this point, we have not sought an attorney simply because #1, we can't afford one and we know we wouldn't qualify for a court-appointed attorney, and #2, we have not done anything.
> I need to know if my mother who is a direct witness and my husband will be allowed to come to this mediation. It is difficult for her to come because of her age but she would like to come. I don't want her to come all the way from Tucson and not get into the mediation. If she'll even be able to come!

All she has ever wanted was for us all to come together and try and resolve this. The defendant is her daughter and has held this over all of us for years now and Mom just wants to see the family try and come together. Of course, I want my husband there for moral support and he has been involved in this mess since it started out. All I'm asking is if it's okay for them to be there.

Sincerely Wendy Adams

More rambling letters followed asking the court to push back the date so as to placate Wendy and the PACT members. In the last letter to the judge, Wendy started referring to it as "re-mediation." She and Ches must have thought a remedy was coming. The mediation finally took place in late September, in the basement of the Yavapai county courthouse in Prescott, a rambling space, protected by many solicitor spiders in the corners in the depths of the law library.

The goal, as laid out by our lawyer, was to get a co-restraining order against Wendy and Bob and not "the re-mediation" ordering us to capitulate to Wendy's demands "to get the family back together." Our lawyer, Daniel DeRienzo, advised us to let him do most of the talking and above all to keep our cool as he suspected Wendy would be trying to push our buttons. Any outbursts on our part would not help our case. "I know it will be hard to sit there and listen to her and take it, but you may need to do some bullet biting. Bring a notepad and just take notes the whole time, that's what I'm going to do. You won't even have to look at her."

We arrived early and were sitting at a table when at exactly 3:00, we spied Wendy and her coterie trailing behind her, coming down the steps to the basement. Sandy whispered, "They look like a bunch of toothless hillbillies." DeRienzo said, "I suspect they will be toothless."

Our two parties sat each on one side of two long tables butted together, while the two mediators, Glenda and Bill, sat together in the middle on the other side. Daniel DeRienzo, Sandy, and I sat on the right half. DeRienzo was our buffer from the PACT and their new member, Bob. Sandy refused to look at Wendy but rather leaned toward me for the duration of round one.

Wendy spoke first. She summarized the incident that prompted her to file a restraining order: "I was assaulted and had done nothing to cause it. I don't know why they were so angry. Mike went to the closet to get something and I honestly thought he was getting a gun to kill us with. But then I saw it was a book. He tried to give me the book. They are writing a book about the whole affair, about the family and about something they said my son did to them. I refused to look at the book. I don't want to see negative things like that.

"After the assault, Mom and I looked into getting a gun and a safety box to put it in, for protection. I was being civil and nice and Sandy and Mike were hostile to me and my eighty-seven-year-old mother who only wanted to see her daughter, Sandy, and the only reason I went to their place was that my mother begged me to take her over there. So, I went with her to tell Sandy that Mom had been in a coma for days and Sandy didn't even know about it. They had asked us to not have contact with them. I asked them: 'What if Hedy needed a kidney transplant and we couldn't get a hold of her?' And then, for no reason, Mike started yelling terrible accusations about my son. My beloved sister Patty, whom I dearly loved, passed away two years ago and Sandy didn't come to the funeral."

I had witnessed Wendy's long conflict with Patty. I never heard Wendy say one positive thing about or to Patty. I never did hear Patty say anything positive about Wendy. Sandy didn't want to create a scene at the funeral. Just the act of Wendy opening her mouth would have caused one. After Wendy spoke of her love for Patty, Sandy whispered, "If that is love, take me to another planet."

Ches said she was having a hard time hearing anything. A hearing device was sent for but none could be found.

Wendy said, "I had a dream that Sandy and Mike were carrying picket signs in front of my church telling the world what my son had done. Three years ago was the first time we knew anything about it. These two have inflicted a lot of pain on our family with their obsession with these allegations against my son. I can't remember where or when Nicki told me that Hedy had done some things to him—we could have gone to the police to report that but we didn't."

DeRienzo had prepared us well. We sat on our hands biting our lips.

Wendy went on. "After the assault, I felt I needed a restraining order because I was afraid that Mike was going to come to our house and burn it down." Wendy must have been thinking: "If someone did to me or my children what I did to them, I surely would want to kill them." The smirk on her face said a thousand words.

She said, "Now my brother Tim has a statement he wants to read."

I said, "Nope, he can't speak here." Mr. DeRienzo addressed the mediators so as not to allow Tim to speak. The mediators declared that Tim had no right to read anything or say anything at that proceeding.

Wendy said, "My brother has been a witness to their harassment. He should have the right to speak. He's come all the way from Tucson."

Mediator: "Sorry, but he's not directly involved in the incident at hand."

She said, "That's not fair. It's a free country; he has the right to speak, too."

"Not here; he doesn't," said Bill. "He can go home and talk all he wants in privacy, but not here."

Then Bob stood up to speak and DeRienzo also stopped him. Wendy said, "Bob is my husband; he should be able to say something."

Glenda, the mediator, explained to Wendy, "He's not a witness and the hearing isn't about anything other than the co-restraining order."

Ches was allowed to speak, "I just want the whole disruption to stop and the family to get back together. I can't hear a thing Wendy is saying, but I agree with everything she has said. I imagine she's covered everything. I really don't have any point to go over that she hasn't already said."

Mr. DeRienzo spoke next. He pointed out that the two women had broken into a gated community where they were not welcome. Wendy spoke out, "It wasn't locked; we drove right in!" She smiled, but her front teeth stayed locked together. Bob and Tim snickered and laughed. Ches couldn't hear and sat blinking.

Mr. DeRienzo said, "My clients have asked Ms. Adams and her family not to contact them since 2003. They let them into their house on July 11th because Ms. Adams said she had important news they needed to hear. So, my clients listened to what Ms. Adams and her mother had to say. When my clients asked the two women to leave, the two women refused to leave. Some harsh words were said on both sides. Ms. Adams wouldn't take her foot out of the door to let them close their front door. If someone did that at my house, I would be very upset."

Wendy said, "That's a lie, I never did that. They're lying." Bob and Tim snorted with laughter. The mediators told Wendy she needed to be quiet and to allow Mr. DeRienzo to speak. No one had interrupted her when she was speaking. "That's because I never told any lies," Wendy said. Tim and Bob snorted again.

We were the first to address the mediators alone while the new PACT went into the law library to wait their turn. Mr. DeRienzo proposed they issue co-restraining orders. I told the mediators, "The incident that Wendy Adams keeps alluding to about her son but never comes out and says is this: Her son raped my daughter when she was six years old. Her son was fourteen when he did that." Both Glenda and Bill seemed shocked at the allegation. "The crime was committed in 1987 and my daughter finally reported it in 2003. We found bloody panties back in 1987 and spent fifteen months visiting doctors while all the while these two women knew about the rape from the day it happened. They steered us away from the truth. Covered it up. They know the truth. They're just pretending not to."

Then it was our turn to wait in the law library. I browsed through the law books and found the Alder vs. Board of Education of the City of New York case from 1952. Alder, lost his case, thus giving school districts the right to dismiss any teacher who advocated the overthrow of the government by unlawful means and also affirmed that it was the duty of school boards to screen teachers as to their fitness to maintain the integrity of the schools as part of an ordered society. Three judges dissented; Judge Douglas said, "Yet it is in the pursuit of the truth which the First Amendment was designed to protect. The framers knew the dangers of dogmatism; they also knew the strength that comes when the mind is free, when ideas may be pursued wherever they lead." DeRienzo came back after a while and said of Wendy, "Boy, she's hell on wheels. I can tell she's full of guilt."

DeRienzo and Wendy both presented requests of what should be on the co-restraining orders to the mediators. He came back and forth between the library and the mediation room to iron out details. For instance, Wendy requested that Sandy and I not be allowed to talk to anyone about these family matters. Sandy said, "I can't agree with that because that would be taking away our freedom of speech." We ended up compromising. We could not speak about it for one year in the public or to use a public forum to announce matters that would be embarrassing to some. We could talk to anyone we wanted in private. Nicki and Patrick would not be on the restraining orders. Tim was on the restraining order but he would be allowed to transport Ches to our residence but only with our permission and they could not show up unannounced. After a year, we could go public if we wanted.

DeRienzo concluded, "This is a co-restraining order for both parties because the Wallriches want to simply live in peace." The mediators declared there would be no hearing because the goal of the co-restraining order was met. On the restraining order we saw later, Wendy had listed only Nicki and Patrick as the people we were to stay away from.

That next week, the movie version of Shakespeare's *Titus Andronicus* starring Anthony Hopkins came on a cable channel. The movie was bloody and graphic but at the time seemed mild to us after the adventure we were having. One main character, Tamora, played by Jessica Lang, could have been the twin of the duplicitous Wendy. We let ourselves feel deeply the ecstatic joyfulness at the end of that Shakespearean tragedy. Sorry, if I spoiled the plot, but then, how can you spoil a Shakespearean plot?

A few weeks later, I was in the class "Autobiographical Interpretations" when a young woman became emotionally distraught during our discussion of a chapter in *Bastard Out of Carolina* by Dorothy Allison. We were delving into the subject of rape when she became overwhelmed. The other girls in class gathered around her to console her. There were ten women in that class. A young man classmate and I sat on our hands as the girl told in detail what had happened to her. Then another woman said, "I was raped when I was twelve," and she, too, told about her rape in eviscerating detail and she, too, had us crying along with her. I put a fist to my lips to remind me to keep my mouth shut. Hedy didn't want me to talk or write about her case. Tears rolled into my beard and dripped into my notebook. Then, one by one, each of the females in the room, except one young woman and the professor, told of being raped at one time in their lives which meant about 80% of the females in that room. They came together in a large huddle around the first girl, touching shoulders, holding hands, and letting loose the wailing sounds of anguish and the tears flow. Ten giant six-year-olds biting their lips and hugging each other, letting the healing wash over them. I had shrunk into a tiny man in a dark little seat, willing myself to become invisible, but my eyes had to be as big as granite boulders. My eyes met the eyes of Ms. Gray, the professor. Her eyes were wider than mine and they said, "My goodness." It was an exceptional moment. That class had turned into an intense rape therapy session.

Later in the week, I had a conference with Professor Gray and we discussed the wondrous spectacle we had witnessed in class. Gray was about fifteen years my junior. She said, "I've never seen such a catharsis."

I said, "I wasn't prepared for that. What a powerful moment that was." I felt I had to say something about Hedy. I said, "My daughter was raped when she was six years old by a cousin of hers; she didn't come forward until she was twenty-two years old. She suffered in silence for sixteen years."

"She must be a brave girl," she said.

"She is. Hedy is a brave and beautiful young woman."

Laura asked, "Why didn't you join in the conversation?"

"I don't know. I was ashamed of my gender for one, I think. My daughter made me promise to keep silent about it, to not write about it. I wish Hedy could have been there in that classroom on that day, to be part of that process. It was an incredible moment, to see what we saw—magical."

"It was unbelievable," Ms. Grey said.

The next spring, we went to visit Tim and Ches in Tucson. God had broken pipe and flooded Tim's house and they were staying at a motel near the freeway. I stayed out in the car and worked on our taxes while Sandy went into the motel where they sat by the pool and aired their news and concerns. Ches requested I not come inside. I stayed in the car and worked on taxes. Sandy said she asked Ches, "When did you first know that Christopher had raped Hedy?"

"Oh," said Ches, "I think it was when Wendy and Chris had first moved to Prescott and they were living in that old trailer. No, it was earlier than that, I—" "Nah!" Tim shouted. Tim, taken off guard, stopped Ches from saying any more about the rape, Sandy said later. He accused Sandy of tricking Ches into saying what she did. He said his mother wasn't thinking straight. Later, Ches remarked, "Sandy, you are ignoring Nicki and Patrick. You never call or write them. It's just awful the way you're ignoring them."

Sandy replied, "Yeah, why do you think?"

They wanted to go to a restaurant to discuss the matter—maybe we wouldn't shout at each other so easily in public. We went to a fast-food Mexican restaurant near Tim's house. Sandy sat in the booth across from Ches. Sandy apologized again for the anger storm the summer before. Ches accepted her apology and they hugged and Sandy kissed her hand. Sandy said, "Ches, you need to find peace with yourself. Forget me. Forget Wendy. Forget everybody. You need to find peace for yourself. Go to that place in yourself and find peace."

Tim's face grew tense and he said, "Your mother is a Christian. She doesn't need to hear the noise from your misguided Satanic religion." Sandy ignored him and continued talking to her mother. After each sentence Sandy uttered, Tim said, "Nah!" After all his years of trying, Ches had never embraced Tim's version of Christianity. She didn't go to the church with him. His mother was being exposed to *another heathen religion* right under his watch.

Tim claimed his turn. He pushed the spin that Wendy had concocted. "Sandy and Mike, you don't understand what's really going on here. You're too close and you're blind to it. The real reason why Hedy is saying these things about Christopher, you see: Hedy is trying to get back at Wendy. You see, Wendy caught Hedy trying to molest Nicki and Patrick years ago when Hedy was a teenager. Hedy made up this rape charge, these accusations against Christopher, and that's all they are, accusations, because you can't prove anything anyway. Hedy did it just to get back at Wendy who caught her in the act. You see, Hedy said those things to get back at Wendy. Your daughter is messed up, and she's created this lie. If you don't see that, then you are blind. Satan is blinding you to the truth."

I said, "You're a dumbass, Tim. That came right out of Wendy's twisted mind, her twisted mouth, Tim. You are being used, Tim. Wendy is lying! She is a liar!"

Ches said, "Wendy was there. You weren't even there, Mike."

"You weren't there either, Ches, and you weren't there either, Tim, but Sandy was there."

Sandy said, "Wendy is a liar! I was there. Nothing happened on that day. The kids were sneaking sesame seeds in the pantry.

That's all that happened. They were pouring sesame seeds into their mouths. Wendy has twisted everything around."

Ches said, "Sandy and Mike, you should face up to the fact that your daughter had made a mistake in a sexual matter, the way kids do."

I told them, "Wendy is lying! It was a fabrication she made up to stop Hedy from telling about the rape!"

Tim shouted, "Sandy, Satan is blinding you to the truth!"

Sandy said, "Wendy is *Satan* and Wendy is blinding *you*, Tim. Wendy created this whole pantry scene and blew it up, just to have something to hold against Hedy, if and when Hedy came forward about the rape. You're such a tool, Tim, to believe her crap. Her lies!"

Ches said, "Awk, I don't believe that. Wendy wouldn't do such a thing."

"Well, Mom," Sandy said, "she did. Wendy apologized to Hedy and Peter about it one Easter, and now Wendy's using it again because you guys are buying into it."

Tim said, "One of them is a liar and I think it's your daughter—she's been out of control since high school. She about wrecked your place with that big party she had. A bunch of cop cars had to come and straighten her out. Peter was in on it, too. Both of your kids were out of control and they still are."

Sandy said, "It was a party, Tim. They were just normal teenagers. You were a teenager once."

"I didn't go around wrecking my parents' home. They had beer and drugs and a hundred kids showed up at your place. They could have torn it up."

"But they didn't tear it up. Everything worked out."

"You're lucky. They should have gone to jail. That would have taught them a lesson."

Sandy said, "You did stupid things, too, Tim. Like causing a head-on collision that almost killed seven people because you were going down the road reading the bible. How stupid was that, Tim? You have a plate put in your head and Jolie had a concussion and her face got cut up and bruised and she was never the same after that accident. And you were an adult and should have known better, Tim. You were out of control. Don't be such a tool!"

    We left Ches and Tim at the restaurant; they were never going to stop supporting Wendy. We suspected that they knew the truth, that they pushed back at us to save Christopher's reputation and keep his name off the child molester list. The PACT had made their stand, twisted the truth into a bundle of lies, and hitched their horse to it. They had held that baby boy in their arms, too, when he was just days old. They admitted Christopher was messed up since he was a teenager and had done despicable things, but if his name was put down on the ledger in black and white, it could spell the end for him. They didn't see they were trapping him into a Peter Pan world, where Wendy could hold her little boy forever.

CHAPTER 21

A family should be a stronghold where truth can come and heal its wounds. Family has been called the foundation of society, but when the truth is eroded, chaos and confusion bring the walls down. History is awash with sick and selfish laws and doctrines that allowed men to molest children; it has gone on for thousands of years. Male-dominated religions led the way blind to the suffering they caused. Change doesn't come overnight; dinosaurs will have to die. I used to think a matriarchal care-for-each-other-world would be best, but after Wendy demonstrated her propensity for malevolence and lying, I doubt that women are really warmer and nobler than men. When mendacity seeps in, society rots.

When Hedy turned three and was beginning to show the signs of an empathetic child by giving hugs to those she saw were feeling blue, Sandy's sister Jolie said, "You know, I bet Hedy will grow up to save the family."

We went to Tucson to visit Jolie and her husband Don in June—ten months after the mediation—just as the valley heat reached scorch. We met them at the care center where Jolie had been a resident for two decades. We took them out to eat at Denny's. It wasn't long before we were discussing the rape. Jolie made the comment, "Well, Hedy was flirting with Christopher, wasn't she?"

Sandy said, "Jolie, did you hear what you just said? Hedy was six years old. Where did you get such a notion?"

"Wendy." She paused, "Gad, I'd like to kick Wendy's butt. That evil shit!"

Don said, "They told us that you attacked them. Pushed Wendy down and slapped her. I said I couldn't believe Mike could do such a thing. Or you either Sandy, to spit on your mother." We told Don and Jolie the two women had known of the rape since it happened and kept it secret all those years.

Jolie said, "I'm never going to have anything to do with Wendy again. I hope she rots in hell. That's where she is going, you know." Jolie and Don belonged to one of the evangelical churches in the city and knew how it worked.

When Sandy was growing up, she shared a bedroom with Jolie for many years. They were less than a year apart in age and were best friends. Sandy made friends with everybody all her life, all through her school years. Jolie made few friends and followed along with Sandy for her social contacts. Jolie married Don Rohrbach in 1979 a few months before Tom passed away; their first child was Isaac (Ben) who was ten months older than Hedy. Isaac and Hedy often saw each other when they were toddlers. Jolie suffered a mental breakdown after Joy was born; Don couldn't function as a parent. Their church helped for six months until two separate families offered to adopt Isaac and Joy. We tried to get Don to allow Isaac and Joy to live with us, but Don wouldn't agree; he said we weren't Christians. We weren't going to the right protestant church. So, Joy went to live with a family in Tucson and Isaac went with the Elliott family that used his middle name Benjamin and moved to Ripley, Oklahoma after the adoption, believe it or not.

When Ben was eighteen and just out of high school, he visited Prescott for two weeks sharing time between our home and Bob and Wendy's. From the moment of their reunion, Hedy and Ben seemed to have more than blood connections; they hit it off and were in tune with each other to the degree of the supernatural. They hadn't seen each other for fifteen years when they were toddlers, but they bonded like long-lost soulmates. They couldn't stop talking about life and the wonderment of it all. Only one person didn't care to see the magic of Ben and Hedy's reunion. Wendy was angry when she saw how joyful Hedy and Ben were together; she pushed her two boys on Ben whenever she could. Ben wasn't giving them enough attention. But Ben was so excited that he came back six months later and he and Hedy laughed and giggled away the holidays. A few months after Hedy broke the secret in 2003, I heard her tell Ben on the phone that their cousin Christopher had raped her when she was six. She was telling everybody.

Hedy was still healing when she left Prescott in 2006. She left her quarreling families to duke it out. She made progress, worked on her trust issues, and she was determined to stay positive. Early in high school, she dreamed of being a musician; "most musical girl of the class of 1999." Many were awe-struck by her spirit and talent, and especially her voice. Hedy was born the day after John Lennon was murdered in 1980 by a Christian terrorist. She was born on December 9 at 11:14 PM exactly twenty-four hours to the minute after Lennon passed away. John was only forty years old and had perhaps his most creative years yet to come. A popular bumper sticker in 1980 was "Question Authority." Lennon lived that message and Hedy embraced it. Hedy was blessed with a mind that could untangle puzzles and an artist's eye that could shine light on worlds. Before Hedy was two, she drew a picture of Sandy holding Peter. She showed a talent for music, too, as a baby, like many babies do, holding her head high, having fun rocking to the beat. The beat was it. I always felt Lennon and Hedy touched when they passed each other coming into and out of the Great Mysterious. From her crib, she heard us play the *Westside Story* and *Fiddler on the Roof* and Johnny Cash, Ray Charles, classic rock, Shostakovich, and an ocean of others. We used to call Hedy the "singing bush" because of the two hundred songs she had memorized by age eight. Hedy and Peter listened to the Disney record books together, ages two to six, and memorized them. Hedy pulled Pete along to embrace this thing called music. Sagittarius is her sign, and those born under it are known to be thoughtful, warmhearted, and easy to love. That's my daughter. She had to stand up to three assaults from family members. What Christopher did to her affected her and changed her at age six; Wendy's lies hurt Hedy deeply at age thirteen; the third attack was from Ches, Tim, and Bob who were but cowards acting as a supply for Wendy. What I hoped for Hedy heading into her mid-twenties was that she could get back to her true self—the thoughtful, empathetic child she started out as.

Hedy flew into this world. I was in the delivery room. When Sandy pushed, Hedy literally flew out and Doctor Cooper had to catch her. The doctor handed the whimpering Hedy to a nurse who brought her to a side table and cleaned her up. When the nurse tried to put eye drops in Hedy's eyes, Hedy wouldn't cooperate and the nurse gave Hedy her first nickname: "Hold still, you little wiggle worm."

In *I Thought We Would Never Speak Again,* Laura Davis wrote about Richard Hoffman. When Richard was in his forties in 1995, he wrote a memoir, *Half the House,* about his tortured life as a boy growing up in Allentown, Pennsylvania. His father came back from fighting in WWII with PTSD and anger issues, and his father often beat Richard. Richard had two brothers with terminal diseases that caused financial and emotional stress in the family. At age ten, Richard was raped by his Little League coach, a secret Richard kept until he wrote his book and named the perpetrator. About the time the book came out and after Richard and his dad had repaired their relationship, his father tracked down the coach (who was still coaching and was still raping boys). The police found a card catalog that the coach used to keep track of his victims—seven hundred names were in that file. Four hundred boys came forward to say me, too. Coach Tom Feifel was sent to prison. NBC Dateline did a story on the case and two days after it aired, Feifel died in prison. The prison officials said the coach died of a heart attack. But isn't that the fate that awaits all of us? We die; our hearts stop beating. The other prisoners knew better what caused his so-called heart to stop.

Hoffman said that he tried to shrug it off, carry on, and be tough like his adult mentors taught him to be. But looking back, by not confronting the coach for the evil he did, other boys were hurt. "I could see that it was a moral shrug as well," Hoffman said. After he and his father confronted their monsters and healed some, Richard became "an amazing optimist . . . there's hardly anything that comes up that I can't deal with." That is what I hoped for Hedy, to become an amazing optimist, tackling whatever problem she faced. Hedy wanted and needed her story to be told, that by not fighting back against rapists and their protectors would be a moral shrug like Hoffman alluded to.

Sandy divorced her family—one of the hardest trials there is on earth. She wasn't invited to her mother's funeral, just as Ches demanded as she kicked the back of Sandy's car seat that one summer afternoon by Thumb Butte. Tim and Wendy made sure Sandy wasn't notified; Christopher was going to have to be at the funeral and they would have to sneak him in under the cover of darkness. There was no easy way to arrange for Christopher to face anyone bearing the truth.

Pete's transformation from gawky preteen to a handsome young man in his senior year in high school was a true metamorphosis. Hedy never had that gangly, nerdy look while growing up; she fit every age well like it was a fine suit.

The PACT needed Hedy to recant and they were pitiful in their call for it. That they could phantom for one second that we were going to go along with their lies is unbelievable. Christopher needed to be on the public's list of sex offenders. When his ex-girlfriend, Betsy, described their sex life to us, she was describing rape. Christopher's ex-wife, Amy, never gave a satisfying reason why she left Prescott with her baby so abruptly. Amy said she was tired of Chris being into drugs and drinking.

Grandma Ches felt she had to play the matriarch of the family; she ordered us to follow her orders, end of the argument. She was not the general she thought she was. No orders to massacre innocent victims were going to be followed by Sandy and myself. Call us insubordinate, Grandma. But actually, it's not insubordination when you refuse to follow illegal orders. In fact, refusing to follow illegal orders is a duty of every soldier and may well be one of the only ways to stop tyranny in its tank tracks. Ches's generation was coached to bury the hurt, shut up, move on, stop whining, and obey the leader.

That so-called family suffered from not only brain injuries but from senility, spinelessness, and hardening of the heart. Hardening forms in a heart that is never open. Protecting the rapists of children produces hard hearts. We never entertained their "poor Christopher" mantra. What we needed was for the two perpetrators, Wendy and Christopher, to admit their crimes, apologize, and make more than a token nod toward truth.

Hedy and Peter needed a written letter of apology from Wendy stating that she had lied about the allegations of child molestations in the pantry incident and Wendy needed to make it clear in her letter why she had made up that story: to blackmail Hedy, to silence Hedy about the rape. For a number of years after the incident, Hedy and Peter didn't want to be near Wendy. They avoided her. In 2002, Wendy took them aside when we were at a park and said she was sorry she had accused them (eight years after the Pantry scene). At least, that's what Wendy told us she said. We should have demanded that Wendy put her apology in writing. Wendy wanted to talk to Hedy and Peter alone, and damn it, we let her. Wendy rescinded her verbal apology as soon as Hedy came forward.

Wendy was never held accountable for her lies. Christopher was never held accountable for raping our little girl. Who knows how many other crimes against the state he committed? He wasn't held accountable for the death threats aimed at our family. We thought Miss Me-Me-Me might grow out of her narcissism, but that never will happen. We failed to take her seriously; we didn't realize how toxic her narcissism was. After the mediation hearing, we knew we couldn't live in the same town. That's what Ches told us when we left Nogales in 1989.

Reconciliation seemed impossible as lines were drawn in the high desert sand, the low desert sand, and the rocky ridges in between. If for reconciliation the best we can get is the seed of peace in our own hearts that can bloom over time, that may be enough. The rape of a child is nearly impossible to forgive even when the perpetrator is remorseful. There is no forgiving the perpetrator who doesn't acknowledge their culpability. An innocent man would work to clear his name, but Christopher fled town. Wendy's image as a jaded reprobate has not faded at least for myself. Wendy was and is an envious, bitter woman who attempted to make her sister miserable by systematically trying to undermine Sandy's pleasure and self-confidence. She declared war on our family because she was feeling bad about Christopher never getting a grip on life. She couldn't stand to see our family progressing while her son chewed his hind leg off in a trap of his own making. Someday, I may have sympathy for the flawed individual that she is, but I could never trust her again. If I was ever in her presence, I couldn't trust myself. I realize she fought hard in the "world of men" to get a foothold, but too bad getting ahead to Wendy meant stomping on those nearest to her. Wendy was so jealous of Hedy and Peter doing well as they grew and explored the world around them that heat rose from her collar and warped her brain and her heart. Sociopaths are made; psychopaths are born. Christopher did crash and burn in the road of life, literally, when in the early 1990s he came back from Texas with a new car after spending two years working with his father. Christopher was home only a month when he had a head-on collision driving the wrong way on Interstate 17 near Cordes Junction while he was drunk. The two cars were completely demolished. No one was killed in the accident; all came away with minor injuries. Christopher and I walked around what was left of his car where it lay in a side lot of a junkyard in Prescott. Christopher showed me the scrape on his forearm and scratches he got. He explained that being so extremely drunk and loose as he had been had actually saved his life. I hope that wasn't the only lesson he took away with him.

For thirteen years, Sandy and Wendy spent half of every year not speaking to each other. Sandy refused to surrender to Wendy's demands and other bully tactics used by malignant narcissists. During those months when Wendy was out of our lives, it was peaceful; we never were in a hurry to patch the rift. Wendy knew how to push my buttons; many times, I had to leave her presence and go for a walk to clear my head of her meanness.

Hedy's story is like a Grimm's fairy tale, one with an evil aunt. Hedy realizes she has nothing to be ashamed of and wants her story to be heard in hopes it will benefit others who have suffered harm from the so-called family. Peter asked me to keep him out of the book as much as possible, and I have.

How could they think we would go along with the family's drivel to hide the crime of the perpetrator, molester, monster, deviate, pedophile, pervert, victimizer, guilty schmuck, shameless rapist, or what else they wanted us to ignore? Sandy and I had a rethink everything near and dear. The giant knot that appeared in Sandy's gut on that long sleepless night eventually shrunk away, though it took four years. One block off Whiskey Row in Prescott was a Buddhist store where I bought Sandy a brass "singing bowl." The shop attendant could make it "sing" and he taught me and I taught Sandy. She found a Buddhist Temple high in the mountains east of Chino Valley near the Sycamore Canyon Wilderness that we went to visit a few times. When we didn't do that, we went church-hopping around Prescott.

Because of the secret, Hedy and Christopher received little counseling in their youth. Hedy got some help but only after she came out with the truth. I never heard of Christopher receiving counseling after he started his rebelling and rampaging at age twelve; Wendy was probably afraid he would say too much. Wendy and Grandma Ches, with all their scheming, strove to avoid at all costs being shamed publicly. That obsession corrupted the fiber of trust that holds any family together. Without trust, no family can survive.

We never knew if Ches told Tom that she was sexually assaulted as a child. He was a main character in the Wolf Under Bed dramas that Ches starred in when Sandy and her older siblings were growing up. "Don't you hear the wolf scratching, Tom? Don't you hear it?" My guess is she did not tell him. We asked Sandy's sister, Jolie, if she was molested as a child and she said no. But she remembered Ches and the wolf under the bed incidents.

How far back into past generations these crimes went, we'll never know. Ches wouldn't share. What were these adults thinking? Who do they really care about? Where is the justice in all this? Accountability is what adults say they stand for, but apparently, many don't. These crooked adults put the responsibility of holding the family together on the shoulders of little girls. The young men were told to grow up, behave themselves, and if they did that, they could stay in this family. Boys need to be taught early that their lust may cause them to hurt those who they should be protecting. It should be drilled into their heads that they have a dual role to play as lifelong protectors and providers, and if they are prepared properly, they will be able to handle and stop themselves before committing vile acts. All people have potential for malevolence. Boys need to be coached that someday, they will be men and they need to work toward the goal of being honorable and truthful men, who can be trusted, and not cheap thrill-seekers who cower behind the skirts of their mamas. A boy-man who runs away from his misdeeds will be running from himself for the rest of his life. If he does a misdeed, he must stand up and face the truth and consequences of what he has done and then recognize the harm he has done, change himself for the better, ask for forgiveness, pay retribution, and realize he has learned a lesson that everyone makes mistakes, and they must stay vigilant. Truly, he needs to be sorry for what he had done and to recognize what is right and what is wrong. If the boy is reached early and instructed in the way of living righteously, he can be saved from himself and become a productive citizen who helps the community prosper and can offer help for the problems that manifest naturally (like hurricanes).

For years, Aunt Neva paid retribution for her son—sent cash in Christmas cards. She so loved Patty, the silent girl. Ches spun it and announced each year that Christmas was being made special because of the generosity of Patty, torturing Patty further. Deck the halls with bloody secrets. Maybe on a subconscious level, that's why Sandy and I wanted to drop the gift parade.

Ches got to act the part of heroine her entire life. Ches saves the family. Ches beats Lassie to the punch. She had no need to run to Hollywood. What choice did Ches have at age six? A Hobson's choice, no choice. Ches put on the face of a pleaser. You can destroy that boy's life or you can be his savior—your choice, my little child. And remember, child, boys can't help themselves. Their nut sacks are swollen with the slime of life and they are forever on the quest to empty them. And you, child, were just another post for the itch. Child, there are two doors in front of you: Behind one door, a wonderful future awaits where you will be rewarded and exalted, but behind the other door, my child, are dark days for the family whereupon you will be reviled and ostracized as a tattle-tale and spat upon for the rest of your life. Child, which door will you choose?

Ches, I guess, didn't really believe in the art of debate. She believed in Ches's way or the highway. We chose the highway.

CHAPTER 22

In late summer 1981, before the whirlwind hit, before trust was strangled behind our backs, before we divorced the family when the family loomed big in our lives, we took a family outing. Truth perched in an Ironwood tree then and sang its song, or at least so we thought. President Reagan was healing from a bullet wound next to his heart, an Arizona woman was nominated for the U.S. Supreme Court, and the Rubik Cube was the rage.

It was Labor Day weekend. Six members of our family got together for a tour-jeep ride into Canyon de Chelly National Monument. We stayed at a motel in Chinle, Arizona. Sandy, I, and baby Hedy, who was nine months old, were living in Ganado where we were teaching that fall. Wendy and Christopher drove up from Tucson and arrived at our apartment on Friday afternoon. It was the weekend of Christopher's ninth birthday; he seemed to be a normal boy. He had just returned from Texas after spending a month with his father, Richard. Wendy was in a good mood, though a bit rankled from her battles with her ex, who had stepped up efforts to get full custody of Christopher. Before we drove over to Chinle, Christopher found the stone arrowhead debris that I had dumped under the trees behind our apartment. We never meant for him to find them. He brought the handful of flint scraps to the kitchen, excited about what he had found. Wendy said, "Wow, look what Christopher found!"

When we told them I had dumped them out of a box, Christopher didn't seem upset and he decided to keep the flint pieces. That incident was forgotten and it was never mentioned again for twenty years until Wendy pointed out in her hate letter that the incident had ruined Christopher's life and turned him into a psychopath.

We drove over to Chinle to meet Ches who was driving down from the town of Kayenta on the Utah border where she taught in the public schools after Tom died. That evening, Sandy, Wendy, and Ches thought it would be a blast to have Christopher and Hedy take a bath together. It was innocently fun and produced lots of laughs. Ches and I took a few pictures of her first two grandchildren together in the tub. Trust sat on the edge of the sink, smiling.

The next morning, we took the rear bench of one of the tour jeeps. The jeeps were two-ton Ford trucks with four-wheel drive, retrofitted with plastic and chrome benches. Our bench easily held five people with a baby. We soon found out that sitting in the back was not a smart idea: you got tossed slightly into the air at dips in the so-called road through the canyon. It was a bright and sunny, short-sleeve, watch-out-for-sunburn day. Hedy was in a yellow bonnet with a matching sweater and she looked like a sweet little quail. We all had jackets or sweaters. The driver was silent but the guide, riding shotgun, spoke to us in Navajo for a minute before he asked, "How many here speak Navajo? Gosh, no one? I'd better switch to English. My name is Ernie. My Indian name is Thunder Toad. People ask if they can call me Toady and I say no, but you can call me Ernie. So, if you want to make it out of the canyon today, call me Ernie. Okay."

The two trucks started down the dirt road into the canyon, each loaded with tourists. When we got to the river, the trucks separated. Our truck veered right and we bounced through a shallow river. Ernie spoke as we drove up the narrow canyon, cracking jokes and laying out the history. "Why don't Navajos like to garden? Because they hate ta Hopis." We passed under the wind-eroded cliffs and Anasazi ruins: Mummy Cave, Comely Rock, and Red Dog Ruins and stopped at Massacre Cave. "In 1792, one hundred of our braves were hiding in those caves when the Spanish fired their guns against the roof of the caves, and the ricocheting bullets killed many of our men and boys. It went on for a long time; it was a slaughter. But, not to worry: we got even with them later."

We stopped below Spider Rock, one of two sandstone spires that rose 800 feet from the canyon floor. Spider Rock has been featured in television commercials because of the awe factor of helicopters landing on it. Ernie said, "The tallest spire is where Spider Grandmother lives. The shorter spire, Speaking Rock, talks to Spider Grandmother about naughty children and brings the naughty children to Spider Grandmother. Then she eats them. The bones of these children can be seen on her top. If the bones fall off, we get people who can throw real good to throw the bones back on the top. Any young people here today? Listen up: If you are naughty, Spider Grandmother will come looking for you." Wendy teased Christopher, "Hear that, Christopher? You better behave or Spider Grandmother will get you." Christopher laughed. We all laughed.

Ernie warned us as we drove back around to the main intersection to watch out for Crazy Danny who liked to throw souvenirs at the tourists. "He's not very fast, so be awake and we'll get past Old Danny without anyone getting hurt." Coming into the next turn, we saw Danny waiting at the intersection with a seven-foot two-by-four on his shoulder. Ernie gunned the jeep and swung wide as Danny launched his missile and fell on his face, missing the jeep by twenty feet.

Christopher asked, "Why is he throwing stuff at us?"

Ches, who was next to me, leaned in and asked, "Is he drunk?"

I said, "Probably."

Wendy said, "It's just part of the show; he's a paid actor."

"No, he's not," said Christopher.

Ernie said, "Crazy Danny is practicing for the Olympics, but as you see, he isn't going to make it. Yeah, his breath is worse than his throw." We looked back at Danny who was picking up his board and getting ready for the next jeep.

At White Antelope Ruins, we stopped and got out of the jeep. High on the wall of the canyon were many petroglyphs. Ernie pointed out a white swastika above the other symbols. "You're probably wondering what graffiti like that is doing up there, that swastika. Friends of Hitler didn't leave it there. That is an ancient symbol. It indicates the four sacred directions: north, south, east, and west. Here in America, that symbol is over five thousand years old. And it was very old in ancient Europe, too, before Hitler took a hold of it. In these pueblos and caves, they have found woven cloth that is thousands of years old. The Hopi men do a lot of weaving and they are always bragging about their weaving skills. But if you venture out on a Saturday night, coming from, say, Window Rock, you'll see Navajo men driving from the bars, and there, you'll see the world's greatest weavers. They'll be weaving all over the road."

We again drove past Crazy Dan who threw at us and made us duck. Christopher said, "They need to stop that guy!" We bounced through the river again. We made it to where the road started its rise out of the canyon, when all of a sudden, our jeep blew a tire. The other tour bus stopped behind us; their two guides came over to help fix the flat. Ernie said to us, "This is the fun part. On foot, our group is going to race their group, up the road, out of the canyon. First one gets the booby prize. On your mark! Get set!"

Wendy said, "That's not fair; we're going to have to carry grandma." Ches was sixty-one and in fair condition, but we all laughed, and she with us. At that moment in history, we were a family, playfully teasing each other, ready to help each other, to go to bat for each other, grow old with each other, help our kids grow up to be happy adults. We drove to an overlook to get a better view of the sun-bleached bones of the naughty children on the top of the rock spire where Spider Grandmother lives.

PART TWO
HEDY'S SONGS

CHAPTER 23

The time could not be better [1]
I know it's meant to be
For time gives all the answers
To those who choose to see

—"No Fear" by Hedy Wyn

Hedy completed thirty songs. Sixteen of her best she selected to be put into an album. Part two of this book has fourteen chapters and each chapter starts with some of the key lyrics to the fourteen songs. Part One of this book covers about four years; this second part covers thirteen years and moves right along—so hold on as I try to render scenes and not all summary. I had many journals to draw from when I wrote the scenes in Part One, but few journals for this second part.

(2007) Hedy worked at the movie theatre the first two years she was in Ellensburg. During that time, she and a co-worker discovered the attic in the old three-story building was haunted. "Seriously, no joke," Hedy wrote, "and it's so exciting. Things creak and things crackle in the air. I won't go up there by myself." They found dozens of old movie posters covered in dust and mud and rotting away under the leaky roof of that old downtown landmark; but alas, few of these treasures were salvageable. They heard strange noises when they entered or when they were leaving the old attic. The noises grew louder each time the two women climbed up there until they decided it wasn't safe anymore. Hedy said she would have gone back but everybody else was too chicken to go with her.

During that time, she fell for and gave her heart to a guy who owned a store just around the corner from the theatre. She thought he might be the one she was searching for who would make a commitment to her, but he didn't want to give up the other women in his life. She came away from that relationship with a broken heart, her first one. Wait, I'll take that back: after her friend Kim passed away, that was definitely Hedy's first broken heart. Hedy had a green four-leaf clover put on her left shoulder blade in honor of Kim. In late 2007, the owner of the theatre sold it. After butting heads with the new management, Hedy resigned and took a seasonal job at Stevens Pass ski resort east of Seattle; she would have free access to the slopes that winter. She wanted to practice her skills on the snowboard, and I have no doubts she would have mastered it, except for the accident. After watching this artist and athlete growing up and getting good at every sport she tested and infecting her teammates with her enthusiasm, I could see her flying down those hills and getting better day by day. But she broke her wrist. Eric, a gay man, helped her out of the snow after her crash and got her to the nearest clinic. He was from Spokane. They became good friends. He more or less persuaded her to get a degree, go back to college, follow her dreams. They would keep in contact for years. He upgraded his computers frequently and sent to her his older models.

That fall (2007), Ches left a message on our phone machine: "I have important news to tell you, Sandy." Sandy didn't call her and Ches never called back.

Sandy felt she was protecting us from more abuse. Sandy and I put the townhouse up for sale and planned a move to Oregon. We couldn't live in the same town as the Big Wen, the big carbuncle. By Christmas, the housing market was tanking in Arizona and Florida, and the buyers went into hiding. Cracks formed in the world banking system.

Hedy started taking classes at Central Washington University in January 2008; she was seeking a graphic arts degree leaning heavily on computers and photography. We hoped she might go back into music. After excelling at viola for seven years and learning to control her voice and wow everyone who heard her, we hated to see her put her talent on hold. But she avoided the music program at CWU in Ellensburg. Hedy told me later that she was afraid Wendy would sabotage her efforts because of the slander lie. Hedy had this fear of Wendy since the pantry incident, maybe remaining under the surface but always there. The secret of the rape was exposed, which lessened its poison; then, it was the trauma of Wendy's lies that infected Hedy. What if she became successful and confident? What if Wendy touted lies to destroy Hedy's reputation and future, out of vengeance, jealousy, and plain meanness? This was the wretched lie Hedy was confronting.

When Hedy was five years old, Sandy and I deemed Hedy our little actress; we could see her heading in that direction with her golden voice, her propensity for memorizing, and the fun she had with play-acting. Hedy was her two grandmothers' girl. My mother, Katie, had that kind of memory, and Ches had a knack for the dramatic. Grandma Katie not only remembered every event in her life; she could tell you the date and year and the day of the week it happened. She was her own calendar perpetual. Ches played some kind of a role her whole life.

At age eight, Hedy had scores of songs in her repertoire. Nowadays, we have Alexis, but in our household back then, we could point at Hedy and say, "Hedy, sing 'My Favorite Things,'" and Hedy would sing it. In her teens, Hedy listened to a wide range of music; one of her favorite genres was punk rock, which inspired her to write songs of her own. Though she shied away from opera, when Hedy was in show choir in high school, she said she had found her calling. And she was also a talented visual artist, building up a portfolio starting in middle school and continuing into college. When Hedy chose graphic arts at CWU as her major, she was mining one of her levels of enrichment. Maybe down the road, she could risk it and follow her voice to freedom and grow stronger to defend herself.

In the spring of 2008, in central Arizona, the raveling of the housing market continued. I subbed in the schools in the Prescott area. Prescott Valley and Chino Valley lost a fifth of their population as the building trades ground to a halt. The new PV high school closed its doors after one year of occupancy and Chino Valley had negative growth for the time in its history.

In mid-March, Sandy saw Bob on his bike at the bank; he hesitated as if he had something to tell her, but he must have thought he better check with Wendy before he did anything rash, like think for himself, so he turned away and rode off. Later that month, we got a letter from my sister, Sharon, and a clipping from the Tucson newspaper: the obituary of Chesna Mae Mitcham, age 88. Wendy and Tim held fast to one of the last things Ches requested. "Tim, don't let Sandy come to my funeral!" was what Ches, the eighty-four-year-old screamed as she kicked the back of Sandy's car seat.

Sandy retired that spring of 2008, but we were not going anywhere; the Phoenix building boom was completely a bust; most of the properties completed their plunge of losing 50% of their value in eight months. The news was full of Barry Madoffs who made off with the hopes and dreams of a lot of people.

I had a number of writing projects that summer, compiling a book of quotes, a book of limericks, short stories, Confucius-say jokes, and a phonic project. Sandy worked on her fiddling and went to jams with her friend, Anita Wells. With Sandy's encouragement, Anita began singing with a country-western band in Prescott; thus, fulfilling a lifetime dream. Sandy was following a dream of her own: getting better on the fiddle. Sandy and Anita went to events together, jamming and singing often. They went to see Willie Nelson.

That summer, with the advice of a counselor, Sandy kept a dream journal next to her bed so she could capture her dreams as soon as she woke up. In the middle of June, she recorded this dream:

> Hedy had been selected from all the young women in the world to go through a ceremony. In order to go through this ceremony, Hedy went to this dilapidated resort where people helped her get ready. It took about a week. Me and Mike, being her parents, were invited. I asked the leader of the place, "Is this a wedding?"
>
> He said, "Yes." Then he told me the young man's name. It sounded kind of Hawaiian. Then the man said, "It doesn't have to be a wedding; it can be a healing ceremony."
>
> I told Hedy. She didn't seem shocked or unwilling. The end.

Hedy loved the music of Israel Kamakawiwo'ole "Somewhere of the Rainbow" and "The White Sandy Beach of Hawaii" especially. Izzy's beautiful voice is what drew Hedy to him. He died young: 38. When Sandy told me her dream, I thought of Izzy as the groom. Hedy's voice would have drawn him to her. There was a singer, Yma Sumac, from South America who became famous starting in the 1930s; she had an extraordinary voice. Hedy was not to the level of Sumac, but she had the tools to get there. Ms. Sumac never had voice lessons and that fact would have won over Hedy. Hedy's first e-mail account in high school was ilovetobreakrules@yahoo.com.

(2008) The schools in Prescott started up in the middle of August and I subbed again and volunteered at the Prescott library a few hours a week. In September, Peter and Hedy visited for two weeks; they coordinated their visits to Prescott to overlap Sandy's birthday; Pete flew into Phoenix a week after Hedy had been in Prescott a week. Sandy played those three weeks with her two grown cubs; they watched thirty some videos and took hikes in the trails around Yavapai County. After Hedy flew back to Washington, we were hiking with Pete on the trails around Granite Lake when Sandy tripped over a root and bruised her ribs. She was sore for over a month. Pete flew back to San Jose where he was working for British Aeronautical Engineering.

One evening, I was at the downtown library researching, sitting at a long table taking notes from a book, oblivious to those around me. I had been working for a while when a dark shadow loomed over me. I looked up to see Bob scowling down on me. He said, "How dare you sit here pretending you don't see me? I won't take that from you; I won't stand for it." I think he wanted to punch me. Apparently, he was sitting at the other end of the table. I said, "I didn't see you, Bob."

He said, "I don't believe you. You're lying."

If I hadn't been well known at the library, working a few hours a week for the last year, I could have caused a scene. But I rose without saying any more and put the book away. Heading out of the library, I glanced back and saw the angriest Bob I had ever seen gritting his teeth and squinting his droopy eyes in a display of faked toughness. That was the last time I ever saw him. His tough act came right out of the mind of Wendy. She pulled his strings whenever she wanted. Bob had pulled stunts like that before on behalf of Wendy. More than a decade earlier (Dec. 1996) the first time I got out of the hospital for the septicemia that damaged my heart valve, we were running low on firewood. Bob got upset with me for going into the Bradshaw Mountains to cut firewood with Tim who was visiting from Tucson. We knew it was Wendy nagging on Bob to get bent out of shape over nothing. She wanted Tim to spend more time with her and her boys and set Bob on us. Looking back, I suspect she also wanted to put more stress on my heart, so she could kill me subtly, and I would die, never thinking bad thoughts of Christopher. Bob was born with sad strange eyes that made him look like he had at one time witnessed atrocities, or his ancestors had.

That winter, my sister Marlys and her husband Marv flew into Tucson and stayed at Sharon and Jeff's for a couple of days. Sandy and I drove down to see them. It was kind of awkward seeing my family and not talking about the hell we had been through because of family. There was a lot of tension created because we were trying to avoid tension. When Marlys asked Sandy how her mom was doing, Sandy told her Ches had passed away. "Oh, I'm sorry to hear that," Marlys said.

Sandy said, "Well, she *was* eighty-eight."

Marlys said, "Oh, then she had good, long life." Sandy glanced over at Sharon who was watching us closely.

Before we left town, we stopped by to visit the gravesite of Tom and Ches Mitcham; it's next to the grave of Vicki Lynn Hoskinson. Sandy said to her father, "If you had been here, I know you would have stood up for the truth. You would have been proud of us for fighting for the truth. You would have forced Christopher to stand up and be a man. You would have hunted Christopher down if you had to. You were a warrior, Dad. You would have never let Ches and Wendy turn this into such a farce. You wouldn't have let Wendy dictate what was true and what were lies." To me, she said, "Kitty, too, she would have been on our side. Kitty would have been so mad at Wendy for hiding the crime, for harming Hedy. Kitty would have never let Mom side with Wendy." Then to her mother's grave, Sandy said, "Mom, I forgive you. You were wounded and taught the wrong way. But the world has changed."

I took a long-term sub assignment at Granite Mountain middle school after a teacher lost his job; he tripped a special education student as she was running out of his class for the umpteenth time. I supervised that class for ninety days and watched gray hairs appear on my head: the principal found a replacement for me in the spring of 2009. They sent me back to kindergarten.

Hedy was determined to stop drinking and partying; she found herself at odds with her younger classmates. She pledged sobriety off and on through the year and couldn't keep the pledge. Another guy broke her heart and no sooner had she said never again than still another guy came along and broke it. She was getting cold sores a lot in Ellensburg. She blamed the climate. She started getting cold sores when we lived in Nogales years earlier. She wondered if Chris had infected her on the night of the rape. Sandy and I had cold sores since we were kids, and Hedy may have gotten them from us. Hedy wrote in her journal: "Okay, I don't believe God wants me to be on this planet any longer. I have a huge cold sore on my lip & I get them so often that I can't enjoy anything—ever! I wonder how many people I've given herpes to—just for kissing. It's not fair that I've gone through this all my life. I really want to die. I'm not angry or depressed. I just believe that I'm destroying the world with my infectious disease. I'm killing people and all they are doing is being innocent. I don't want people to hate me because I kiss them. I don't deserve that and they don't either. I can't do this anymore. Oh, man, he even asked me if I was clean and I lied."

Sandy and I went to Peoples Valley in June to an Old Time Fiddlers campout event; we stayed at a motel. We met a lady who made tipis for a living; she had set up a tipi at the fiddle camp. We admired her tipi and talked with her for a while; she gave us a print of Black Elk's Prayer.

We accepted an offer on the townhouse in June and drove to Ellensburg to visit Hedy and scout Oregon. In Idaho near Boise, we ran into the fiercest rainstorm we had ever seen; we pulled off the freeway and stopped in a little town, aptly named Bliss, while the storm pummeled our car for a half an hour. Hedy was living in a ground-floor studio apartment, part of a two-story house. She had just finished stitching a quilt by hand, which she proudly showed to us. She said, "I have something exciting to tell you. I'll tell you when we get to the river." She took us to one of her favorite spots on the Yakima River and we had a picnic on its bank. It was a beautiful summer day and songbirds could be heard everywhere; something Eugene lacked was songbirds. "So, what's new?" Sandy asked.

Hedy hesitated, then said, "I've switched my major to biology. I thought it would be better telling you face to face. So I could see your expressions. Ha! I think that's where I should be. It's so interesting, so exciting to me. I want to help take care of animals. I think that would be so much fun. I'm so into photography, too, and it won't be wasted; I can see using that for whatever I do in the future. Everything is tied together." Also, she told us she was volunteering as a late-night DJ at the campus radio station two nights a week. She got to explore music all night long. "At that time of the day, I can play songs that I couldn't during the day, you know, real cutting-edge stuff. But I did got in trouble once playing something that was totally off-limits. But no one complained and so it was cool." The next morning, we ate at a café near the downtown. She said, "I feel a bit out of step being one of the oldest students on campus. My classmates are so young. They don't know what they want to do. All the girls I meet, all they want to do is get married and have babies. I'm never getting married, and I tell them that and they think I'm crazy. And I ask them, 'You're going to trust a man to bring you happiness? That's the craziest thing I ever heard.' They stay away from me. They don't want to hear anything else but getting married and having babies and acting like eight-year-olds. If they see me coming, they turn away." She showed us again the tattoo of a four-leaf clover on her left shoulder blade. In her journals, Hedy sometimes talked to her friend: "Kim, if you are out there, send me someone to love, someone who will love me back."

We left Hedy and her books and drove into Oregon. At Corvallis, we headed to the coast and camped near Florence. It was cold and windy walking on the beach. We drove into Eugene the next day. We checked out the University of Oregon; near the campus, we found the most unusual drugstore on the planet and wondered around inside it for quite a while. Later that day, Sandy started getting a rash all over her body. We put Eugene on the top of maybe move-to list because it was about halfway between Ellensburg and San Jose. The next day, as we neared the bay area, Sandy's rash turned into misery. The more she tried not to itch, the more she groaned in agony. When we got to Pete's place in San Jose, she cooled her burning skin in the tub. Pete took us hiking in a reserve. We cut our stay short to get Sandy to her doctor; she groaned all the way back to Prescott. Her doctor said it was poison ivy; she could have got it anywhere between Ellensburg and Eugene. For a whole month and a half, Sandy didn't do much more than cover her body in calamine lotion, and watch the news about the death of Michael Jackson. I liked his music since he was a kid wonder but I never followed the sordid tales that he might be a child molester and not just a lover of children that he claimed. It's hard to unwrap the packaging after you've trusted someone for so long to be doing right by the world and then be presented with a different but probable reality. It fogs your senses. From the novel *The Crossing* by Cormac McCarthy I found this quote: "…that while the righteous are hampered at every turn by their ignorance of evil, to the evil all is clear light and dark alike."

CHAPTER 24

Ring, ring, ring, ring, Hello [2]
Would you like to come over an' chill a while, yo?
'Cause we're all here, chillin' out, chillin' out, chillin' out

—"Chillin" by Hedy Wyn

(2009) We sold the townhouse in late July and packed up. Pete came to help us move to Eugene. During the day, it was over a hundred degrees during the entire trip: 110 in Bakersfield and Redding; 108 in Medford and 105 in Eugene. The stores in Eugene ran out of fans. We thought we were moving to the cool pines.

That fall, I subbed in the Eugene area schools and landed a long-term gig for the shop teacher that divided my day at the Springfield middle school and Thurston high school. Thurston was where a student gunman, Kip Kinkel, shot and killed his parents and four of his classmates in 1998, a year before the Columbine shootings in Colorado. The building trades class turned into a personal projects class and we brought in materials as needed. The Springfield middle school was three woodworking classes and I assigned simple boxes, puzzles, animals, and lastly, a small catapult. Some of the eighth-grade boys, excited about their catapults, turned the corner of the room into a battleground. I didn't let it get out of hand and we all learned something.

I wrote a letter to Hedy to say hi and she wrote me back:

Hey Dad,

> Nice utilizing my address! It's very rainy here, no sunshine—cold and wet bike handles and seat. I liked your stationary. I found this at the Dollar Tree. You know, at the highest point in my life, in Bend, OR, I accidentally stumbled into a hidden bar, mistaken for a store. I noticed that the three guys at the bar were all working on projects. It was mid-day on a weekday and it seemed out of place. I scooted closer to the older gentleman who was closest to the door and looked at his drawing. The other guys were doing projects, too, drawing or writing—it was dark inside, so I couldn't see them from afar. His drawing was the perfect rendering of a cowboy atop a horse—beautiful. He, the artist, was dressed in brand new clothes. I assumed these men were local artists, together at the bar, sipping slowly on the dark brown liquor, stirred with ice cubes. My point: get away from distraction and screeching violins. Maybe there are others in Eugene for you to join. Spend a little money to enjoy life. Don't waste time, do it today. You need a unique environment.
>
> My writing class is taking up too much of my time, am contemplating dropping it—it won't effect my financial aid—and I could concentrate on important classes for my major—I love chemistry—almost better than biology—I can switch majors—I'm better at it, too—it's more definite than bio because of the math—even though the classic equations are still considered theories, but that's everything in this world—well, pretty much. It seems there is more opportunity in the chemistry field. I dreamt that I made a snow-boarding pant material and also designed them—I wonder if chemistry would guide me there. Or making plastic stuff & objects for

companies—if I really start understanding compounds, I could make machine parts (quality of course) or just working with raw chemicals—I just don't know—he, he!

I'm excited to see where it leads me. I'm very excited about being on the radio, too.

My DJ name is Merry Kate—my show name is Radical Sabbatical—I'm going to start playing techno music next quarter—I get to make my own commercials, one-liners, posters & stuff. It's another fun-ness in my life. Okay, I'm going to blow out my candle and bid you adieux {my spelling sucks!) Bye—I love you daddy. Hedy

I didn't get many letters to me personally so this letter I treasured. She was as good of speller as me, but I would have never gotten "adieux" on the first try. Pete was laid off at BAE in San Jose; he moved to Eugene to look for work. We bought a house and Hedy came by bus at Halloween to help us move in. We took Hedy back to Ellensburg. Hedy, Peter, and Sandy sang harmony pretty well so we had lots of music on the way. We drove down into Yakima to check out that town; it was a sleepy town the day we visited. On the many hills in the area, wind turbines churned wind into electricity.

Our house in Eugene was a fixer-upper. The previous owners had careless pets, the carpets stunk, the kitchen vinyl was ruined; their teenage son had redecorated his room in part Gothic and Jackson Pollock and the fence in the backyard needed work. Pete and I started on the teen's room by tearing out the rug and stripping paint from the window jambs, replacing some casings. We laid down a ceramic tile floor and painted the room. Pete had always had strong olfaction sense and he wanted desperately for the smells in the living room carpet to go away. So, he led the tearing out the carpet in the living room and we discarded the padding that was the toxic source; we left the carpet loose on the floor until we could replace it with something. Next, we redid parts of the backyard fence and rebuilt the big double gate. Then, back inside, we tackled room number two, which the previous owners had started to turn into an office. That was the easy room. We installed new closet doors, put down new flooring, and painted. All this while I was subbing during the week and Pete was sending out resumes. Mid-semester Springfield Board voted to close the middle school, effective for the following year, and they stopped the shop classes after spring break. Pete moved into an apartment across town. I subbed for the Bethel district more. The Eugene District had a thousand subs and a waiting list of hundreds more and I couldn't get on the waiting list to the waiting list. I subbed for the track coach at Springfield High School on Fridays; he happened to be the woodshop teacher and requested me often. I subbed at Hamlin Middle School for a man who taught three hours of English and three hours in the woodshop. They were in the middle of building trebuchets, not to be confused with catapults. Pete helped me to build a trebuchet about six feet tall that could toss a baseball a considerable distance.

Sandy spent her second year of retirement by practicing her fiddle and playing in jams four or five times a week. In June, we went to an Oregon Old Time Fiddlers Association (OOTFA) jamboree in Burns, Oregon where we met the McLain family from Lakeside, a town near the California border. They were a musical family; they told us their yearly jam at Silver Lake. A month later at Winchester Bay, we met Bob Huffman who was born the same year as Ches Mitcham. He was turning ninety in August and he was still flying his plane, still playing a jazzy guitar that he learned as a teen when jazz was new. We met so many people who were into music in Burns that Sandy thought she'd been reborn into heaven.

Hedy worked the summer of 2010 with a crew that cleaned, painted, and made repairs on the dorm rooms throughout the CWU campus. As the summer slipped away, Hedy called Sandy to say she had switched her major again, this time to art. She was taking beginning sculpture, art history, a class on fabrics and fashion, and a jewelry class. She had a hundred hours of credits by then, including the Yavapai College credits, but she was looking at another two years of classes for an art degree. She said the biology program had put too much pressure on her and triggered her PTSD constantly; she wasn't coping well in the program. The only thing she enjoyed that last quarter was her Deejay gig with the campus radio. And it was about this time that a number of her original song ideas, melodies, and lyrics started presenting themselves as gifts from the universe. She worked on these songs for a number of years, improving on them as she found time. She was meticulous and kept track of every beat and note that went into each song.

During the summer of 2010, Springfield and Eugene each closed middle schools and the laid-off teachers went to subbing that fall. The sub-jobs came so slow that in late September, I started driving for Oregon Taxi. Pete couldn't find work in Eugene and moved to The Dalles on the Columbia River for a Wind Turbine Tech program. Oregon and Michigan had the highest rates of the unemployed.

I drove four days a week, twelve hours a day, got into my cab at 3:30 in the morning and dropped it off by 3:30 in the afternoon. To drive a taxi, you have to have the ability to fall asleep quickly and wake up at a start. And you have to have patience. I thought I did. It's tough to sit in a cab for twelve hours and make twenty dollars. Especially when a fare you take to the airport is telling his clients on the phone that he charges six hundred dollars an hour. That happened to me one day while I was already feeling sorry for myself. The next day, I brought home three hundred dollars and was on top of the world again. No profit one day, followed by a huge profit the next, was par for the course. Putting up with that is what Jim, the man from whom I leased my taxi, called patience.

Hedy sent me a note: Driving taxi was the perfect job for you, Dad. You can work on your projects while you're waiting. I thought, Yeah, wishful thinking.

I had hailed taxis in Mexico a few times, but I had only ridden in a taxi in the States just once. I was a young man then, walking across Phoenix in the middle of summer and hurrying to the Greyhound station to catch my bus to Kansas when I called for help. An old cabbie in an old beat-up cab picked me up and got me there on time.

Cabs from many different companies were parked at the station. The fare came to four dollars and my lowest bill was a ten. (This was at a time when the minimum wage was $1.60 an hour.) I asked the cabby if he had change or I had to run inside and get some. He mumbled, "You don't have time." He was missing teeth. He snatched my ten, stuffed it in his pocket, and turned away into a group of cabbies standing in a circle. They let the old cabbie in and tightened the circle—a team huddle. I came behind my cabbie and tapped him on his back and said, "I need my change." He didn't respond and I heard snickering from the other cabbies, heads down, men of all ages. I ran around the huddle to see if it would crack but it held firm. When I came around again, my cabbie lifted his head slightly and said, "Your bus is leaving, you better go! Get out of here!" I said, "This is low—you're a bunch of low lives." More snickering, and then some bursts of laughter. I ran, found my bus, and I got on, swearing to myself that I'd never hail a taxi again. From the window on the bus, I saw the drivers strutting around, wild with excitement.

In Ellensburg, Hedy bought a small pickup with a shell and said she was planning to sleep in it and spend all her waking hours at the art labs at the campus and taking showers in the gym. She put all her furniture and boxes into storage.

On my first taxi fare in an Oregon Taxi, I took a young woman to a door at the back of the city jail in Eugene where her friend was being released at four o'clock in the morning. I drove the two girls to their car parked at the Gateway Mall in Springfield. They didn't have any money. They begged me to not file charges. Just released from jail and committing a theft, that doesn't look good. I didn't call the police. They were lost women the same age as my daughter. And so, my new career began with a stupid act of kindness. As Christmas neared, I wrote a parody to the song "Up on the Rooftop" about cab-driving; I called it "Up on the Freeway." Jim thought it was fun.

Hedy wrote. She was excited about a sculpture she had just completed. It was a giant handsaw, *Saw of Thor*, over five feet long (before bending) and a foot wide, composed of beat, bent, and blued iron with a wooden handle. After the bending process, it stood about two and a half feet tall. More pieces, welded and forged, were to follow the theme of Thor, the mythic Viking.

(2011) Sandy and I went to the Burns Jamboree again in June and onto the fiddle contests in Weiser, Idaho on the border. On a hike, I tripped over a root and bruised my ribs and Sandy called me a copycat. (It was three years after her bruised ribs.) When we came back from Weiser, I found out my sister, Marlys, had passed away from cancer. I sent some flowers but we had missed the funeral by a few days. I couldn't get service on my cell phone in Weiser. I really wanted to get to Marlys' funeral and I felt doubly guilty for a while. In 1986, Marlys had gotten irate toward our Uncle Bernard, mom's brother, because he missed mom's funeral.

We went to the Silver Lake jam and when we returned, Sandy and three of her friends started *Back Porch Soiree*, an eclectic Americana band. Hedy wrote a note: "Way to go, Mom, a band! Oh, yeah!" Hedy mentioned she had been to a number of concerts in the Gorge Amphitheatre overlooking the Columbia River. She said she wanted to start a band, too.

I picked up a truck driver who was having his semi impounded; he was cited for driving under the influence of painkillers. A patrolman caught him "drifting around" on the freeway. His name was Abbas Shahi; he was from Iran. He fled Iran in 1979 when militants overthrew the Shah. Abbas said he was a governor of a state in Iran, a wealthy businessman, and his ancestors were of Persian royalty. He was driving trucks out of Dallas. He called for rides numerous times over the next two months as he was hold up at the Motel 6 in Springfield, trying to shake his addiction and regain his license. He had broken his back in 2010 in an accident in Nevada that was caused by another driver. He started taking drugs for pain. His oldest daughter was Sarah Shahi, an actress in Hollywood; he said she had disowned him and he hadn't talked to her in years. We went out to a movie one Friday night while Sandy went to a jam. Abbas thought it was the stupidest movie he had ever seen. It was forgettable for sure.

CHAPTER 25

> Hey, where did you get those crystal eyes [3]
> Lighting up the night skies?
> Tell me, where did you get those crystal eyes
> Twinkling in flight?
>
> —"Four Leaf Clover" by Hedy Wyn

(2011) That summer for the second year, Hedy worked on the dormitory crew on the campus of CWU. In early September, Hedy visited Eugene via Greyhound. We had just bought a pallet of veneer oak flooring and had rented a hammer-stapler. Hedy volunteered to help set the floor. It took us a little trial and error but we soon had a system. She chose boards for their color and tones as we progressed and she also manned the hammer. The groove and tongue boards were five inches wide and of random lengths. I held the boards in place and positioned the gun while she smacked the gun-head with the hammer. Bang. Bang, we shot it down, my baby shot it down. She laughed at my teasing and silly jokes, and more importantly, she never hit me once with the mallet. It took three days. I had a few places to cut and fit in corners to finish up, but it was down. And it turned out great. "Hey, hey, oh yeah, Dad! Give me five!" she celebrated.

When Sandy was gone for a day to an old-time meeting, Hedy helped me clean out the pond in our front yard, put in a new pump, rearrange the rocks, and cover the pond with netting. Hedy picked out six goldfish as the final part of that birthday present for Sandy. Hedy and Sandy sang to the fish and taught them to come when food, manna, was about to fall from heaven. They were just tiny little fish but they responded. I would sing, "There were six little fishes and a momma fishy, too, and they all swam together and they called it fishy school." Sandy soon discovered the fish's favorite tune: "Midnight in Moscow."

We planned to stop by The Dalles to say hi to Pete when we drove Hedy back to Ellensburg. Hedy brought along a jar of snails she had found on the rocks around the pond. She talked to the snails and they seemed to open up to her and listen to her wisdom. Instead of taking the freeway, we took an alternate route through the Cascades. On the map didn't look any further but because of the winding roads, it took twice as long: six hours instead of three. In the town of Maupin, we stopped at a park to use the bathrooms and Hedy threatened to run away. It was dark and we were grouchy when we arrived in The Dalles. Pete was expecting us hours earlier. Pete was renting half of a small house on a hill and although it was only mid-September the house was cold. Hedy wasn't friendly to Pete and they got into a spat. Frustrated, Hedy screamed a few times at the top of her lungs which made the house colder. The other half of the house wasn't being rented, so no one came knocking. Hedy's PTSD had come to the surface. Sixteen years of hiding her secret had taken its toll for sure. Maybe all along, since she came out, we were ignoring the signs, hoping and praying that she was healing, when in fact she had been hanging on by a tenuous string for the years following the secret. She was good at hiding her feelings. Hiding secrets. Hiding that she was stuck. Maybe she was trying to protect us from the turmoil that was roiling inside her. She had told us earlier that she preferred living by herself, that the umpteen times she had shared apartments never worked out because the girls were either crazy or insecure. People with PTSD can get irritable for no apparent reason. Dennis in Prescott was Mr. PTSD. People not afflicted with that disorder don't understand it, especially if the sufferer hides it and only shows it in fits. It was eight years then since the sixteen-year-old secret was out. Would it take another eight years to find balance in her life? When a girl is raped at such a young age, as Hedy was, it knocks her off the path of who she was meant to be and the only way back to her true self involves struggling upstream, fighting her demons, and clawing up the bank and back to the path. The longer she keeps the secret, the longer it takes to heal, the deeper the ditch. In 1995-97, researchers with Kaiser and the CDC had been able to show that **A**dverse **C**hildhood **E**xperiences (ACE) affects the developing brains and bodies of children. Children with high exposure show high risks for heart disease, cancer, and a shortened in life expectancy. They lose twenty years of their lives on average. Two out of three children in the United States have at least one ACE, and one out of eight children are considered high risk of developing serious illnesses. Dr. Nadine Burke-Harris did an insightful Ted-Talk on the subject. Many of these high-risk children turn to substances to help with their suffering. Many become addicted and start on the merry-go-round of shame and emotional pain that traps these people in hell. Dr. Gabor Mate says our medical professionals are trauma-phobic, that they are trained to deal with biological and mental wounds with pills. He says few are asking the right questions to help these people heal. He says you cannot cure someone that's suffering from trauma but you can help him or her heal themselves.

Hedy frequented two different counselors at CWU during the first three years: a woman named Lana was the latest and counselor Randy, who Hedy started seeing when she started school. It was Randy's office door, one day, that Hedy slammed and broke the glass. She still was invited back to talk with Randy for the next year. He gave her many tools to carry on and helped her explore the deep struggle that was her life.

We invited Pete to accompany us, to see Hedy's place in Ellensburg, but he declined. When we drove into her college town in the early afternoon, she made us stop at the outskirts and we let her out by a gas station. She was going to call someone to come pick her up. I couldn't guess what that was about, but we honored her wishes and left her standing on the side of the street with her suitcase, boxes, and snails. Sandy told me later what that was all about: Hedy was sharing a house with four guys. They were brave and true and Hedy told Sandy that she felt safe living at their house, safe for the first time since she moved to Ellensburg, the safest in a long time.

On the way back, we coaxed Pete to go out to dinner. He told us all about the big burg of The Dalles and the museum in town that was worth seeing, and we put that on our bucket list. I asked Hedy when she was four, "What is a museum?" She said, "A place where they keep old musical instruments."

Hedy wrote Sandy:

> "Hola, Mom. Can you make your handwriting a little more legible? Thanks. You know what? I feel like a college student from the past—no phone—like in the classic novels where they get shipped off to a distant land to study and where the only form of communication is a rare letter. You know? Like Frankenstein. He, he. I'm totally doing good being a vegetarian. It's been about a month. I've lost three pounds and my skin has cleared up. I've almost stopped eating sugar. I started being sociable again. I knew I had to build up my skills again, but I didn't know it was going to be a snake pit. God! It's like a whole bunch of muscle, resembling brains, slithering around, and fighting for their piece of the pie. A leader at work said that socializing was so important to get a job and so I'm building my skills back up. It seems like no one at this school knows how to joke around. They're just trying to prove every else wrong. Too serious. Being in science classes proved to me I don't know everything. It's nice to be around people like that. Love, Hedy"

Hedy made it into November before the freezing weather drove her into an apartment. Her truck blew an engine and she took up the bike again. At the Christmas break, Hedy went to Spokane and spent a couple of days with her friend, Eric, and his partner. Eric was the guy she met when she broke her wrist. She commented: "Every girl should have a gay male friend, like in *Will and Grace*. Yes, that is the only way a girl can survive the craziness of having a boyfriend or being married to a man. Gay guys are so important, so cool. Isn't that sad or what?"

On the first day of spring of 2012, I left the house that morning like usual, at 3:00, and stepped into ten inches of snow that had fallen silently during the night. I made it to the lot where my taxi van was parked, but the tires were so bald that I slid into a curve and flattened a tire instantly. My day ended before it started. I changed the tire and called Jim and he wasn't too happy with my opting out. Later that afternoon, Jim talked me into taking the #28 van to get a new set of tires. We put 80,000 miles a year on that '94 Previa van. At that time, the #28 was on its third engine and transmission and had a total of 940,000 miles chocked up. We started watching it for when it would hit a million miles.

In May, Sandy and I went to the old-time fiddlers' jamboree at Silver Lake for the first time; we slept in the back of the truck, and we froze. We booked a room at the little motel in town for the next year. Sometime in early summer, Hedy had her senior show and kept it secret from us; she won a monetary prize for a soapstone sculpture she called Teardrop. She used 1200 grit sandpaper to make it shine. She came home in June and said she had a couple of projects to complete before she could sign out of her classes and receive her degree. She could've marched with her graduating class but she said she felt out of place.

Sandy took Hedy to the jamboree in Burns and they camped out by the fairgrounds. Sandy said Hedy seemed kind of lost while they were there. Sandy brought a fiddle and a guitar. Hedy brought her viola and joined the jamming. After Burns, Hedy went back to Ellensburg.

It was a busy summer jamming. Sandy and I visited the coast near Astoria and Three Arch Rocks; Sandy played in three bands—String-a-Longs, Back Porch, and Big Foot Lane. In the garage, I made space for Hedy's boxes. In August, Hedy finished her classwork, paid off her fees, and rented a U-Haul truck. I volunteered to drive it back but she wanted to do that herself. On the phone, I could tell something wasn't right. I asked her if she was okay. "I'm fine. How are you, Dad?"

"Is there something wrong? Something you want to talk about?"

"I'll be alright. Eugene is fine. I'll be all right. Eugene is fine."

But everything wasn't all right. She called hours later from the town of Sweet Home and said she could not drive any further, that she was getting dizzy and wasn't sure if she was lost or not. She didn't have a map and she wasn't listening to me explaining how to proceed. We went there to help her out. Hedy had pulled the truck into a lot by an abandoned gas station. It was starting to get dark. She was sitting in it when we pulled up. She stepped down from the cab of the truck as if she was in a trance. I asked, "Are you on something?"

"No, I don't think so," she said. "It's just that I don't want to live with you guys. It's so depressing. Not Eugene, not this way. But I'm broke and in such debt. So much debt." Sandy said, "Make that your goal: pay off your debt as fast as you can." I drove the truck to Eugene and we unloaded her stuff into the garage. That next weekend, we turned the house over to Hedy and went to an OOTFA jamboree at Diamond Lake and drove to Crater Lake National Park and around the highway that skirts the lake. We forgot our tent and slept in the camper shell; the mosquitoes ate us up. When we got back to Eugene, Hedy was feeling better about the move and thankful to have had the house. The next weekend, we went to Bend's High & Dry Blue Grass Festival; we came back to an even happier Hedy.

It was during that fall that Hedy registered a number of her songs with the Copyright Office in DC. She had written twenty songs by then. She received a letter from a publisher asking for money to publish her songs. I gave her a copy of *Music Publishing* by Randy Roe and told her to read the part about song sharks. She read the book and avoided that shark. I worked on a book *The Savvy Dictionary* and made plans to self-publish it. Sandy's band, Big Foot Lane, played at the Emerald Valley Opera at Willamette High School that fall.

The summers are dry in Western Oregon and on the first good rain, usually after mid-September, the roads get slick because of the accumulation of oil on the surface. That night on the 105 near Thurston, the night driver lost control of the #28 taxicab and totaled it. It had 990,000 miles on it.

Hedy said she had gotten an apprenticeship with a sculptor in Monterey, California. So, she drifted away in her Jeep Cherokee; she was gone a week. She made it as far as Eureka, California on the coast. On her return, she confessed she didn't have an apprenticeship but just needed to getaway. A few days later, she drove her vehicle to the Target store on west Eleventh Avenue and hitchhiked to the coast. She left a note telling us where we could find her jeep and asking us to take it home; she was heading to California again. We didn't find the note until later that night. In the morning, I drove over to the coast and made my way south, down Highway 101, inquiring in all of the communities about her. Winchester Bay, Dunes City, Reedsport. A little afternoon, on a hunch, I stopped at a house in Lakeside where a man was working in his yard. He asked me to describe her. I did and he said, "She spent the night sleeping in my chicken coop. She just left an hour ago. She needs some help; she's not all there."

I said, "She's trying to work it out. We're trying our best. It's a long story."

"Well, we talked for two or three hours last night. She's a bright girl."

I thanked him. A couple of miles down the road, I found Hedy walking on the side of the road. She came over to the truck and said, "I surrender." She was glad I had come for her. She had walked forty miles, she thought. She wanted to see the Redwoods, but that would have to wait. We drove east out of Reedsport on Highway 38; we had burgers at a café in Elkton. She was talkative and happy to be going home. "You know I can't stand your guitar playing and Mom's fiddle. They sound like dogs and cats being killed. I'm going to get a job and I'm going to get those bills paid off." A break in the fog.

Later that week, we offered to pay off her credit card bill; most of the balance came from university-related expenses. She promised never to abuse credit cards again. And we promised to never help pay them again. She got a full-time job as a manager of a KFC and a part-time job as a waitress to tackle her student debt of $20,000. She joined the Friday evening art walk in Eugene and had some of her art up for sale at the galleries and businesses along the route of the walk. She read *The Seven Spiritual Laws of Success*. She wanted to make fashion her life's calling. She bought a sewing machine at our neighbor's yard sale.

The three of us walked to the United Methodist Church ten blocks away for the Christmas Eve candlelight service. Hedy dressed Brian up in some old doll clothes and she didn't go out and party on New Year's Eve; she said it was the first time in a decade she stayed sober on that day.

CHAPTER 26

Now you're in front of me and never were my lover   [4]
I tried to tell you patiently: you won't win Red Rover
You're a chain break, a gate flake
But my heart's a pumper,
I guess I'll fake what I did discover

—"My Playground" by Hedy Wyn

(2013) Hedy drew forty illustrations for *The Savvy Dictionary* including the cover during the first month of the New Year. She got a little carried away on the letter D and had five illustrations crowding the pages there but other than that, she graced the pages of that book with delightful black and whites, her first art gig out of college. All this while she rendered drawings to expand her portfolio. She took thousands of photographs throughout the area. She experimented with making videos to accompany her completed songs and covers of popular songs. When an African lion named Cecil was killed in an illegal big game hunt that made national news, Hedy had a color pencil lion drawing up the next weekend at the gallery. She was forging ahead.

Peter came back from The Dalles and accepted a job from a wind turbine company in Eastern Washington. We played tennis and went bowling before he was scheduled to leave. Then the head of a helicopter company in Eugene made an offer and Pete stayed in Eugene designing parts for them. Pete's first job at Raytheon was designing guns; at BAE, he worked on designs for armed vehicles; then on to helicopters. Our perpetual wars were keeping him busy. Since the mid-seventies, many cities in America have been hurting for lack of good-paying jobs. Eugene used to have about fifty small cabinet shops until 2009 when the recession knocked most them out business. Hedy worked fifty hours a week and ground away at her student loan debt. She had worked in the restaurant business since she was sixteen, so in 2013, that made half her life, or sixteen years. She said she hated it. Some restaurants in Arizona she worked for only paid waitresses $2.00 an hour because they claimed tips made up the balance. On good nights, she might make money. Hedy said she was making good per hour on such nights. In March, I drove a student in my taxi to Portland and the boy jerked his collateral (two cellphones in a backpack) out of my hands and ran into the dormitory and out the other side and disappeared in the darkness. The dispatchers warned us not to leave on a long trip without money upfront. The kid had gotten down on his knees in Eugene and pleaded with me to take him to Portland or his parents were going to kill him. I chose wrong: his parents should have killed him.

We went to the OOTFA gigs throughout the spring and summer. Then in June, Sandy's band, Big Foot Lane, played at the south lodge on Odell Lake in the Cascades. The Pacific Crest Trans-American trail passes by the north end of the lake. As payment, her band got free rooms. I went with Sandy. The lodge was old and rooms came with a double bed with a bunk bed and a dresser tucked to the side. There was not much floor space remaining. A musky smell had seeped into the pores of the logs.

Hedy experimented on the barbeque behind our house; she brought smoky tastes to an endless number of foods. *The Savvy Dictionary* came out that summer. We gave Hedy the house for a few weekends as we went to Burns, and the southern coast of Oregon to see the Redwoods, and to High & Dry in Bend. In July, we heard on the news that nineteen firefighters with the Granite Mountain Hotshots from Prescott were killed in a fire near Yarnell, Arizona. One of the young men was one of Sandy's former students in Prescott. He left a wife and two children behind. That week, I picked up a young firefighter in my cab and took him to the bus station; he was heading into the Cascades to fight a fire near Crater Lake. He had heard the news of the unlucky hotshots, and was planning to be extra cautious.

In July, as an artistic statement, Hedy got a butch haircut. She found a black and blue wig and started parading around in it. Hedy made a few more avant-garde films that summer and wrote more songs. She worked in the evenings and often got Peter to help her stage scenes and play the mysterious stranger. After a huge argument with Hedy, Peter moved out of our house and into an apartment.

In August, Hedy left the fast-food industry (forever she hoped), as she landed a job at Odell Lake. She said she was going to get to learn the jobs necessary for the operation of the lodge. But alas, one of them was waitressing. Willamette Pass on highway 58 is one of the more friendly winter routes, in that it's not as high in elevation as others further to the north. I drove her up the lake; she brought her bike and a suitcase. On the way down the hill, a cougar crossed the road in front of my truck. I pulled over to the edge of the road. The cat was eight feet long from the tip of its tail to its nose and it seemed to pad across the road in slow motion. I had never seen a cougar in the wild before. When it hit the shadows, it disappeared. A six-year-old human child would look tiny next to one.

On her time off, Hedy caught fish, cleaned and cooked them, or pedaled a boat across the lake or she pedaled her bike down to the little town of Crescent on Highway 97; she would struggle back up the hill for an hour. She worked forty hours a week or more. Her boss was a lanky man named McDougal who was about a decade older than Hedy.

In September, Sandy's band played at the Odell Lodge again; I didn't go that time. During the band's performance, Sandy said McDougal showed up in a Big Foot costume and brought some laughs. Hedy showed up a short time later extremely drunk and falling all over the drunk McDougal. After the show, Sandy confronted Hedy while they were alone in Sandy's room. "I've never before felt ashamed of one of my children, until tonight. Don't you ever act like that again in front of my friends. What were you thinking?"

Hedy slapped Sandy and almost knocked her down. "I'm not your little girl anymore," said Hedy.

"You're not acting like a responsible adult either."

"Good! You don't control me. Not anymore." Hedy left the building by a back stairway. Hedy was living in a small travel in an area of cottages nestled in a stand of small trees, fruit trees, and the like. Her trailer was next to McDougal's trailer, end to end. Sandy knocked on Hedy's trailer but there was no one there. Sandy heard music coming from McDougal's trailer; she followed the path of the beaten-down grass to the area beside his trailer that was covered with empty beer cans and empty bottles. Sandy knocked on the door. A staggering, red-eyed McDougal answered the door. Hedy was yelling in the background, "I don't want to talk to her!" McDougal told Sandy this. Sandy begged Hedy that they needed to talk. Hedy pushed him aside. "What?"

Sandy said, "Please, come out so we can talk in private." She motioned to the ground beside Hedy's trailer where there was a break in the sea of beer cans. Hedy came down the stairs and they moved up the path. Sandy said, "I know you're not yourself when you drink. But when you come back home, you have to see a counselor or you can't live at our house."

"I don't want to live at your house. I can make my own life."

"Well, if you change your mind, that is the condition of your living with us."

"Fine!"

Sandy considered calling the sheriff to come out to the boondocks, but she didn't want to cause a scene. Sandy didn't sleep all night. When she got back to Eugene, she looked into finding a therapist for Hedy. Sandy also talked with the group called SASS, Sexual Assault Support Services, and got some literature from them. Hedy apologized by phone but stayed up at the lodge all winter. It was a destination for snowmobiles and cross-country skiers. McDougal was a bad influence on all his workers, but especially Hedy. He drank himself to sleep every night. Before she went to Odell, she had quit drinking, at least around us. Hedy would say later that McDougal "was a bad, bad man." He had stashes of every drug and he partied almost every night.

In early November, with our musical friends from Bend we rented a house in Yachats for a weekend and we drove over to the coast and played to the rhythm of the surf. There was a small cave at the shore where the waves crashed and sent a spout of water straight up twenty feet.

(2014) We went to our regular music get-togethers that year. Hedy called in in early May and I drove up to Odell Lake and moved her back to Eugene. She had saved enough money to pay off a large portion of her debt. Her hair had grown back. The first thing she did was to lease an orange Toyota hatchback. Hedy looked into getting into the Navy. McDougal had suggested that to her. She talked to a recruiter and she came back with a handful of brochures. Because she had a degree, she could start at a higher grade and she was excited about that. In the news that month were stories of rape in the military. Hedy said she might be too old to join anyway. Sandy and Hedy went for a walk in the neighborhood just to discuss that issue.

"There are bad things everywhere, Mom. Around every corner. I can't roll up into a ball and hide from them. I'll carry a knife with me." But over the next few weeks, Hedy didn't say any more about the Navy and the idea faded away.

We took Peter with us to a Bluegrass Festival in Fossil, Oregon. It was a hot weekend. In the hills, above Fossil high school, we dug in the dirt looking for fossils and found some; we didn't stay long—there was no breeze. To get to Fossil, we passed near the town of Antelope. In the 1980s it made international news on a daily basis. Antelope was where a rich maharishi from India tried to force his will on the stubborn old cowboys in the area. It didn't turn out well for the fellow and his cult followers. He went back to India or to prison in Oregon; I can't remember which. He left forty Rolls Royce automobiles in Antelope. Not enough for every cowboy, but enough to bring joy.

In Eugene, Hedy landed jobs at a barbeque restaurant and at Denny's by the freeway. Hedy told me that it was the Denny's where Jack Nicholson performed the chicken salad scene in the movie *Five Easy Pieces*. The sign "We Reserve the Right Refuse Service" was still on the wall. I took a couple who worked there, to and from work at that restaurant often. I waited for calls in the parking lot and got to spy on Hedy. She really worked hard with that big pleasing smile.

Sandy and I made a mistake when we did not demand Hedy get some help for her depression or anger issues. In July, when I was working in the backyard, Hedy and Sandy had a disagreement in the kitchen, and Hedy slapped Sandy. As Sandy stood there in shock, Hedy slapped her again. Hedy drove away in her car before Sandy called me into the house. Hedy had been drinking, we suspected. We demanded she get counseling, no more alcohol in our house, no more drinking, or she had to find another place to live. She found a counselor a few miles away on River Road. She went to this counselor for a few months before we all started seeing a family counselor together. Hedy had become adept at getting her counselors to take it easy on her and it wasn't long before she had the family therapist, Susan, eating out her hand. Sandy and I looked in awe as Hedy bent Susan to her will. Susan, an elderly woman, was nearing eighty years old and didn't seem to suspect a thing. I was hoping it was a ploy by Susan, but it wasn't. Hedy's anger at us was upfront and foremost. We rationalized that Hedy had slapped Sandy and not me because first, Sandy was physically smaller, and second, Hedy blamed Sandy for being from the family that had attacked her.

Hedy lived with the secret for so many years and the damage caused by the secret's toxic effects never did let her heal; she and we pretended she was healing. She made it through college, but only with the help of her counselors who glued her piece by piece back together week by week. As Blume said in *Secret Survivors*: "Adult incest survivors have so much to be angry about. She has been hurt. Her needs and feelings have been disregarded. She has been forced to take care of those whose job and moral responsibility it was to take care of her. She had no childhood. She never got the chance to develop into a healthy adult. And now she must maneuver through the world handicapped by emotional deficits and a history of trauma and pain that is often buried beneath the consciousness. Yet, she is often robbed of her anger by fears, family rules, and social injunctions."

Hedy started to understand her anger better during her last year at CWU, that it wasn't necessarily a bad thing but a tool to use. In the sculpture studio, in the jewelry processes, in the fabrics, in the fantasy world of her drawings, in the music she was creating, she was getting herself back. In college though, she was living a sheltered life, working in hope toward a future where she would finally be free. Living in Eugene with the people who failed to protect her as a child was not the future she imagined. Her hope had shrunk to fit into a glass menagerie.

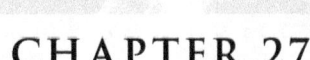

CHAPTER 27

Every need, every want, every desire   [5]
I have plunged, I will fall, but I want to fall higher . . .
To know that I exist
I wanna sleep, I wanna lay, next to your fire

—"Your Fire" by Hedy Wyn

In the fall, Sandy hurt her wrist in a bicycle accident and stopped playing the fiddle for more than a month. We shared another house with our musical friends for a weekend in Yachats, one with a ten-foot totem pole. Sandy's wrist was better by then. Hedy was delighted to have the house.

Back in 2002, in Prescott, just months before Hedy broke the secret, a counselor that Sandy was seeing suggested that Sandy and her sister, Wendy, come to a session together. Wendy said she would go, but only to a counselor of her choosing, a neutral person. Wendy chose Nancy Burns, a counselor Wendy said she had never met. Burns couldn't get Wendy to be quiet and let Sandy speak; Wendy would constantly talk over Sandy. The counselor asked them to start over and to state their concerns and asked Wendy to restrain herself. Sandy learned then that Wendy had seen Burns many times before. Sandy said, "Wendy is always criticizing my children. She puts them down like it's some kind of a game with her." Wendy stood and said, "This isn't going to happen; I'm not going to listen to her lies." Burns kicked them both out of her office. As they walked back to their cars, Wendy was happy she had sabotaged the meeting. Looking back, Sandy could see that Wendy was afraid the truth was going to come out. Just a few months later, Hedy told the secret.

(2014) We went to a jam in Powell Butte near Bend at a house some friends said we needed to see. The owners of the house, Dennis and Ellen, who frequented the central Oregon jams, had a few acres in the country, not unlike the high desert around Prescott. They had decorated their house to look like a bar. The large living room in ranch style home could accommodate sixty musicians. Dennis took Sandy and I outside to see the newest critter to his little ranch: an Emu that had wandered onto his land a few months earlier. When Dennis tracked down the Emu's owner, the man gave Dennis the big bird. The stars in that area of Oregon shine bright; as bright as we remembered the stars in Prescott.

We met one Friday at the house of Susan, our family counselor. Hedy came straight from work; she was waiting in her car in front of Susan's house. This was our third session with Susan. During some small talk, Susan said she knew the owners of the café where Hedy worked, had known them for years, and that the cook lived right behind Susan's house. At least we could see the roof of the man's home. Hedy told Susan she was considering joining the army and had talked to a recruiting officer. Susan said that sounded good. Hedy said, "I probably won't join. I think it's too late. I'd be too old. I would feel out of place."

Susan said, "Sounds like you don't want to go. Maybe it's best you didn't pursue that." Susan asked Hedy what she thought she needed to do to move forward with her life. Hedy said, "Well, you know I have a new car. I'm just leasing it but it feels so good to not worry if your car is going to work."

Sandy said, "I hate car problems more than anything."

Susan said, "Enough about fixing cars; let's work on this family."

Hedy said, "Well, I would feel better if my dad would stop copying me."

Susan said, "How does he copy you?"

"He's writing songs now, but that's my thing. If I get a drink of water, he has to get a drink of water. If I go to eat something, he has to eat something."

Sandy said, "He copies me, too. If I get up to go to the kitchen, he follows me."

Susan glanced at me to explain myself.

"They never said this before. I do drink a lot of water. To get rid of headaches like the one I'm getting now. If we're watching a show, we all get up during commercials, get something, do something. I wrote songs ten years before you were born, Hedy. I'm not copying you. That's a stupid thing to say."

"Don't call me stupid."

"I don't copy you, Hedy."

Susan said, "She thinks you do. You have to consider how she feels."

(2015) In late January, we got the news that Sandy's friend and former teaching buddy, Anita, had been killed in Prescott Valley. Her son, addicted to opioids, went into a drug-induced fit and murdered Anita and a man and a woman who were renting a room from Anita. We drove down to Arizona for the memorial. We asked Hedy who had Anita as a teacher for two years if she wanted to come with us. She was too excited about having the house to herself.

I teased Hedy, "No parties!"

She laughed and said, "Oh, we'll see. No! I promise: no parties."

On the trip, we stayed in Bakersfield the first night and got into Prescott the next evening. At the high school, the auditorium was packed. Sandy got to see a number of her teacher buddies and reminisce. We kept an eye out in case we would run into Wendy or Bob. Nicki and Patrick probably had Anita as a teacher, but we saw no sign of them. The boys had gone to the same college in Ohio. Bob had bought a different house. Then, we were off to Tucson to visit Sharon and Jeff. We told Jeff he looked more than ever like his grandpa Pancho Villa. Sharon's friend, Henry, had just laid ceramic tile through her whole house. They were in the process of grouting. We headed toward Oceanside, California and our next stop, my oldest sister, Arlene, and her husband Ray. Arlene had lost a lot of weight. She was struggling with Alzheimer's that had been diagnosed a year earlier. Ray, the super caregiver, helped his wife of nearly sixty years at every turn. They asked about Hedy's situation and we told them more than they wanted to hear. They paled, listening to it all.

By summer, Hedy announced she had paid off her school debt, was debt-free. It seemed like quite an accomplishment, so we had a celebration barbeque. Pete came for the cookout. He told us his helicopter company was moving to Canada. So goes the life of an engineer. He was moving to Corvallis for a short program to get certified for Electrical Engineering. That summer involved running to and from music festivals like the previous years. John Hancock, the man who created the Bluegrass Festival at Bend, had passed away from cancer and the land was being sold and that was to be the last year of that festival.

That summer (2015), I came across a memoir called *College Girl*. The author was the professor at NAU who taught the class "Autobiographical Writings" that I took in 2007. That was the class where eight out of the ten girls in the class testified to being raped sometime in their life. Proclaimed, rather. Only one girl and Ms. Gray didn't join the testimonials then. *College Girl* tells the story of Ms. Gray's rape in her freshman year at Syracuse University in New York. So that upped the percentage. When Ms. Gray and I had talked in her office about the catharsis of healing we had witnessed, she must have been considering her memoir and the approach she would take to break her secret. When I told her about Hedy, she had said, "Your daughter must be a brave girl." I told Hedy that summer that I hoped she would write her own memoir but she pushed the idea aside. She asked me again to not ever write about it.

In the fall, Hedy recorded some of her songs at the Don Ross studio. She put her tracks on her computer's Garage Band program and added more tracks to that. She also bought an electric guitar and got serious about learning it. On the first of December, she moved into a tiny apartment in downtown Eugene.

We had seen Susan, the counselor, about every other month during the year; she announced she was retiring. We were the last of her clients. "You could continue to see me, and that would be alright and I would love to see you, really, it will not be a problem to continue seeing you here. My husband will have to wait. And you were always welcome here and I would be fine with seeing you from time to time, unless of course, you could find another counselor and by all means, that would be fine with me, and you all for sure would have my blessing if that was what you really wanted to do."

Susan never liked me. I never liked her. As a parting shot, she asked if I had ever been tested for Asperger's Disease. I told her I didn't know what that was. Sandy didn't either. Hedy perked up. Susan said, "It's a type of autism and I believe you exhibit the true signs of it. You've never been tested? Are you sure?"

"Should I have been?"

Hedy chimed in, "Dad, it makes so much sense. I always thought you were weird. But now we know why." At first, I thought she was teasing me, but when she didn't crack a smile, I knew I was in for a long week.

Susan asked, "Have you ever heard of echolalia?"

"No, I don't believe I have," I said.

"It's a condition associated with autism and I believe you exhibit it."

"Really?"

"Really."

"Really?"

On New Year's Day (2016), we were fifteen minutes late for a meeting with Hedy in the Rose Garden at the end of Jefferson Street. She was on her bike. It was cold and she was angry. I told her it was my fault; that I had to retrieve something I had left in the cab. But she said she didn't want to hang out with us anymore. "You guys could probably stay out of my life and that would be for the best." As she rode away from the park, we watched her disappear behind the roses.

Peter was allergic to the solder used in his classes at OSU; he broke out rashes all over his body. He moved back to Eugene. When Hedy heard about Peter's rashes, she was reminded of an incident from her childhood that happened not long before the pantry scene. When Hedy turned twelve, Wendy told us a neighbor gave a pet rat to her boys. But Wendy decided her boys were too young for such a pet and she offered it to Hedy. We had just moved into the Bridle Path house, and the first night Hedy had the rat, Hedy broke out into a terrible rash all over her body. We gave the rat back to Wendy and what Wendy did with it, we don't know. It was over twenty years later that Hedy wondered what really caused that rash. "Did Wendy dust that rat with poison to torment me? "She was doing crap like that to me my whole life. I bet she gave me that rash on purpose."

In February, Hedy started a band called Splunk with a drummer and a bass player. They played a dozen gigs at the downtown bars and at Old Nicks in the Whitaker district; we went to see her. I filmed most of one concert. She sang her original songs. The bass player, Nathan, was in his first year of college and she said he didn't drink or do drugs. The drummer, Garrett, she met at Hole in the Wall when she waited at his table and started up a conversation with him about making music. Splunk went into the studio soon after they formed and recorded a couple of songs.

About six blocks from our house was Emerald Park where a skateboard pit attracted a lot of young people. In early April, a young man, just out of the military and suffering from PTSD, was living in the house next to the park. He got into a shouting match with some skateboarders. He came to the skateboard commons with a gun. When one of the young men tried to defuse the situation, the soldier shot and killed the man. The young soldier went into his house and killed himself. They were both in their late twenties. Hedy walked by the skaters for years on the way to the indoor pool at the park and she would cheer them and chat with them.

That same week, in my taxi, I picked up an older man in Springfield, a grandpa, who was going back to the doctor to have his bandages changed on his hand. Days earlier, he had shot off his index finger while cleaning his gun, and all the while taking swings from a bottle of whiskey. He said it was the fault of an electrical transformer in his alley—that had popped and startled him—that caused him to pull the trigger. He was going to sue the power company, he said.

In May, Hedy dropped off a black Subaru hatchback at our house and I drove her back to her apartment. Later, she walked four miles to our house from the dealership where she left her orange hatchback. Sandy was at her band practice. Hedy and I had a long conversation. I should have filmed her. She was excited about her life, about her future. Her band was one of the greatest things she had ever done in her life, she said. She gave Brian, our fat cat, a good rub down as we talked. Brian was in seventh heaven because Hedy, his favorite human being on this planet, tickled him for an hour.

CHAPTER 28

> Bite your tongue with your blatant teeth　　　　[6]
> You know that I could drool forever . . .
> The ones forced to the bottom must rise to the top
>
> 　　　—"Rise To the Top" by Hedy Wyn

(2016) In early June, I got a pain in my lower intestines and after throwing up a few times, I went to the emergency room. Seven hours later in a CAT scan, they found that my gut was twisted. The surgeon, an Asian-Indian man, performed emergency microsurgery. He said later he had never seen a case like mine and that they caught it just in time. It appeared to be congenital, he said. When I got home, I called Sharon in Tucson and said, "I think I've solved the mystery of mother's cancer. See, Katie must have had a twisted gut and because she didn't go to the doctor immediately, the back-up caused her intestines to bulge out. When the surgeons in Iowa cut her open to drain her because they thought cancer was causing the blockage, they found the twisted gut. But by then, the pinched area of the gut had died and the doctors mistakenly called it cancer. It wasn't cancer. Katie didn't have cancer. She never healed right after surgery. What killed her was her not going to the doctor right away.

You might have this twisted gut syndrome, so watch out. Get right into the doctor. Don't hesitate."

"Okay, I'll try to remember that when the time comes," said Sharon. "Are you feeling all right?" I only stayed on opioid painkillers for a day.

The next project at the Old Casa was painting the outside and I started prepping. We went to a jam at Crane Prairie Reservoir where Sandy swam in the cloudy water. The next weekend, we volunteered at the Northwest String Summit in Portland where our friend, John, got us free tickets for helping at the Alcoholics Anonymous Booth; we pretended we were recovering. It was a crowded campsite and Sandy may have come down with it there or at the CP Reservoir, but she was diagnosed with mononucleosis later in the week. So plagued with the low energy blues, she missed out on all the prep work and the priming of the house, the trim, the chipping, the scraping, the sanding, the spraying. Brian, the cat, pretended to be sick, too, and spent a month lying around with Sandy. Sandy said she was sorry, but she was smiling when she said it.

Joe Canady, a close friend, died from cancer in August. He was a guitar picker in his eighties; everyone at OOTFA was sad to see him go. The key word in OOTFA was "old" and a lot of our members were disappearing. Some friends in Arizona told us the last of the old time fiddlers in the Prescott passed away and the organization disappeared from the area that summer of 2016. We found out that Ray Gardner had passed away the previous year.

That September, Hedy said she tested positive for HPV and also that she had a cyst. She claimed she didn't have cancer. Sandy called Hedy's doctor and by mistake, the office gave out Hedy's confidential information. Hedy had not tested positive for cancer but she missed an appointment to remove the cyst. Sandy thought she knew why she missed her surgery. Ever since Hedy started her period when she was twelve, she would faint at the sight of blood. And if a doctor examined her private area, she would faint. During such appointments, Sandy accompanied her, holding her hand. This was the norm all through middle school and high school: Hedy fainting in doctors' offices. When more women pediatricians began showing up, it took the pressure off Hedy's visits to the doctor, but she still fainted. Hedy wrote in her journal that when she started bleeding at age twelve, she tried to hide it from Sandy. But by the third day, a worried Hedy told Sandy something was wrong with her. Sandy took Hedy out to a restaurant to explain the facts of life. Sandy told Hedy that the beginning of her periods meant she was a woman, that now she could get pregnant. Still baffled, Hedy said, "Where am I going to keep all the baby diapers? In my room? In the hall cabinets?"

Sandy laughed, "No, honey, you don't understand. You've started your menstrual cycle; it will happen every month from now on. Starting now, if you have sex with a man, you can get pregnant."

"Yuck, that's disgusting."

Hedy's doctor's assistants also told Sandy that the cyst could turn into cancer. Sandy talked to Hedy about the missed appointment. "I'll come and hold her hand during the surgery. If you reschedule, I'll help you." Hedy was angry after she found out that they gave Sandy any information. Hedy told Sandy to never contact her again. She texted me also in an angry tone.

On the Friday after the 2016 election, we were getting ready to go to the coast for the annual musical get-together; I was wheeling the garbage can from the curb when a little beater of a car drove by and someone yelled, "Nigger!" at me. I turned back to see an arm out the window flipping me off. There were four young people in the car. I was stunned. I hadn't been called that since Sharon and I were kids; we were two of the few black-haired kids in our small town in Iowa.

Hedy's apartment lease was up in December and we noticed her car had disappeared from the parking spaces by her building. Her landlord wouldn't give us any information. There was a KFC across the street from the restaurant where Hedy worked and we ate at the KFC a few times to try and see her. A fierce ice storm hit the area in the middle of the month and knocked out the power after tens of thousands of tree limbs and trees came crashing down the night of big freeze. All night long, we listened to the trees groan, pop, and crash. I parked that night at the elementary school down the street. That morning, I bought the last generator at Bi-mart and I had been home only five minutes when a huge limb fell and wiped out my camper shell without putting a scratch on the rest of my truck.

In January (2017), we didn't see Hedy's car parked at the restaurant. We called there and asked for Hedy but they told us she didn't work there anymore. It snowed the first week of the year. The roads were slick and half the cab drivers went home. Drivers never made money on days like that; the company mad money because they still collected their leases. The computer tablet in our cabs lit up red with dozens of waiting calls, but the customers, angry with us for our slowness, were seldom there to be picked when we finally arrived. I was sent to Elmira, a town west of Eugene, to pick up a gentleman for a Ride Source run and the traffic was crawling along highway 126. On the way back, I took the Clear Lake Reservoir Road that had turned out to be all ice. The Beltline was iced over, too, and I avoided siding into a stopped car ahead of me by inches. The car behind me was able to stop, but the truck behind him couldn't and nailed him; luckily, I began moving seconds before the crash. There were over five hundred accidents reported around Springfield and Eugene that day. Our company received so many complaints that they had no choice but to blame the drivers. Our leader wrote a scathing e-mail to us saying how disappointed he was in us. Many of our drivers had gone home as soon as the roads iced over; they were the smart ones. Those who stayed to help were the dedicated, the stupid, and the insane.

Hedy e-mailed Sandy on February 8, 2017, the fourteenth anniversary of her breaking the secret:

> "I am so angry with you for not fighting for me and Peter when we were young. If we are going to have any kind of a relationship, I want you to post-camp with me in Arizona, you need to pay for a lawyer unless I can get

one pro-bono and I want to fight against Wendy Adams for what she did to our family. She has defamed our family, listed as slander because she was malicious about it—blackmailing was her intent. I know we can win this because we didn't do anything she claims. Also, there may be other charges we can use against her. Our entire family is breaking down because of the domino effects of her deviant acts. Peter and I have stayed so strong this entire time. I can't hold on anymore. I will change my name after this and that is how I will move on.

We will be stronger together. I know we have a case. I will have my own case, as a direct hit, Peter can join me. I am also suing Nicki for what Wendy said he claimed. This is the entire basis for the lawsuit. Either Wendy has brainwashed him or he is an evil seed. Patrick may carry the golden key if Nicki lies. Patrick didn't accuse me or Peter of anything. He might remember the sesame seeds. I'd like to hear what they have to say. You will have your own case. Pop can join, too.

If this doesn't work for you, I will never talk to you again because I am so angry that I cannot even look you in the eye. I will have a restraining order against you for stalking me and defaming my character against my employers and landlords. Think about it. Let me know. Hedy."

Later that same day, she e-mailed again. Hedy reiterated the points about the case for slander and blackmail and she brought up another incident that she still remembered—an incident in which she believes Wendy tried to kill her and Peter. The incident happened in Nogales in September 1986; Hedy was five years old and Peter was four. It was about six weeks after Wendy and Bob's marriage; it was six months before the rape. I was at work. Sandy had to be at work and she was going to take Hedy and Pete to daycare, while Wendy and Christopher, who had just turned fourteen, were going to explore the shops across the border. But then, Wendy volunteered to watch our children and we said okay. Wendy drove them to a Patagonia Lake outside of town. Wendy rented a rowboat. According to Hedy, Wendy and Christopher pushed the boat out into the choppy waters with Hedy and Peter in the boat and then, Wendy sat on the bank eating KFC chicken and laughing as the boat nearly swamped in the choppy water and Hedy and Peter, terrified, screamed for help. After a while, Wendy got Christopher to swim out to the boat and row it back. Hedy remembered crying and Peter crying and Wendy laughing in their faces and calling them big babies. Hedy said Christopher didn't join in on the laughing. This was the story Hedy remembers. But Wendy told Sandy and I a different tale that evening. Wendy said then: "You guys were so lucky that Christopher was there today. He saved Hedy and Peter. He's a real hero. The boat drifted away from shore with Hedy and Peter in it and a storm was coming up and I said you got to do something, Chris, and Chris jumped in the water and swam to the boat and climbed inside and rowed it back to shore. The wind was blowing hard and the waves were high and the rain was really coming down by then. Chris was a real hero today. Isn't that right, Hedy?" Hedy said she remembered Wendy telling that version to us. Hedy was afraid to disagree with Wendy's version of events and afraid to tell the truth; Hedy didn't say anything that night.

We called around Eugene found out we could not file a missing person's report on Hedy because she was over eighteen. One day, Sandy was browsing the Internet and came across some information about Nicki and Patrick. They were living in New York. They were musicians, had a band and were teaching music.

CHAPTER 29

> Turn around, don't look at me, [7]
> No need to know that I exist . . .
> Turn around, don't look at me
> No need to see my apathy
>
> —"Umbra" by Hedy Wyn

In mid-February, Hedy called and Sandy met with Hedy at Terry's café. Sandy said Hedy was depressed and could barely talk. Hedy had been living in her car since the first of December, over two months. She had lost a lot of weight. She had been camping in the hills above Dexter Lake all through the ice storm and the snow that followed. She drove into town for five weeks to work at the restaurant. Dexter is twenty miles out of Eugene. She said her car was actually warm at nights and she slept well.

Sandy and Hedy left Terry's and drove back to our house. As they were walking through the garage, Sandy mentioned that she had found Nicki and Patrick on the Internet. "They are in a band and were working as musicians in New York."

When Hedy heard that, she fell to her knees crying for mercy. She said, "That's what I've wanted to do my whole life. Wendy destroyed my dreams. They've stolen my dreams. Wendy must have pushed them into music to destroy me. I was finally getting there, then this? This can't be, this can't be." Sandy helped a trembling Hedy to her feet and held her as Hedy rested her head on Sandy's shoulder. When Hedy reclaimed some composure, they came into the house. Sandy found the site where the cousins had their band posted. Hedy spent the hour going through their site, their pictures, and postings.

Over the next days, Hedy called numerous lawyers for information for lawsuits for slander. She and Sandy compiled a list of the terms associated with slander—libel, lie, misrepresent, smear, defame, malign, make false statements, denigrate, cast aspersions, scandalize, discredit, and malicious gossip. All the lawyers said no. One firm said we needed to file a suit in Arizona. Hedy said she would try to get help pro bono but to no avail. She called down to DeRienzo in Prescott and he said it wasn't a strong case and couldn't help. Sandy and Hedy went to the office of SASS and asked if they could help, but they said they didn't deal with legal aspects.

When Hedy was staying in her car, she spent a lot of her days working with an acting studio downtown Eugene. She helped to build sets and performed with the black puppets for a Shadow Theatre Show. The troop was just finishing up their performances and Hedy spent the first week home working nights at the theatre. She didn't want us to come see them perform.

About that time, PBS aired a documentary called *Tower* about the 1966 shootings on the campus of the University of Texas in Austin where a lone gunman killed fourteen people and wounded thirty. We tuned in mainly because we knew Claire Wilson James, one of the survivors of the tragedy. Sandy worked with Claire at an elementary school when we lived in Nogales in the late 1980s. Claire's husband Brian James worked at the Conn Instrument Company that had twin manufacturing plants on the border. We had hung out with Claire and Brian for over a year before Claire told us she was the young pregnant woman that the gunman Whitman shot; she was one of his first victims. Detectives in Austin believed Whitman purposely aimed at Claire's pregnant belly, and that it was no accident when he shot her there. Claire told us that because of her internal injuries she could never have children. Hedy was seven and eight years old and Peter was five and six when we shared meals with Claire and Brian. Claire was drawn to our children and I think she would have kidnapped Hedy if she thought she could. Claire and Brian came up to visit us in Prescott.

After two weeks of being turned down time and time again by the lawyers, Hedy had an anxiety attack, trashed the hall bathroom, ripped stuff from the walls, and left a mess. Hedy was angry one evening and confronted me when I was reading in the back room. I wasn't sure if she was drunk or on drugs. She said, "I just wanted you to know that I think you are the worst father in the whole world, for not protecting me. For not protecting Peter and me against Wendy. The only protection I got was from myself."

I said, "Well, thank you very much for that. You should have told your secret. We could've helped you."

"You know, I'm so angry at you right now."

"You know you're a mean person when you drink. When you get drunk."

"It's not the alcohol. It's the truth."

"Hedy, I don't know how to help you. What do you want me to do?"

"I just wanted to tell you that. It feels good to tell you that. I never told you that before."

"You've said that before. When does it stop? Around and around, we go. Where it stops, nobody knows."

I was going to take a shower that night, but I heard Hedy in the small bathroom taking a shower and feared if she heard me go in after her, she would blow up and accuse me of copying her. If I went to the bathroom for a bodily function, I was copying her. If I ate dinner after she did, I was copying her. If I was alive, I was copying her. I had enough of it one day and said, "I'm not copying you! Stop saying that."

She fired back, "You are autistic! You copy me, you follow me because of your autism. You should've never had kids. Mom should've never had kids with an autistic man. Dad, I hate you so much. You were never a father. I'll never think of you as a father. You were just a sperm donor. You should have never had Peter and me—you ruined our lives. And now we're all fucked up and it's because of you. I hate you. I wish you were dead."

I said, "Sorry to hear that, but I don't have autism. No one ever suggested that before Susan. She said that because she hates men. Good night and joy be with you all."

"Don't put Susan down. I really liked her."

"We saw you manipulate her like a piece of clay."

"I don't want to talk to you." She slammed her door.

That week, I took one of the tests on an Internet site to see if autism was in my cards. The result: negative. I told Hedy this. She bet she could find a test that proved differently. "You have to be tested by someone who knows what they're doing."

I said, "I knew what I was doing. I passed it, didn't I?"

She said, "I don't want to talk to you. I won't argue with someone who has autism."

"Good, that means we can argue some." She left the room and slammed her door. Many times that month I had to realign the doorstop. The door had numerous glass panels that also had to be attended to because they became loose and rattled in their casings.

At 2AM one morning, I went down the hall to use the bathroom and then to the kitchen to get a drink of water. I had just settled back into bed when I heard an explosion in the kitchen. Hedy had opened the refrigerator and shook everything on the door onto the floor. Glass jars and bottles broke. Hedy was screaming that I had awoken her on purpose. Sandy ran in the kitchen as I started down the hall. "Why does he hate me?" Hedy cried, "What have I done that he hates me so? Why does he hate me? He's just like Wendy. He woke me on purpose because he hates me! Why is he doing this?"

"What's going on?" I said.

"Ask your daughter," Sandy said, "She thinks you hate her."

Hedy screamed, "I have to work in the morning! Why did you wake me?"

"I didn't mean to wake you. I'm sorry," I said.

"Why are you attacking me? What have I done to you?"

"I just got a glass of water," I said. "I'm sorry. I don't hate you."

"You're a liar!" she screamed. "You woke me on purpose. You're lying! You're trying to bring me down, but you won't beat me down. I can hate you as much as you hate me." She ran to her room, screaming, with her hands over her ears. "Ah!" Sandy went back to bed; I cleaned up the mess. Deja vu.

Later that day, after work, Hedy and I had a talk. I swore to her that I had never awoken anybody out of spite. She apologized. We talked about her PTSD that had kicked in when she was half-awake—she was trapped in a personal hell.

Not long after that, Hedy had a miraculous turnaround after a session with her River Road counselor. She started concentrating on her jewelry designs and other projects. She awoke one morning and decided she needed to get back on the horse, stop getting trampled by it. The ones forced to the bottom must rise to the top. She said it was like an epiphany she had a few years earlier, back in Ellensburg one bright sunny morning where for the first time since she was a little child, everything seemed so crystal clear.

She got involved in the Saturday Market in downtown Eugene and set up there for weeks straight. She got a job at KFC again and brought in money. She awoke every morning at five o'clock and worked on her copper and silver jewelry. She designed a display case and I made it. She turned a number of her colorful pencil drawings into greeting cards and miniature cards, had an exceptional day at the market, and finally made some money. She was named "Find of the Day" and got a bonus.

Her band, Splunk, had disbanded but she created LuvBlud, a one-woman show of her original songs that she orchestrated herself. She had recorded those songs during the last few years, making many tracks. When she performed her songs, she sang live; her computer played back up. It sounded great when she ran it all through good speakers. She performed on the last day of May 2017 at Sam Bonds Bar. Sandy and I went to see her. Hedy called her show that night "A Wretched Lie" and a few of her autobiographical songs were aimed at a mendacious ant. "A Wretched Lie" referred to the pantry incident. She did the original art for a poster for the show that featured a big-eyed fawn in shackles with a padlock on her ankles; on a tree limb above the fawn was an evil red ant holding the key to the padlock. Hedy's song, "Red Ant" was aimed at Wendy. "Shut Up the World" was aimed at the rest of us. It was a provocative show especially for those of us who knew the story behind some of the songs. She totally nailed it; I regretted that I didn't film it. Her show lasted an hour and left us in awe.

Sandy and I planned to go on a road trip after the Burns jamboree in June that would take us through five states. Our destination was to visit Utah, the Camp Floyd Museum, Salt Lake City, Dinosaur National Park, and Fort Bridges in Wyoming. We found Christopher's address; he was living in Nebraska and we thought we might swing over to visit him. When we told Hedy our plans, she begged us not to go near him. "He's dangerous! He probably had his gun. He probably has a big dog named Cody!" We met with a private detective to see if he could get Christopher's juvenile detention records in New Mexico and Tucson. We were hoping his records might show that Wendy was instructed to keep Christopher away from young children in the 1980s. The records might help in a lawsuit. Records would show if Wendy snubbed her nose at the court. The private eye said it was doubtful those records existed anymore; states usually expunged the records of teenagers. He would need to get a court order. He, too, suggested we should not go near Chris. We told him the lawsuit wasn't about money it was about justice. He said justice and pride are expensive. He wouldn't take any money for his time.

Sandy was never overweight and she went through a stretch of time in 2017 where she lost thirty pounds and looked emaciated.

A year earlier, her doctor had put her on PPIs for acid reflex; the medication was tearing up her stomach. When she complained, the doctor said, "Oh, I've had patients on those pills for years and years." She switched doctors. She found a nutritionist who weaned her off the pills and saved her stomach. She gained her weight back. Sandy started on a ketogenic diet. We started cooking for ourselves. Brian was feeling under the weather; the vet diagnosed him: diabetes. No more fruit for him. He had been eating fruit all his life. It's not good for a cat.

Sandy and I went to the jamboree in Burns and then on to Utah via Nevada. We hit most of the stops we had planned. When we were at the most eastern point of the trip, at the Dinosaur Park, we contemplated going to bother Christopher, to let him explain himself. Maybe we could get him on our side for the lawsuit against his mother. But we chickened out. We wouldn't bother the once-upon-a-time baby that we held in our arms.

We ended the trip with the interpretative Oregon Trail Museum outside of Baker, Oregon. Sandy said her favorite place on the trip was Fort Bridger. She asked me what my favorite stop was. I said I liked them all. Upon returning, I read a book I borrowed from Taxi Jim about the mountain men of the early 1800s. Sandy and I went to see *The Revenant* movie that told of mountain man Hugh Glass getting chewed up by a grizzly bear, left for dead, and left seeking revenge.

For the next eight weekends, through the months of June, July, and into August, Hedy continued to work on her art projects, to set up at Saturday Market, but she made almost nothing—enough to pay for her space—and not much more.

She wrote in her journal: Depression. I hate society. I question everything. I feel like a hopeless slave. Life had been awful to me and I am too exhausted to stand up to it anymore. All day, inside ugly buildings, wearing ugly clothes, for a stupid paycheck. This isn't living, this is worse than death. I don't know how to break free. I will most likely quit again without notice—if I accept just any job. I need a break. I've put in my time as a slave. I'm exhausted. I need to have a job where I can wear what I want and have a chair.

The first week of August, Hedy quit her job at KFC, signed up for an improvisation acting class in Los Angeles, and left town on a bus.

CHAPTER 30

> Going down the middle track this way and that [8]
> As fast as I can in my pussycat hat ...
> Waves, waves, waves, waves, wash it away
>
> —"Bitten" by Hedy Wyn

A full eclipse was expected in mid-August; it wouldn't be seen again in Oregon in our lifetime. I wanted to drive north, closer to Salem, to be in the direct path, but a crowd of people was predicted to head to that area and Sandy wanted to stay out of the traffic. So, we viewed it from our backyard. I pricked cardboard with a pin and we set up for the heavenly show. Brian was sitting on Sandy's lap when the eclipse occurred. He was down to twelve pounds from his fight with diabetes. It didn't completely turn dark in Eugene, though the streetlights came on. The image coming through the cardboard pinhole showed a crescent moon. Brian looked perplexed as the sunlight dimmed. He was a smart cat. A few days later, Sandy's band played in Lebanon, Oregon for a hundred-mile bicycle race the city was hosting.

That week, I exchanged e-mails with the Scottsbluff, Nebraska Police Chief and the Scottsbluff County sheriff's office. I warned them if they had any unsolved cases of rape in the area, they should get a DNA sample from a character named Christopher Johnson who had moved there. I told them to approach him with caution, as he liked guns and dogs. They wrote me back and thanked me.

Hedy returned two weeks later. She had worked a couple of times that week as an extra in Hollywood. She said she felt she had found herself, making money and having fun. She returned her black Subaru to the dealership. She tried one more Saturday Market and sold as much merchandise at slashed prizes that she could and gained some cash. She had over the years accumulated a lot of clothes from the thrift stores; she had wanted to be a designer and took pride in her tastes. She selected a wardrobe for acting her work and piled it into a rental car and headed south again. A week later she called when we were out and left a message that was saved on STAR99, a service we forgot we had. She was irritated but teasing at the same time. I transcribe them here:

"Hi. Umm, I'm just calling to ask you guys if you're okay. Can you please let me know that you're okay; somehow. Cause, yeah, if you're trying to ignore me, I feel like, that that's not very adult-like. I guess. You know, Mom, I texted you back the other day after I left the house when you were in a bad mood. So, I would, I would appreciate this favor, yeah, we all get in bad moods and I don't know, I don't know what's going on. And keeping me in the dark like this is just ripping our relationship apart. I mean it helped me at first, but now I need you to communicate. I'm on my way home; I'm going to be there tomorrow morning. So please let me know you're okay. That's just how relationships work. So, we work things out. I'm calmed down. I'm going to be fine now. I hope, I hope to hear from you. If not, I'll see you when I see you, yeah. But that's not very adult-like. [She laughed] All right, Bye."

An hour later, she left another message: "Umm, why aren't you guys picking up? I was wondering if you could help me get to Highway One, so I could at least see the ocean on the way back and enjoy the ride. So, could you give me a callback?

Please. I know you are not picking up on purpose and for some reason, that makes me feel like you guys are super evil. [She laughs] But whatever, if you could give me a call, that would be great."

We were home when Hedy called again. Sandy picked up. Sandy gave the phone to me to give Hedy directions. She was stuck in traffic. I looked at the map. I tried to talk her out of going to the coast, but she said she was already on a road heading to the coast, by the town of Fillmore. "Don't lecture me, Dad."

"Well, in about fifteen miles, your road is going to merge into the One-oh-One. Follow that all the way up to San Luis Obispo, and when you get there, you can decide if you want to take the One, on the ocean, or stay on the One-oh-One. The One is a lot slower than a freeway. You need to get a map."

"Why should I when I have you?"

She returned in the morning, which was a fete in itself. She stayed a couple of days and left by bus, trip # 3. She was gone for close to a month. She stayed in the dorms that were available for extras on a temporary basis, and got around via the subway system I didn't know they had. The sitcoms and dramas kept her busy. She went to a Jimmy Kimmel show one day and sat behind Zach Galifianakis, which thrilled her to no end. That week, she asked me to go with her to a used car lot in Junction City where she bought an older Taurus sedan. In early November, Hedy left for California in the Taurus. Trip # 4.

My nephew Jeff passed away in Tucson the day after Thanksgiving 2017. He was on dialysis for over a decade and his health had been deteriorating for the last few years. They had told him five years was about the maximum time on dialysis. I took a lot of clients in my taxi to dialysis over the years. What can you do? Hold your head high and your shoulders back and live day by day. Sharon postponed the memorial for Jeff until a time when his friends around the country could come together. Hedy came home after Thanksgiving. Brian passed away in December; Brian and Hedy had a soul connection. We buried him in a corner of the backyard and set a big obsidian rock for the headstone. Hedy and Sandy left little gifts on it.

On a December 2017 cover of Time magazine, the person of the year went to The Silence Breakers, the thousands of women who lent their voices to the #Me-too Movement. The downfall of Harvey Weinstein and others was big news; the movement was powerful. "It began with individual acts of courage," the article began. Tirana Burke first used that Hash tag #Me-Too in 2006, when she encouraged women to show their solidarity with one another against sexual violence. Individuals in other countries took up the call; in France, it became #Balance-Ton-Porc which means Expose the Pig. With true courage, Hedy exposed her pig in 2003. Her act exposed the cowardice of the deniers of that family, the pettiness of their self-proclaimed righteousness.

Sandy was into making her own ice cream with no sugar and a lot of butter; ice butter she called it. Her concoction was heavy on egg yolks with the leftover egg whites left for Hedy and me. Throughout January 2018, Hedy experimented with making different foods with the whites: baking the whipped whites like cookies, freezing them, making tortillas, and a number of other attempts. On Sunday nights, Sandy and Hedy came together to watch their favorite show: The British Baking Show. They sounded like college roommates excited about the big dance.

In March, Dylan Talbot, the son of a good friend of ours, passed away from cancer at the young age of fifty. We always hoped that one day, Dylan and Hedy would discover each other and watch out for each other. Dylan worked as a nurse for over twenty years, and maybe he could have helped Hedy heal.

Hedy brought her wares to the Saturday Market as soon as it started up that spring and again, she spun her wheels. But she went back religiously and made some friends. One was a grandfatherly man named Wayne who was a potter. He happened to own the rental house next to our house. He was remodeling it that summer after a longtime tenant had moved out. Hedy would go over and talk to

Wayne about the challenges of making it as an artist. "Useful" was the word he gave her. "Everything I make is useful. People will buy if they can use it." He made a decent living selling his wares at different venues throughout the state and ventured into California every once in a while. "Pretty pictures don't sell that well and there are so many people who can do that." Hedy started looking into making her art more functional.

Pete was working as a salesman for a crane company. We played tennis whenever we could get together. He went with us to the coast on Mother's Day and out to eat in Florence. Hedy didn't come because they still had a feud going on with him that she wouldn't abandon. I wondered if Pete was passing up opportunities in his employment so Hedy could have a chance to catch up, to get ahead, or at least find some happiness. I know it was hurting him to see his sister struggle as she had. He might have been feeling survivors' guilt. At four years old, he was sound asleep when Hedy was attacked. He had seemed to brush off the pantry incident without a second thought. Hedy's obsession with the false allegation never landed in his back as it had for Hedy. But after the pantry incident, Pete didn't want much to do with Wendy either.

Hedy was praying for justice. After all those years of carrying the burden of the secret, justice eluded her. In *Secret Survivors,* E. Sue Blume writes: "On the one level [the secret keeper] is relieved that they don't ask, because she doesn't have to tell them. She tries to not cry out in any way. She tries not to act upset ever. Thus, she is trapped in the reality of her pain. Which is worse? If they don't know or if they know? Like the rat in the *learned helplessness experiment* who gets shocked if she pushes the lever, and gets shocked if she doesn't."

We went to the 2018 Burns jamboree and took another road trip. We drove northeast across Idaho and into Montana where we visited a sapphire mine. We bought two bags of gravel taken from the banks of the Missouri River. We visited Glacier National Park and the disappearing glaciers. Highway construction dampened the fun of the trip, but on the way back, we found the community of

Hot Springs on the Flathead reservation and soaked in the mineral waters.

On our return, Sandy wrote a two-page letter and sent it to her family, to her many cousins, to Nicki and Patrick, to Christopher's father in Texas, to four of Hedy's high school teachers in Prescott, to the assistant pastor at the Prescott Methodist church, to cousin Marvin who molested Patty; twenty-two copies in all. Hedy and I helped to edit the letter. Christopher's name was mentioned four times and Wendy's name and her mendacity eighteen times—just to give a feel of the magnitude of how Wendy affected Hedy compared to Christopher. We mailed the letters on the Fourth of July in a gesture to help Hedy regain her freedom.

Sandy and Hedy found an Asperger's group that met downtown and they bugged me for months to check out. To appease them, I went in June and sat in on a meeting. I sketched portraits of the members and took notes as I listened to the leader. I thought there might be the seed of a story there, along the line of *One Flew Over the Cuckoo's Nest*. The group seemed a bit ill at ease; they thought I was a spy. I was more disjointed than they as I had subbed dozens of times for special education classes where I kept severely mentally challenged children from hurting themselves and others. A girl three chairs to my left sat hugging her knees and rocking in her chair during the length of the meeting. She was creating the most of the ill-ease. I knew this wasn't going to work out for me. But I did score a ticket to the Country Fair in Elmira.

One afternoon, Sandy and I had just begun to sift through the Montana gravel on a light table in the back porch when Hedy came home, wandered outside, and stood watching us. Hedy reached out in front of me and plucked a sapphire out of the wet gravel—the first sapphire we found. "Is this one?" she asked. We whooped and said it was and that she could have it. She put it down and said, "Maybe later, but if you guys need help finding more, let me know." She walked into the house with her head high as easy as catching a fly with chopsticks.

Hedy took realty classes in August, aced her tests, and got a license to work with a realtor. She did that for three weeks until she got disillusioned because she wasn't making any money. And she said her male colleagues in the office and at the open houses kept hitting on her. Her antennas went up during those unwanted advances and she said her PTSD kicked in and that she wanted to flee. She wrote in her journal: Anxiety. Men seem to get offensive when I ignore their non-work-related questions to me. I feel if I talk to my bosses about my fears, they may see me as someone wanting to file a sexual harassment claim and will see me as a company liability, losing their trust when all I want to do is protect myself. Men have delved into my personal life so much at my new jobs that I almost don't want to work anymore.

Depression is sometimes described as apathy, where nothing matters. Apathy was showing in Hedy's life. She was trying; she was struggling. So many times, her voice sounded like the voice of a little girl. And she knew that and she wished she could move forward, find her bearings, and grow a deeper voice.

Eugene city busses went to Elmira every hour the week of the Country Fair. The Fair started in 1969 by some artists and craftspeople on a large wooded farm. Sandy and I had never gone as it was usually at the same time as the High & Dry festival. I ventured about and I saw demonstrations on flint-knapping and how to start a fire with a bow drill.

The first week in September, Sandy had pains in her lower torso which turned out to be a distended bladder. Hedy helped wait on Sandy who was laid up for a few days. Hedy was upbeat and happy all week. She did a couple of dog sitting jobs after she advertised online. Our three birch trees in the backyard were dying; we had a tree service company come over to take them out. The trees were ninety feet tall and produced tons of firewood. Wayne the potter hauled it away in ten trips to his home near Vida which is near the community of Nimrod in the middle of the thick Willamette National Forest. Hedy bought a little golden Toyota Echo, parked her Taurus, and headed south for Los Angeles for more work as an extra. She stayed there for three months and slept in her car. Agents for Scientology Center in Hollywood lured Hedy into their meetings and she said she attended the training sessions for the free food.

On a Saturday afternoon while I waited for the barbeque coals to get hot, I made a bow drill fire starter and after two hours of cranking on it, I produced a little coal that I dropped into my "bird's nest" and Presto! I invented fire. That same week, I built a "shave mule" for shaping wood, making handles and dowel rods, a project I had procrastinated on for years. I had serendipitously accumulated a box full of bolts and odd-sized hardware that lent itself to that project.

Hedy came back from LA in mid-December. Shortly after returning, she brought a shoebox into the living room and said she had something to show us. She said, "You might not know what this is. It's a chastity belt. I wanted to tell you what this was about in case you see it in my closet; I don't want you to think I'm into kinky sex, or stuff like that. I bought this in LA to keep me from getting raped. When I was walking to my car one night, I thought I was being followed and it freaked me out. There are so many people living on the streets, so many creepy guys. I got this thing to let me feel safe being there."

CHAPTER 31

Nothing can make this current stop [9]
No logic can make our magic cease
Don't fix my leash I want it to break
So I can feed on sugar steak

—"Sugar Steak" by Hedy Wyn

When she came back, Hedy restarted the dog-sitting service. She spent a week at a couple's house in Veneta watching over a pair of boxers. While at their house, Hedy wrote a letter to Wendy:

> Wendy (the manipulative mother of Nicki Adams, Christopher Johnson, and manipulative wife of Bob Adams)
> I remember you.
> I remember that you were always laughing off my words.
> I remember that you never congratulated me in my successes in any way.
> I remember your backlashes when I would say things that mattered.
> I remember you were the first person I freaked out on, when you slandered me for the horrendous crime of

harming your children. Then you interrogated me with Nicki's blame—your scheme to hide Christopher's crime of rape.

I can't believe I ever loved a monster like you. The only memory I have of a time alone with you is when you and Christopher let the boat—that my brother and I were in—get caught in the current next to the lake and we almost died. The boat drifted into rough waters after you saved your bucket of Kentucky Fried Chicken from our boat.

I believe that you will laugh off these words.

I believe you are so angry with yourself and are still trying to falsely blame me for something.

Your entire family is living a lie because of you.

In your household, you are the only one that knows the truth of these events.

I guess you like to raise families that lie.

Your minion sons and your minion husband eat out of your bloody palms constantly.

You know nothing of nurture, only motivation to appear worthy.

I have put my lawyer on standby. If anything happens to me or my family because of the truth concerning this broken secrecy (no matter how far-fetched it seems that you may not be the cause) all we have to do is snap our fingers and the case will open like this: snap!

And everyone in New York and Arizona will know, plus a few important others. The distance to New York will not keep Nicki's friends from knowing the truth about you. My family deserves complete happiness now, like all. Unlike other families, we have to fight evil to accomplish life at all. Wendy, you, Christopher, and Bob are all evil entities. Wendy, you have made your entire family one evil entity. And you have made an enemy. It takes only one hurt person to be the devil's downfall, only one person. You have 4 people here advocating the truth.

My family no longer supports monsters and their manipulations.

Thank God I have a kind family. Without them, I would be so lost because of the simple fact that evil was once in my life. I believe my family's love and kindness have helped me rise from the ashes that you created from an evil fire a long time ago (the concealed rape). Now, I am like a fresh tree—from my own will.

I was voted most musical in my high school class. Like in The Little Mermaid, you are the evil queen who stole my music and handed it to your sons, raised with nothing but manipulation. But I like who I am now, for I am not jealous. I applaud your boys for their success. I only long to know what it is like to get along with my brother as much as your boys get along: as best friends, not ripped apart by blame and deceit from a once trusted, very close relative who turned to evil.

You treated everyone else much, much, much better than we.

—Hedy

She never sent this letter.

The next week, Hedy brought home a Cavalier King Charles setter named Bentley; he made himself right at home for a week. Bentley was a lucky dog and Hedy spoiled him. Years earlier, we made a mistake when we brought home a lost dog, a small terrier, we found by Fern Ridge Reservoir. Brian saw it and growled and hissed. Hedy got between the angry cat and the terrified dog and she was scratched and bitten by Brian. The punctures on her thigh were deep, they got infected and it took a while to heal.

Before Christmas, Hedy took a job delivering for the Eugene daily newspaper, The Register Guard. After a week, she was going to quit because two men were stalking her on two different sections on her route where she walked through the neighborhoods. I had stopped driving taxi after the icy roads dictated so, and I volunteered to be her bodyguard. She got up earlier than I was used to; we left the house at 1:30 a.m. to pick up her papers. Hedy was in the best physical condition I had ever seen her and I told her so when we were jogging through the neighborhoods and I was trying to keep up with her. She said she had found some really healthy places to eat on the main boulevard in Hollywood. When she was able to eat at the buffet some companies had for their extras, she ate healthily. She delivered a hundred and fifty papers a day and over two hundred each day on the weekends. She pointed out the two houses where the stalkers lived: first, a guy who left his house on his bicycle every morning at three o'clock who tried to strike up conversations with her, and second, a guy who sat smoking in front of his house like he was waiting for her to come by. She was supposed to have her route done by six. We split up whenever she felt safe and she easily made the deadline. The smoker changed his habits after the first morning; we never saw him again. Days later as I covered the left side of Hemlock Street and Hedy on the right, I came through a tall hedge at the last house and I saw the guy on the bike stop in the middle of the road in front of Hedy. He said something to Hedy. I shouted, "Hey! I'm all done!" I hopped out of the hedge behind him and the guy about shat his pants. He fumbled with his pedals and raced away down the street. Hedy said to keep the noise down. She said, "Whoopee! We took care of him. Give me five, Dad. But don't wake up the neighborhood." He never bothered her again. I went with her for the next seven weeks and we made a game of it to see how fast we could finish. We only missed the six o'clock deadline two times and that was because the company was late getting the paper out. Hedy kept meticulous records; her books showed she was making about four dollars an hour. If she missed delivering to an address, and instead of letting her take care of it, the company charged her a hefty fine. The owners of that paper made millions; the motley crew that delivered it made peanuts.

 Hedy had been driving her old Taurus because her gold Toyota lacked current tags. One night she switched the plates on the two cars and a police car pulled behind her parked car. I was on a front stoop putting a paper in the box when an officer called, "Hey, you! Come here!" I couldn't run across the frozen lawn without killing the grass with each footprint, so I started to run around the lawn. The officer yelled at me again. But I got to the driveway and ran straight to where Hedy stood with the two officers. The officer said, "Didn't you hear me calling you?"

Before I could speak, Hedy said, "He's got Asperger. He doesn't know what he's doing." I took it as a cue, so I hung my mouth a bit as the policemen looked me over. I pinched my mouth shut and forced myself not to laugh. To them, she pleaded that she planned the switch plates for a day only. They only gave her a warning. We laughed about her quick thinking. I got a bit carried away with my part as Rain Man, until she told me, "Stop it, it's getting old!" Then we laughed some more. Her last day with the paper was the last Saturday in February. The next day, it started snowing Sunday evening. By morning, there were twelve inches on the ground. Three days later, it snowed six inches more. We felt sorry for the new guy who took over her route.

Sandy got it in her head that we needed a trailer to go to the jamming sights around the state. She was done with tent camping. I was against a trailer and said I preferred dumpy motels. She bought a twenty-foot trailer and we set it up in the backyard. It was too big to pull with my truck. Hedy donated her car to a charity that gave her a weekend stay at a resort at Lake Tahoe. She was excited about that.

In March, Hedy trained for and got certified to be a fire fighter. She would be called as soon as the forest fire season started in late summer.

In April, Hedy went to LA and worked as an extra for two weeks. When she came back, she dog-sat, drove delivery, and kept ahead of the penalties on her credit card bills. Sandy and I went to the Silver Lake Jam and stayed in the motel there.

A week later, Hedy complained of pain in her gut; she told me she thought she had constipation; she went on a fast. The pain in her lower abdomen worsened and Sandy took her to the ER on a Saturday night. The nurse looked at Hedy's file and said, "You do know you have cancer."

"Yes," Hedy replied. Sandy was shocked. Hedy had been ignoring it, hoping for magic. The ER doctor scheduled an appointment with an oncologist. The day before the appointment, Hedy left for California; she got to the Oregon border where she had second thoughts and turned back. Sandy went with her to the appointment. Hedy wanted to see the doctor alone, so Sandy walked the hospital grounds and said prayers. Cancer confirmed; they suggested Hedy start chemo and radiation immediately; they set her up with a cancer clinic.

When she returned to our house, Hedy called around to everyone she could think of, trying to find a room for free. She couldn't find one. "I can't stay here!" she screamed. She crashed a lamp into the hardwood floor. She knocked more stuff off the wall. She asked Sandy, "Any of your friends have a room I could stay at? I can't stay here!" Her PTSD was on display: nightmares, emotional detachment, rage, and desire to avoid people and places that might trigger memories of the trauma. She took off in her car and was gone for three days.

Sandy accompanied her to the cancer clinic. The cancer clinic suggested chemo and radiation. Hedy refused. They told her it had already metastasized and it was spreading. She wanted to look into other options. The cancer had already run over her and she was looking for ways to get out of the way. Hedy started on a diet of grass-fed beef and shitake mushrooms and cut out sugar and grains.

Hedy asked me to go away for a month. My presence was triggering her PTSD, she said. It was a "free fishing weekend" and I left for the coast that afternoon. I camped in Nashville, Oregon and played my guitar for a bunch of trees with standing room only. The next day, I fished on the Siletz River at Sunset Landing south of Lincoln City. I talked to another fisherman who told me tales about the area. In previous years, he had seen sea lions eating salmon on the banks across from the boat ramp. "Otters showed up, too," he said.

"Siletz Bay rises and river backs up and fun things can happen." I got a couple of nibbles but that was about all. I dropped breadcrumbs on the millions of tiny fish that called home the dock by the boat ramp.

I drove down the coast and walked the rim trail at the Devil's Punch Bowl; visited the lighthouse at Yaquina Head. On the beach at Newport, I saw a young man cast his line out into the waves and catch a fish instantly—the first time I ever saw that happen. He threw it back. I didn't try to fish there. I camped that night about twenty miles up the Alsea River below a little hill called Stony Mountain—the other Stony Mountain.

I stayed by the coast for a week and came back to see if I'd be welcome. I wasn't, so I left again for the coast. I camped by the sand dunes near Florence and then another night by Winchester Bay. I followed the Umpqua River inland and camped at Loon Lake for two nights on a ridge above the lake

Hedy got a job as a taxi driver with my old company. She only worked a few weeks because the cancer was making it hard for her to sit up in the cab. She told me she loved driving a taxi.

Hedy moved into the trailer in the backyard. We got the water hooked up for her and strung a power line. Hedy warmed up to me somewhat. She helped me pick out and lay cement stepping-stones from the trailer to the backdoor of the house; it led directly to the small bathroom. Hedy cooked her meat and mushrooms and drank her herbal Essiac tea.

Sandy and I went out to dinner and a show organized by Addison and Peggy for a group of OOTFA regulars. Family style at a Chinese restaurant was followed by the play, *Harry*, about the invisible rabbit. I went back to the coast in August on a charter fishing boat with Addison and two other friends, Prentice and Von; the captain of the charter boat said his was Dylan. For some reason, Prentice was curious about the captain's last name. He asked. It was Talbot. Dylan Talbot, the name of Addison Talbot's son. We couldn't believe it.

It rained enough times in July and August that there was a very slight fire season for 2019. Hedy would not have been called to fight fires, something that only happened once in the last decade.

Peter sent Hedy a book called *Outsmart Your Cancer*; Sandy read it, then passed it to me. Hedy didn't want to have anything to do with new remedies. Sandy took Hedy to the cancer clinic. She had lost thirty pounds since starting her new diet; she was down to 124 pounds on her five-nine frame. The cancer had spread through all her organs. On 9/11, Hedy screamed in her trailer that she wanted to die, to get it over with. Members of a team from Cahoots, a crisis center, came to talk to her. They were able to calm her down.

Hedy started on a quest to paint everything black. "No colors anymore I want them to turn black." Lyrics from the Rolling Stones song came to life in our backyard. Over the years, Hedy had saved and collected every small box that came her way and we had stored them in the garage above the rafters. She took them to the trailer, set up an assembly line, and painted black a hundred or more boxes and sheets of cardboard. She went through a gallon of black acrylic paint. Her art project took over the trailer. Items were set to dry on every level surface.

Hospice House came to see Hedy in November for the first time. Hedy had a long discussion with John, the chaplain. She said she enjoyed arguing with him about religion and the afterlife. He encouraged her to write about her beliefs and how she saw the realms of the universe. She had talked to him of the pearly gates; she should start there. John told us that Hedy was having visions of dark beings stalking her in her dreams and stalking her even during the day when she closed her eyes. He gave her some prayers she could say to keep them at bay. Sandy printed out a familiar one end put it on a card: Now I lay me/Down to sleep, and I pray the Lord/My soul to keep/Angels watch Me/through the night/And wake me with/The morning light. The prayers worked because a week later, the Black Song was out of her head; the demons had disappeared; she transitioned back to her colored pencil drawings of stylized flowers. She wanted to do a children's book about foxes so I found a children's book at the library about baby foxes and made some photocopies. Before she started that project, she became obsessed with "Seven Deadly Sins." She set up the paper cutter and she made a thousand bookmarks, listing the *seven sins* with the description of each of the seven and the cures for each. These she did in bright colors:

LUST: Strong desires, especially sexual
CURE: Self-control, leverages that energy for a better humanity
GLUTTONY: Excessive eating of food or drink
CURE: Temperance, nourishes health for salvaging the earth
GREED: Excessive pursuit of material goods
CURE: Charity; desire to help or stop hoarding treasures
SLOTH: Excessive laziness, not utilizing your talents
CURE: Diligence puts interests above your inner zombie
WRATH: Strong anger and hate toward another
CURE: Patience comes from understanding before acting or speaking
ENVY: Intense desires to have someone else's possessions
CURE: Learning to appreciate rather than supersede
PRIDE: Excessive view of self without regard for others
CURE: Truth removes ego, boastfulness; one must live with a great attitude

CHAPTER 32

Your majesty, keep hunting me [10]
Your consequence: my propensity
Thanks for the platter you put me on . . .
A tree without wind could never grow strong

—"Red Ant" by Hedy Wyn

Hedy had heard or read somewhere about the afterlife beliefs of the ancient Egyptians and she explained some of these ideas and teachings in her journal. "In that culture when a person died, his or her soul was sent to purgatory to wait to be assigned to a living physical being, usually an animal or a plant. If you were a corrupt person, dishonest, mean, and harmful to others, you would be sent to live in the body of an undesirable host like a worm or a red ant or toxic fungi. If on the other hand, you were a loving, trusted, and righteous person, your assignment to the next life could be a beautiful plant or a brave animal. Wendy is destined to live her next life as a red ant."

Hedy asked Sandy if she knew the story of the Little Mermaid. Not too well, said Sandy. Hedy explained, "Well, in the Disney version, the Little Mermaid, Ariel, is born with the most beautiful voice and an old sea witch steals her voice. Ursula, the old witch versus Ariel—that story is my life. The old witch Wendy stole my voice when she falsely accused me; she stole my voice to keep me quiet; she stole my voice and kept it for her sons. Ariel's father gives up his life to save his daughter." She asked me later if I had heard that they're making a new version of the Little Mermaid. She said, "It's to be like the new version of the Lion King, with life-like animation instead of cartoons. I hope I get to see it."

A bad case of edema attacked Hedy's legs in mid-December, weighing down her legs and making it hard to climb the steps into the trailer. She texted me and asked me to bring her some toilet paper one afternoon. I brought along the copy of the cancer book Peter had sent. I read to her testimonials about a product called Protocel and asked her if she wanted to give it a try. She said yes. She moved into the house and slept on the couch for a couple of days until hospice sent a hospital bed. Hedy started taking Protocel every six hours around the clock. One of the reasons her all-meat-and-mushroom diet wasn't working is that Hedy cheated on it. She stopped driving when the edema appeared but before that, she would drive over to Costco and come back with a pumpkin pie and other sugar-laden foods. She was supposed to avoid sugar and grains. She had gotten too skinny on that diet of meat and mushrooms. She was starving and couldn't help it, she said. On New Year's Day, we watched the movie *When Harry Met Sally*.

The early results of Protocel on her cancer looked promising. She switched to a ketogenic diet, the same one Sandy was on; Hedy could eat a lot of her favorite foods. The Protocel works on the theory that cancer cells are anaerobic and healthy cells are aerobic, and by keeping a continuous stream of the medicine in a person's system and avoiding sugar, the anaerobic cancer cells will die of starvation and leave the body as a waste product—phlegm, urine, feces, and sweat.

Every night, we boiled three gallons of water on the stove to add to Hedy's bathwater. Those hot baths were allowing her to sleep through the night (at least until the 4 am dose of Protocel). I installed a showerhead with a hose in the bathtub. Hospice sent over a shower bench for the tub in case she couldn't get in and out of the tub easily.

I still didn't grasp where this was all headed; I was in a fog. I didn't want to face it, I guess. Hedy was facing it.

One evening, we planned to watch an old classic movie *When a Stranger Calls*. Sandy was baking a chicken and during a break when Sandy went into the kitchen, I called her on the landline from my cell phone. When she answered, I growled, "Have you checked the chicken?" Hedy was delighted. That evening, we couldn't stop laughing at the characters in that movie. They were too serious.

Chaplain John told Sandy and I that Hedy's attitude toward us had improved exponentially from the first time he talked to her. Her demons had gone away. She had stopped painting it black. Hedy created a term to help her forgive us, her parents, our foibles; the phrase was: asinine innocence. It related to our propensity to trust people unconditionally and not be aware when dark acquaintances and/or twisted family members were plotting, scheming, and preying on our good natures. Hedy would always be irritated and baffled by our "asinine innocence." John said Hedy could now better appreciate her mom and dad for what they had done and were doing for her. Hedy tried to overlook our shortcomings but flare-ups still occurred.

I was doing a lot of the cooking for Hedy as she became bound to her bed. She was on a steroid we called Dex that made her hungry and irritable about half an hour afterward. One day, Sandy cooked Brussels sprouts with cream sauce, steak, and sugar-free ice cream, a meal Hedy said was the greatest meal she had ever experienced. She loved it so much she broke down crying. It was emotional nirvana for a plate of food, tears of joy, and epic compliments to the chef.

But the morphine Hedy was taking was not keeping up with the pain. Her sleep patterns were disrupted; she stayed up all night watching movies, going to sleep after four in the morning, and lashing out if we made a noise during the day. Hedy slept not by routine but necessity. Sandy would whisper Hedy awake when medicine time came around. Oftentimes, Hedy greeted her with a smile, but other times, not so much. Hedy was up and down, positive one hour and angry the next. She accused me again of stalking her, of copying her.

We were warned that Hedy's cancer might have metastasized to her brain. She began to get bad headaches during the fourth week on Protocel. We expected that; it was supposed to mean the cancer cells in her brain were dying and since removing the dead cells from the brain was harder than other areas of the body where waste escapes naturally, the dead debris caused pressure on the brain. Her urine became bubbly and her stool showed signs of pale, glossy cell debris, but her headaches were hitting her hard. And her night sweats got worse, drenching her sheets. Her pain ratcheted up and she was often miserable. During an episode of pain, Hedy warned me if she ever heard me clearing my throat again, she would stop taking Protocel. I left for a day and drove past the town of Stayton to hike the Seven Falls Trail. When I came back, I did everything I could to *not* clear my throat, but I failed. She stopped her medicine. Happy one day, threatening suicide the next. I cried a lot that week. So did Sandy. Hedy was clearly saying that she didn't want to live any longer.

There was a guest opinion column in the Register-Guard earlier in the month of January penned by a man who had been on the sex offenders list for a decade, ever since he was a teenager, and that "living with a label" had ruined his life. He felt it wasn't fair that he should be punished long after the crime, long after he had paid his dues, and that what he got amounted to a life sentence that was poisoning his future and his opportunities. Three weeks later, a grandfather of a girl, five, who was raped by a twelve-year-old boy wrote an opposing opinion. His little granddaughter will probably have to be in counseling because of her wounds for the rest of her life. There's not much chance for justice and retribution—the boy's parents fled town with their son; thus, teaching the boy to be a liar and a lifelong criminal. Wendy taught that to Christopher: run, son, run, and forever be evil. Christopher needed someone to tell him to stand up straight and face the consequences. When he was fourteen and wanted to become a man; because of Wendy's supervision and intervention, he never would. Oedipus' mother claims another victim. Ches and Tim helped put Christopher stay in his private hell.

WOLF UNDER BED

A nightly ritual of the hot baths became a bonding moment for Sandy and Hedy and harkened to a time decades earlier when the two took baths together before Hedy started walking. After Peter came along, the two girls continued their baths and added Pete once he was old enough. Hedy looked forward to her hot baths.

Hedy's edema for the last month had not gotten progressively worse. But once she stopped Protocel, her legs swelled hugely and the edema spread into her lower torso. Her arms, her neck, and her face stayed thin. Her better angels were battling her worse angels and her upbeat self was fighting to hang on.

During one calm interlude, I asked Hedy if she remembered an incident that happened about three months after the rape in 1987. She was six. To this day, this incident weighs heavy on my mind. At the end of June that year, Wendy coaxed us to come visit her and Chris and Bob in Truth or Consequences. We could tube down the Rio Grande River, Wendy said. We had engine problems on our van on the way over to T or C; it was hot and Sandy and I quarreled. We brought along a spring-loaded rocking horse that Hedy and Peter had outgrown; Wendy and Bob were trying to have a child and Wendy wanted the horse after Sandy offered it. When we arrived at their house in the early afternoon, Christopher was not there. We were in the living room, chitchatting with Bob and Wendy when Hedy climbed on the riding horse for one last gallop. "Isn't she too big for that?" Wendy said. Hedy continued to rock slowly. Then Christopher came in through the living room screen door; he proceeded into the kitchen for a snack. Hedy started rocking the horse harder and harder. Wendy said, "She's going to break that!" Hedy then rocked it all the harder, she was angry and trying to pound the horse into the floor. Christopher watched Hedy as he chewed his food.

I said, "Hedy, stop that!" Sandy asked her to stop, too.

Bob said, "Mike, you better stop her!"

I went to Hedy and took a hold of the horse. Christopher quickly crossed the living room and out of the screen door and ran off down the street. Hedy stepped off the horse and she began pleading, "I don't want to sleep here tonight."

"Why not?" Sandy said.

"I can't sleep here. Don't make me sleep here." She made a dash out the front door, and we followed her outside. She said, "I want to sleep in the van. Let me sleep in the van. I don't want to sleep in the house." Bob and Wendy had followed us out of the house. Intensely, Wendy was watching this unfold. I'm sure Wendy was ready to intervene if Hedy said too much.

Sandy said, "You can't sleep in the van. It's not safe out here."

"I can't sleep in that house!" Hedy screamed. "I can't sleep in that house! Let's all sleep in the van." Hedy screamed, "Ah!" She ran to the edge of the lawn as if she would run down the street. I ran and took her by the arm.

"Stop it, Hedy, stop it," I said.

Bob scolded, "You need to control your child, Mike."

"Hedy, settle down. Do you want a whack on your bottom?"

Wendy said, "She's acting like Patty."

Hedy continued to fuss. I steered Hedy into the house and into the bedroom. She pleaded that I not spank her. I gave one hard whack on her bottom. In the living room, I heard Wendy gasp, "Oh, my!" I sat on the bed and Hedy sat in my lap and sobbed into my shoulder until she calmed down. That was the last time I or Sandy ever spanked our children. Hedy said in 2020 she did not remember that incident. The four of us all slept in the van that night.

CHAPTER 33

> Whip it up with meringue, put it in a pie, lemon pie   [11]
> Taste the sweetness of your lemons, heaven's sake
>
> —"Egg Yolk" by Hedy Wyn

Hedy watched a videotape to learn Chinese. She said she had that desire her whole life and she was going to finally do it. She loved the Chinese characters as an art form. Every little detail was important to the artist in Hedy. After a few days of climbing the mountain of the Chinese language, Hedy tired of the challenge, and realizing there was no one in the house who was ever going to communicate with her in Chinese, she stopped. Time wasn't going to wait for her. She did add "Wa eye nee" to her collection of phrases in different languages that said: "I love you."

The hospice nurse invited Hedy to come to the hospice house for a week to balance her pain with her meds. Two days before the transport van was to come, Hedy had one of her worse days; she was grumpy; she lashed out at us. All week, Sandy had problems with her eyes; she went to bed early and she was listening to a book on tape in her bedroom when Hedy got irritated at hearing the voice on the tape. She threw a fit. "Stop the noise! It's all about them. No one gave a shit about me!" She threatened to kill herself if we bothered her again that night. She cried herself to sleep, moaning, "No one ever protected me. No one protected me from that evil family. What were you thinking? How can you live with yourselves? I just want to die!" I peed in a can that night, so as not to bother Hedy, not to move in the hall, not to face the truth.

The next day, a calm Hedy asked me to fetch her art portfolio out of the trailer. Sandy joined us looking through the artwork. Hedy broke down crying, "I never got a chance to live my life. I could have done so much more."

Sandy said, "You've done a lot of beautiful things, honey."

"But my life has been cut short. A half-life is what I got. Now I understand what they meant when they talked about the half-life of an isotope."

Next, we helped her sort through the jewelry she had made, labeling it and packaging it. Later she asked, "What are you going to do with my art when I die?"

I asked, "Whatever you want us to do, we'll do it."

"I don't know. I'll have to think about it."

The hospice ambulance came on a Monday morning. The high that I was on for the past few weeks came crashing down when I helped Hedy walk out to meet the two men and their gurney. Our little girl. Our hurting child; sweet pickles, Rosy, petunia, sweet buttercream, kitten, singing bush, songbird, kibbles, dolly. Her head held high and smiling and talking to the two men like she was going to an amusement park. I felt we had discovered a miracle in the Protocel product, a secret that the Big Business Cancer Industry didn't want to get out to the public. I could see conspiracies everywhere that negated real cures if they hurt the profits of Big Cancer. I imagined myself mounting a white horse to fight them with the sword of truth. I could see Hedy starting a new life after surviving her cancer, on another horse, promoting a real cure, touring the country, telling the world the secret, that a cure of cancer that had been drug out of secrecy was available, and she was finally making a living for herself, singing the song of the cure. But, alas, we were to never know if that brown liquid was a miracle cure: Hedy had stopped taking it. Going from months of torture and desperation, praying for a cure, and then believing your prayers being answered by a miracle elixir that began working immediately, then having that sense of hope ripped away, was an excruciating punch in the gut. I hid away the bottle that remained. Maybe if I got cancer, we could find out if it worked.

The week at the hospice house gave Hedy a much-needed break from our innocent asininity. The nurses there loved Hedy and she loved them in return. They were able to help get Hedy's pain under control. Sandy and I went to a round table discussion with the nurses and other members; they explained Hedy's new regiment of painkillers. A young male nurse during the meeting looked right at me and Sandy and said in a threatening voice, "So, you don't believe in western medicine?" That was kind of out of the blue and I was a bit taken aback, not aware we were on trial. We had allowed Hedy to make the decision whether she wanted radiation or chemotherapy. Her cancer was well advanced when she was offered that option. I never tried to persuade her one way or the other. I had ten sisters in my life if you include Kathy, my brother's wife, and Sandy's four sisters. Four of these women died from cancer and in my mother's case, cancer might have been the culprit, too. So, add my mother, and that makes five dying from cancer, and most had radiation and chemo treatments to no avail. My sister Eva, the only cancer survivor, won a battle with breast cancer using conventional methods. After the guy attacked us, I fumbled around for an answer, "Don't know about that." He said, "Well, nothing better has been found." I'm not good at thinking of the top of my head and didn't reply. He acted smug the rest of the meeting, and I tried not to think of ways to kick him in the ass. I liked the hospice house and didn't want him to spoil my relationship with them.

After Sandy and I returned home, I found a box of cassette tapes from when Hedy and Peter were little and singing their hearts out. We listened to those tapes for hours and didn't get through half of them. One of my favorites was Hedy singing "Beauty and the

Beast" at age nine. We were trying to find her "Somewhere Over the Rainbow" that we remembered taping, but we couldn't find it. Peter at a young age loved to sing as much as Hedy. We tried to have a family night every Friday or Saturday night where we turned off the television, and told stories, or drew portraits of each other, or our pets, or played board games or cards, but we gravitated to singing and playing music most of the time. Hedy started piano lessons early and had a good ear. Hedy liked to point out every time I sang off-key. It's a little unnerving to have a ten-year-old tell you that your singing is out of tune using the word, ooh, like she was viewing an open sore. Sandy's voice came out strong on those tapes.

As the week went on, I began to worry that hospice house was not going to let Hedy return to our house. I regretted letting her go there. If it weren't for John the Chaplain and the many wonderful nurses, I would have lost all trust in the world. But still, I obsessed that someone there plotted to get her away from us and keep her locked up in a little room and to end her life quickly at the bequest of some insurance company. Another conspiracy. Our whole family had trust issues from the piling on of lies. Hedy said many times she had a knife stuck in her back from Wendy; she said that we all got stabbed in our backs. The beginnings of Hedy's cancer can be traced to the conspiracy of the PACT: Wendy and Ches conspiring to conceal Christopher's rampage of rape during his early teens. Hedy's secret had a devastating effect by weakening her immune system from the daily stress caused by the secret she was protecting. Her PTSD and depression kept Hedy from taking care of herself when the cancer showed up in 2016. I mentioned earlier "The Learned Helpless Experiment" where the rat gets shocked whenever she pushes the lever and she gets shocked if she doesn't push it. The worry and the fear drive the rat into stress hell. This poor rat is more prone to cancer. A human secret survivor is always worried about accidentally betraying the secret. The stress keeps zapping her, day in and day out. Damned if you do, damned if you don't; that's the gift of the secret. That's why secrets are deadly. If Hedy had gotten help immediately after the rape, if Wendy and Ches had stepped forward to do the right thing and helped Hedy after the rape, Hedy would have been able to heal enough to have a normal life. Ches knew what needed to be done. When Ches was raped at age six, she got counseling from her mother and grandmother, and that might have been enough. Ches didn't have that secret to weigh her down to zap her constantly. And Ches didn't have the constant fear that the perpetrator and his mother would kill her to silence her or that he'd rape her again. Ches had the support of her family; her perpetrator paid remittance for his crime for many years in a deal fostered by the justice system of the family. He sent Ches to college. He could keep his good name in such a system, apologize for his crime, make promises to become a man the family wanted to keep around; he paid retribution. Hedy had none of that. Wendy was not going to allow that. Christopher had already run amok with the law in several jurisdictions and another transgression like raping a child would have sent him away for a long time. Wendy chose to turn her back on honesty and morals, but in doing so, she also trapped her son in a pit of venomous lies. I suspect Ches was open to her family's kind of justice in dealing with Christopher's crime, but Wendy wasn't going to have it. If there was a chance Wendy could make Hedy bear the secret, then that would be the way they'd set it up. Hedy never got the early counseling she so desperately needed to heal herself.

 The following Monday, a transport brought Hedy home from hospice. That night, Hedy wanted to call Aunt Sharon in Tucson and wish her a happy birthday; they talked for a long time. Jeff had been gone for over two years. When Hedy and Peter were young, they loved to go visit their Cousin Jeff. Jeff was seven years older than Hedy and nine years older than Pete. Jeff made it to Hedy and Peter's high school graduations. Jeff wasn't confined to a wheelchair until he was twenty. About that age, he had his heart broken by a girl he had fallen for; she was about two years younger than him. The girl broke it off and devastated him. In 2003, when I talked to Jeff about his childhood friend, Christopher, raping Hedy, Jeff said, "He is no friend of mine. If I ever see him again, I'm going to tell him what I think of him, that he's scum, that he's lower than low. And I'd be on the firing squad that shoots him."

Sharon overheard him and said, "Oh, you wouldn't want to do that."

"Watch me. I'd blow his head off. Forget shooting at the heart—he doesn't have one. Ha!"

Hedy was drinking gallons of liquids and was peeing a pond. The weight in her legs from the edema made it hard for her to get out of bed. The edema was now moving up her torso and she gained a lot of weight because of the retained liquid. Hedy said that the edema was worse than cancer. In late February, while swinging her left leg onto the bed, Hedy hurt her knee. The hurt knee made her take more pain meds that caused the balance to be upset. She couldn't think straight from the increase in meds. She accused me of slipping Protocel into her food; I was fixing most of her meals at that time. I showed her the seal on the new bottle wasn't broken. She accused me of stalking her, of stealing her ideas, of setting off her PTSD on purpose, of being like Wendy, out to torture her. But once again, the nurses helped her regain med-balance. I had finished off the first bottle of Protocel a week earlier by taking it myself—regularly for five days—an experiment that seemed to help the color in my left ankle.

Hedy wrote in her journal for hours. Sandy brought home from the library DVDs by the bagful. They started with a show called *Portlandia,* a sitcom, about the foibles of a couple living in Portland, Oregon; they watched episode after episode. A masseuse from hospice came by for the first time for Hedy. The lady was from Kazakhstan; she spoke good English. Hedy was seeing a counselor too every week and John, the Chaplain, came often. Hedy fell asleep halfway through many of the shows. She stayed awake for a new version of *The Lion King.*

Hedy and I had a talk about the afterlife. She wanted me to tell her what I knew about Jesus and Buddha and Native American religions. I said, "Follow the Ten Commandments, do good on earth, don't hurt others, follow Jesus's example and one should be able to get into heaven. The great mysterious is what the Lakota Sioux called the afterlife. Babies being born, coming out of the great mysterious, people dying, returning to it. People have near-death experiences; they come back and tell what they've seen. But no one knows for sure."

Hedy said, "I see it that we go to a kind of purgatory, and we are judged. I've led a good life. I haven't done harm to anyone, only myself. And I will be able to return to do good things. If I survive, I'm done living in fear. I'm going to comfort some people. If I get through this, I want to help people." She closed her eyes and licked her lips. "Or when I come back, I'm going to help people." Sandy said Hedy said that numerous times to her. She wanted to help people.

CHAPTER 34

Only clowns surround me now [12]
I need the silence from their painted smiles
I can't taste my cotton candy
I can't stop this Ferris Wheel

—"Glass Menagerie" by Hedy Wyn

The three birch tree stumps in our backyard were nine feet tall. I asked the tree cutters to leave them that height. I was planning on doing some chainsaw carving, that is, until Sandy stopped me. I had made some nice sketches of some beautiful totem poles but, alas, Hedy agreed that I should leave them alone. Around Eugene, they like to grow their birch trees in groups of three, so the roots will intertwine and hold each other up. The squirrels in the neighborhood grew to love our tall stumps. They chased each other around the base, hopping from one stump to another—flying varmints with fluffy tails. The younger ones would play with intensity unimagined. Many a peanut was eaten at the top of those stumps. A female squirrel came by most days and stood against the glass door in the back, leaving smudges with her wet paw prints, begging. Who can say no to that?

It was the wettest winter (2019/20) we had seen since we moved to Oregon. A year ago when the snowstorm hit, old-timers disparaged our complaints and talked about the winter of 1969 when it snowed four feet in one storm stranding hundreds of cars between Portland and Grants Pass. We were glad we were in the land of the tall cacti. In Eugene, the ice and snowstorms had come every other winter and 2019/20 was an off-year. Three decades ago the Eugene area averaged forty-three inches of precipitation a year, but in the past decade, the yearly average was at thirty inches. The drought years they called it. Compare that to Prescott, Arizona that had nine inches in a normal year.

Hedy told me she put three of her songs on an Internet site called Reverb-nation. I was able to get into the site. I asked her if she wanted to see the video that I recorded of her singing with Splunk at Old Nick's in 2017. She said no. Hedy asked the nurses what kind of music they liked. Hedy's counselor, Mariel, and Nurse Jenna said they liked all sorts and even punk rock. When the two of them were over, I showed them Hedy's sculptures that lined our mantel. "Amazing!" they said. I proudly mentioned that Hedy had written some good songs; Hedy got angry. After they left, Hedy said I had sparked an episode of PTSD, and it took all of her strength not to scream at me in front of them. She said, "Please, do not tell anybody else about my songs."

The last week of February was hectic; Hedy requested meals that put my cooking skills to the test. I made double-baked spaghetti. Baked salmon. Enchiladas. Omelets. The masseuse stopped coming because of the pandemic that was getting the attention of everyone in America. Hedy hurt her other knee and she had a hard time rising out of bed. I helped her to stand up. The nurses attached a catheter bag. Sandy found some pop-sickles at Market of Choice sweetened with stevia and with natural flavors and brought them home to the delight of Hedy.

We worked together to go through her boxes as she designated what to keep and what to send to charity. She wanted her art supplies to go to help an art and craft store called Mecca. Hedy had a hard time letting go of most of her stuff. When it came to clothes, it was almost impossible. She had collected a great deal of her clothes just since 2017 when she started working as an extra.

Hedy bought a ring one day on the channel that featured jewelry 24-7. She used a pre-paid card that had some money left on it. She was excited, "Dad, I bought a ring! It's so pretty. I can't wait for it to get here." It arrived a few days later by mail. I watched her open it. It fit her finger perfectly; she cooed over it. Sandy for years had called Hedy's fingers wing tips, like the wingtips of angels. I could see why Sandy called them that as Hedy flaunted her ring. She took it off and handed it to me. It had a little weight to it. It was silver with a golden tint finish and it had a heart-shaped pink zircon stone. I handed it back. I asked, "Daught, how did you know it would fit?" Years earlier, we called each other Dad and Daught, and started doing that again at that time.

"Duh, dad. Geez, maybe I know what size I wear. You think? Dad, you should know your ring size. Everyone should know their ring size—in case a cute ring shows up. You never know when one will show up. And Dad, just why is it you don't wear a wedding ring?"

"Duh, Daught. I don't do rings. Working around machinery, remember?"

"I used the drill press a lot and I always wore rings," she said.

"You were lucky. But on the drill press, it's more important to get your hair out of the way. Remember—"

"Oh, yuck, I know, Dad—that long-haired person whose scalp was wrapped around a drill bit; they put it on the cover of shop safety."

"No, Daught, I was going to point out the landscaper in Tucson—the one who got pulled into the chipper because a branch caught on his ring."

"Yuck! And all they found were pieces of him?"

"That's the guy, Daught. Or at least they think it was him."

"Why don't you wear a wedding ring? Don't you like being married? You should put it on when you go out with your wife. Or are you playing the field, Dad?"

I said, "I never look at people's hands."

"I always look at people's hands. If they're married, I just like to know."

"I don't think I've ever looked at a person's hands to see if they're married."

"You're weird, Dad."

I looked at her hands. Hedy has the most beautiful hands that any human can have; she could give the hands of angels a run. Her long slender fingers allowed her to play with the wind and feel her direction her way forward during the dark times of the secret. Her hands coaxed the catgut to make the hair of a horse purr; her hands ran over the piano keys, like lovers racing down a boardwalk. Hedy must have thought so too because she sketched her left hand a number of times. She had hands that Leonardo would have been drawn to.

When Nurse Jenna showed up that day and saw Hedy's new ring, Hedy told her it was an engagement ring.

Jenna asked, "Oh? Who's the lucky fellow?"

Hedy said, "Me. It's an engagement ring to myself. I always wanted to get engaged, so I thought why not? So, I asked myself to marry me and I accepted."

"Oh, I'm so jealous. You're so lucky."

"Yes, I know. It feels so great to have me. Isn't it pretty?"

When the hospice counselor Mariel came by moments later, they told her of the big announcement. Mariel said, "Wow, Hedy! Engaged!"

"I know," said Hedy. "I know." And she displayed the ring with a limp wrist, with her fingers pointing down. I remembered Sandy's dream from a decade earlier where Hedy was marrying a young man with a Hawaiian name. Somewhere over the rainbow, bluebirds sing.

In our living room, we had a large picture window through which Hedy could see the world. In our front yard, was a pond surrounded by big rocks and tall water plants. A big sycamore tree grew near the street. We lived on a busy corner so cars and pickups, skateboarders, dog walkers, joggers, and other busy people passed by frequently. The motorcycles were not yet out. Across the street were two more huge sycamores in front of a gray house; behind the gray house, another big tree. The neighbor in the gray house was Bobby, a retired lady, who Hedy had met at the mailboxes. Hedy liked to watch those scurrying about the neighborhood in the picture window of her world.

I saw Bobby at the mailboxes and told her of Hedy's condition. Bobby started stopping by to say hello to Hedy. Hedy's true self came out when Bobby came to visit. The little girl who was so comfortable in herself at age three that she reached out to those not feeling so well—this spirit in her showed up. This giving spirit went into hiding those many years ago, and we only saw glimpses of her every once in a while. How could we not recognize that she was holding back, trapped behind a veil of secrecy? From the time Hedy learned to walk, she would reach out and run to every dog or cat she saw. She couldn't get it in her head, the concept of an animal wanting to harm her. Why would a furry creature want to do harm? It made no sense. She inherited *some* of our asinine innocence. We left an angry animal sleep in the room with our children and our babe got hurt. In Scotland and in other countries across the world, they have superstitions about children who show early promise. A widespread tradition warns that precocious children are doomed to premature death, which is presumably why they reach wisdom and refinement so early. Hedy's early trauma kept her from becoming the person she was meant to be.

On the first Monday in March, the hospice house sent a transport van again. She could go there for five days once a month; a new month had begun. I helped Hedy to stand. Leaning on me, she was able to step down the two steps of the front porch and we walked out to the van. The first time she had been at the hospice house, she didn't want us to bother her; we didn't go except for the meeting with the staff. But this second trip, by Wednesday, the third day, Hedy asked Sandy to come over and spend the night. I took Sandy there. Hedy asked us to pick up a super burrito on the way over. When we got to her room, Nurse Jenna and the counselor Mariel were throwing a surprise engagement party for Hedy. There was cake and streamers and non-alcoholic champagne. Other staff members were coming by to say hello. As we stood at the foot of her bed, sipping bubbly, Jenna said of Hedy, "Look at her, she looks like a little girl. Just like a little girl."

"Our little lady," I said.

Sandy brought some clothes and she stayed over; the room had a chair that turned into a twin bed. The next afternoon, I met them there again. After a while, Hedy wanted to go out on the patio terrace, just outside the back door, and watch the sunset. She had been lying on her bed for three straight days, which concerned me. I helped Hedy to sit up on the edge of the bed. I helped her stand and take a step or two. An aid helped us lower her into a wheelchair and we wheeled her onto the patio.

The patio was on the north side of the hospice building. To the west and to the northwest were pastureland and fields. Directly to the north was the pond, about twenty feet wide by forty feet long; it was about one hundred and fifty feet out from the patio. To the west, scattered golden clouds above the horizon blocked the sun, keeping the sun out of our eyes. A long gray blimp-like cloud hung closer in the sky between the distant clouds and the blue-gray sky above us. The sun was hitting the backside of this long, gray cloud; a golden ring of sunlight encircled the edges. Connected to the nose of the blimp was a jet trail-like cloud. That thin vapor came down at an angle to our left and it grew longer as we watched. Hedy commented that the color of the sky was surreal. At this time, a flock of noisy geese flew into view from the south. They landed in the pastureland northwest of the pond where they began feasting on grass and noisily talking to each other. The geese stopped chatting when a frog on the banks of the pond began to sing a slow song. The geese fixed on the pond. We couldn't see the frog. A minute later, a second frog with a deeper voice joined the first. Seconds after that, more frogs and other critters, insects with grievances, joined in. The song became a racket.

Then a chorus of frogs, waiting in the wings with lower voices, joined in and turned up the volume; the racket became a roar. Night on Bald Mountain meets screaming sirens meets Rachmaninoff. My eyes searched the rocks on the bank above the water for a crazed conductor leading that fury, expecting to see flailing arms or legs or wings, but I saw none. This burst of life went on for another few minutes. And just when I thought the pond would explode, the frenzied orchestra abruptly stopped. Poof! All was quiet. The geese were in awe as much as we were. The sun by then had dropped out of the clouds and below the horizon.

Hedy said, "That was so cool." I stood with my mouth at half-mast and couldn't say anything. Sandy pointed to where the cloud blimp had been. "Look, that cloud is gone." Only fragments of the ramp jet trail remained.

Sandy stayed over again and came back in the early afternoon on Friday. Hedy hadn't had a bowel movement for five days and she was bummed out about that. In the late afternoon, she called and asked me to come back and watch a movie with her. We were still on the phone when her bowel movement called to her and she had to get off the phone in a hurry. She called back a little while later and said it was a success. Hurrah! I remembered her first week back from the hospital, the week she was born, and remembered her first stools coming black and sticky like all newborn babies. She had all her bowel movements when I was holding her that week. And our rule was: if you are holding her, or if you discover it, you get to change the diaper. That was a rule Sandy made up that week. I like to think Hedy felt especially safe and relaxed in my arms; why she unloaded then. Her face would turn red when she started pushing and we knew what was coming. During the first three months of her life, she gave me more gifts than anybody else.

It was overcast and there was no sunset that night, so Hedy and I watched *Jeopardy!* and shouted out answers. Following that, we found *South Park*. I warned Hedy that the humor of that show was a bit off-color. She scolded me, "I know that, Dad. You don't have to tell me. I thought you like shows like this?"

"I like them all right. I just thought you might be shocked at kids cussing."

"I'm not nine years old, Dad. I've been around. I know more about life than you. I've been out there living it. Everybody cusses. Don't try to protect me from this. I bet I've seen more crude stuff than you."

"We used to make you and Peter close your eyes."

"Dad, that's nothing to be proud of. You were protecting us from the things we should have been learning about—that there are bad people everywhere. That you have to protect yourself if you want to survive."

Hedy came home from hospice the next day.

CHAPTER 35

> I hear the darkness calling me   [13]
> Under the shade of the movie theatre glow
> I feel the lightning about to strike
> Take me, I've chosen death row
>
> —"Death Row" by Hedy Wyn

Back in February, we had gotten in contact with a lady who helped hospice patients connect with mellow cats and dogs looking for homes. A cat named Claudia, a nine-year-old brightly colored calico, came to live with us. Hedy spelled her name Clawdia. The cat had just gone through eye surgery and was missing her left eye. Years earlier, when I was driving a taxi cab early one morning, I picked off a road barrier a stuffed toy cat; I threw it in the washer when I got home, dried it, and stuck it away in the garage on the shelf with my tools where it sat for eight years. When Clawdia came to us, I remembered that toy cat, and I went looking for it. As I suspected, it was a calico cat. But I wasn't ready for what I saw next: the toy was missing a button eye, not the left eye but the right eye.

    That week, Hedy begged Pete to come and see her. He was planning to come that weekend when snow blocked the Santiam Pass. Hedy prepared a list of things she wanted to tell him on the phone. She was getting forgetful and so she wrote down things when they came to her. Her list of topics: Call Peter! What kind of storm? We're playing Nintendo when you get here! What kind of pizza should we order? Do you have any preferences where we get it? Do you like Chinese take-out? Are you going to stay two nights? We got a kitty, a calico! Do you like incense? Hippies wouldn't use any incense with chemicals.

They talked on the phone for an hour until Hedy tired. Peter came that weekend. He brought along a natural remedy for Hedy, but her cancer was too advanced; she didn't want to look at it. Pete was upset that he couldn't help his sister and left the next morning.

I went out to Hedy's Toyota parked in our backyard and tried to start it; it hadn't been driven for months. The battery was dead. March Madness, was canceled that week because of the pandemic. Hedy went on a liquid diet. She was six days without a BM again. The masseuse didn't come again. Chaplain John did. Hedy told John that she was getting so weak that she didn't think she had but a few days. John prayed with her for a while. Hedy called Pete again and tried to get him to come back but it snowed in the pass again. I had been working the previous year on a wooden archery bow made with yew wood from the Cascades; when Hedy saw me carrying it through the living room, she told Sandy that she was afraid I was going to use it to shoot Christopher.

Hedy texted me on my phone at five in the morning to say her catheter bag needed emptying. She wanted me to go to Starbucks and get her some coffee. When I returned, she had taken a double dose of her steroid because she could not remember taking it earlier. She had a nervous breakdown because the med-balance was so disrupted. Nurse Jenna came early to help her out of the episode. Jenna held her hand and talked her calm. Nurse Jenna was also a trained therapist. We limited Hedy's access to her medication.

We gave Hedy back rubs and shifted her position numerous times a day. When we did, we could see the green shamrock she had on her back. Kim was watching.

It was twelve below zero in Santiam Pass on the weekend.

One afternoon, Hedy wanted me to bring her a small drawer containing jewelry that she had bought over the years mostly secondhand stores and fairs. She separated out what she wanted to keep; she stored it in a little box. A few days later, she complained of something hurting her back; she wanted me to rub her back. Hedy got on her side and I started rubbing and behold, I found a small cross, a crucifix, stuck in her back. It caused an imprint that soon disappeared. John had inspired Hedy to study the Bible, but she just ran out of time. Well, maybe the cross did replace some of the hurt because soon after it was found, Hedy let go of a lot of her anger. For a week, she enjoyed teasing Sandy and myself.

As she was leaving Hedy's bedside, Sandy said, "I'm going away now, I'm going into the kitchen." Hedy said, "That's not far enough." Then Hedy grinned and laughed.

Another time as I stood beside Hedy's bed watching Sandy wipe Hedy's face with a washcloth, Hedy told Sandy, "Wipe his face now." When Sandy hesitated, Hedy said, "Come on, play the game!" I leaned forward and Sandy wiped my face as Hedy chuckled with laughter.

When I came up to her bed later, Hedy said, "Dad, you stink." I asked her if I needed a shower and she whispered, yes. When I left the room, I said, "Daught, I'll take a shower." Hedy laughed. I did take a shower.

Another time, she called me to hurry to her only to whisper, "Dad, you're so obnoxious," and then she laughed. She told me with a serious tone, "Dad, I wonder about you. What are you going to do with your life?"

"I have millions of projects," I said.

"But you never finish any of them."

"Oh, finish enough. I'm never short of projects."

Once she whispered to me Sandy and me, "Thank you guys for helping me."

Hedy stopped watching videos, but we left some running for her at night, and she fell asleep to them often. One of the last things she watched was a sitcom called Silicon Valley. One of the episodes ended with Izzy singing "The White Sandy Beaches of Hawaii." Hedy broke down and started crying when she heard it. She had at that time pretty much stopped talking or commenting on anything.

Another time she whispered to me, "How is it that you're still alive and I'm dying? Don't you think that's wrong?"

"I'd trade places with you if I could," I said.

And she whispered to us, "You're killing me. This is so cruel."

Sandy said, "Honey, I would trade places with you in a second."

Sandy and I worked to keep the bedsores away from her back. Every three hours, day and night, we helped her shift her position. Hedy called Pete once again and begged him in a whisper to come back. "We never had our pizza, we never got to play Nintendo." She could hardly whisper. Hedy hadn't eaten anything for days, except a pop sickle once or twice a day. I read to her from a joke book and Sandy would laugh and Hedy would smile. Sandy read the beginning of *The Princess Bribe* to Hedy; when Sandy realized that she had read thirty pages of the introduction, she cussed, "Darn it!" Hedy smiled widely. Sandy started playing a nonstop classical music channel that came on our cable service. Day and night, 24-7 classical pieces filled the house. At first, Hedy would ask what a certain piece was but by the last day of March, she wasn't responding too much to anything.

Peter came back to Eugene on a Friday night the first weekend in April. It was too late for any Nintendo or pizza. We were not sure if she realized he was there. Sandy said to her, "Hedy, tighten your eyelids twice for yes, and tighten them once for no. Now, do you know Peter's here?" She blinked her eyes twice. That Friday night and Saturday night, her breathing was congested and we heard her both nights breathing rattle through the monitor that the nurses had lent us.

At noon on Palm Sunday, Pete and I went to the Owosso Bridge and planned to walk on the other side of the Willamette river, but as soon as we got there, I had a feeling we should go back. We got back just as nurse named Holly arrived at the house. As we stepped through the door, Sandy called for us to hurry to Hedy's side. Hedy passed away at 1:47 PM with Sandy holding her left hand and I holding her right. Pete was standing at the end of the bed. A violin was playing a tune by Claude Debussy. Peter read the title, "The Girl with the Flaxen Hair." Hedy was thirty-nine years old. Death by secret.

CHAPTER 36

Go ahead and chase the scared up the stairs   [14]
I'll keep tapping my wooden finger . . .
I bled for you, almost died for you,
Someone had to make up for all the lies you people hide

—"Shut Up the World" by Hedy Wyn

Hedy started keeping a journal when she was a sophomore in high school. That first journal told the story of a girl obsessed with becoming a singer, to make her living as a singer. By the beginning of her senior year, she discovered marijuana and the calming effect it had on her and the healing it affected. She had found a way to soothe her PTSD. She worked harder at being with her friends than pursuing her dreams. Her viola playing and her singing were put on automatic pilot as she searched for who she was and who she wanted to be. She didn't pursue any scholarships, which she could have easily earned; she wanted to take a year off from going to school. Even with her drifting, she was voted the most musical. Hers was the first voice to begin the singing for the "O Sifuni Mungu" that her senior class performed on graduation night.

Many journals later, as Hedy lay in her hospital bed in February 2020, she was determined to put down some of her lessons in life and explain some of the detours that she took. She rewrote this short essay numerous times; even after she gave it to someone to type it out, she rewrote it. Her unfinished symphony.

It starts: Once upon a time . . . 2007 took place. I love him! What? Damn it! A guy I barely knew triggered my emotions enough to burst open my chained heart. He just happened to be there at that particular time in my life. Poor sap. I'm sure he barely knew of my existence, and that's okay. But for those who understand how crazy impossible it is to stop that love or heartbreaking feeling, that lust, obsession, confusion—it's totally embarrassing, Ah! It was my time to give love, and I was surprised by the powerful feeling, even if it was based on purely fleeting feelings of nothing. The huge question here is: Was I trained or raised to fall for just any man? I feel—even now in retrospect—it was a rancid parallel of sorts. Boy, that hurt.

But I kept trudging on. Even though much of what I seemed to know at age 26 was humiliation and self-mutilation. So, what did I do then? A lot of that. Self-mutilation helped me forget about a consistent pattern of humiliation from unhealthy thoughts, which I was replenishing from my store of memories, and recycling the more problematic memories over and over. This storage box must have had a beautiful life and unique love, awesome enough for my survival for another decade and a half. Because how I was able to battle a gargantuan amount of stress, deceit, blames, false accusations, failures, and ridicules is beyond me. Either that or my personal convictions and strong will saved me. Some of these burdens have branded a dark stamp of shame—unjustly—upon my childhood innocence. And still, I kept smiling and laughing at my own expense, oblivious to my own reality, the only one I knew.

So, the year 2007 was significant for me. This love feeling, this love giving, is what I like to call my soul awaking. I think I stumbled upon it as love because no one in my family had introduced any form of its righteousness to me before. It came robust. Not refined. That was part I had to work out. And this is the practice I will have to bring with me through all my lifetimes. It may have been the only thing I had at that time of reflection in my life. That was also the year I could get in-state tuition and had already embarked on a future for myself by placing myself in college.

Thank goodness, a college roommate studied psychology and encouraged me to seek professional guidance. Talk therapy helped me realize my destructive ways and thank goodness I was able to preserve the teensy bit of myself that I had left and tie up many loose ends. At that time, I turned from extrovert to introvert and started working on myself.

Around 2013, I guess I convinced myself that I would be able to grasp the reality of life. Still, little did I know that wounds like mine are too deep, and cannot be reckoned with, no matter how badly I wanted to start new and fresh. A certain compulsion from my immediate family started to strain on my personal power and left me shocked and cornered many times, while mimicking my ideas, stealing them for themselves. They would abandon me, and go off and do fun stuff, with little regard for my feelings and considerations. I felt punched in the stomach. I began to verbally express and silently wish to rid my existence. I believe I got my wish because of the unselfish nature of the wish. I was so mixed up with deep anguish and suffering I endured through the years; my mind, body, and soul could not bear it any longer. This wish was granted almost immediately because of the timing. Jupiter was hanging around 2013-2014. Because of the deep anguish I suffered, the wish was answered in my favor, just unraveling before my eyes now in 2020.

Apparently, I didn't know how to find my place in society as a well-rounded adult. More importantly, I held a deep sense that awful parts of my childhood kept superseding my psyche before I had much chance to realize my opportunities. My psyche was wrestling myself into my daunting unforeseen future and stinking it up. I was so tired I could not battle its stench any further. This lifelong constant evoking of a lie-not-of-my-own has drained my avenues of survival tools. I felt a dark force stalking me, trying to shake me to the very core of my being, watching me, wanting me. I will not bend. I will not cross the line. I am not a puppet. He cannot have me.

Presently, in 2020, my body is consumed by cancer. My physical and mental exhaustions have depleted me and my willingness or desire to deflect my current existence. I guess this is my non-apology to anyone who may need more than I can give. As I write this letter with hospice behind me, I'm going to enjoy the time I have left. I have tried time and time again to experience some wholesome goodness from life, even if it is just some great food; I know I will be a little happy at the end. The kind of wholesome goodness attained through patience and unconditional love; the kind of wholesome goodness that brings beauty and relaxation; the kind of wholesome goodness that softly and gently brings and soft and rustic yellow glow into my atmosphere so that I can continue to practice leaving behind all the negligence and evil of the world.

I have to say there were great times within my semi-short life. A person striving to keep a low carbon footprint says so much. A semi-short life also allowed me to distain from adult compromises. I was able to explore life like a child in a big shiny candy store and milk a playful and youthful nature, which we all have inside ourselves. But I am an adult now and so these basic survival skills I gathered from childhood can only get me so far. I want nothing more than to know where I stand from the tests of time. And I do believe it is my time. I will find this on the next step of my spiritual journey at the pearly gates!

I wrote a diagram of my thoughts on what the pearly gates have meant to me for the last few years, as I was pondering my wish, or wishing my cancer scare would go away. I don't know, but death has never been a fear of mine. I cannot believe I lasted this long on earth: a rebellious, self-mutilating athlete and artist. I don't know how anyone can be scared of death if you're on a planet with so much to do, whether it is to save a species or to fly in one of those neat-o flying suits. Death, that will be my freedom day; the last day that I am judged by any human. That will be the last day I have to worry about being harmed by another human, by protecting myself with a very expensive chastity belt. The last day to compete for a frigging dollar, to diminish myself to survive a simple day in the life of a starving artist.

As a spiritual person, I believe I am one step closer to a new life. A life in which I get to serve more important purposes with higher standards and processes for exploring other varieties of life or beyond life—into the stars of righteous kingdoms. My limited scope of the kingdoms: plant, animal, etc.

Wherever I am needed, I would be honored to be part of it all in the future. Currently, I have to succumb to the temptations and demands as part of the animal kingdoms. I don't know . . . I think I want to be a tree or a flower for a while.

I found this next sentiment in one of Hedy's notebooks. There was no date on it, but it was in Ellensburg. She wrote:

I really understand what love is now. I don't know if I can actually love someone right now—I mean a boyfriend. I love my family and friends so much though. I know the main part of love, for me right now, is about sharing. That means sharing experiences, sharing secrets, sharing entities—anything! Sharing the little things in life is so important. The big things in life are important, too. Gosh! Love is great!

As of spring 2021, Sandy has found help, solace and support with the Seventh Day Adventists, free of politics and strong on the truth.

This poem was found in Hedy's 2009 journal:

> As I walk along the beach
>   I look back to see if the waves
>   have washed over my footprints
>   that I made in the mud
> Then running, running,
>   as the breeze slaps against my skin
>   and my dress blowing,
>   and my hair in my face
> Again I look back
>   for my prints
>   and with a whisper of the sea
>   they are gone
>
> XXX

APPENDIX #1

Family Relationships

Wilson Mitcham & Mary (Coward) m.1917/children: Thomas, Robert, Betty
Wm. Dillinger & Sylvia (Trexler) m.1915/children: Arnold, Harold, Neva, Chesna
Thomas Mitcham and Chesna Mae (Dillinger) m. 1946/6 children: John Timothy, Patricia, Jolie, Sandy, Kitty, Wendy
    Greg Wallrich & Katie (Poss) m.1932/ 7 children:
        Arlene, Marlys, Madonna, Anthony, Eva, Sharon, Michael

Jolie (Mitcham) married Don Rohrbach 1979/ Benjamin and Joy
Kitty (Mitcham) married Craig Loveridge 1975/son: Sean
Wendy (Mitcham) 1st marriage to Richard Johnson/ son: Christopher
    2nd marriage/ Bob Adams/ two sons: Nicholas and Patrick
Tim and Patty (Mitcham)—both unmarried, no children
Arlene married Raymond Peluso/ Mark, Daniel, John, Anita
Marlys married Marvin Auchstetter/ Steven, Susan, Lori, Karen
Madonna married Tim Vanek/ Timothy and Randal
    Tony married Kathy Fisher/Pam, Pat, Barb, Rich, Jim, Michele, Dianne, Amy

Eva married John Whitten/Lisa, Joseph
    2nd Marriage/Jim Prendergast/Paul and David
Sharon married Robert Dolen/a son: Jeffrey
Michael married Sandy Mitcham 1972 / Hedy and Peter

APPENDIX #2

Dates connected to this story:

21 March 1987—The night of the rape
April 1987 to summer of 1988—Trips to doctors in Tucson
June 1989—Wendy/Christopher move (from T or C to Prescott)
July 1989—Wallriches move (from Nogales to Prescott)
March 1990—Christopher drops out of school
September 1991—Wendy depressed, locked in her room
March 1994—Wendy's Pantry Blackmail Scheme
Summer 1995—Hedy wins first of 4 yearly music camp awards (viola)
June 1999—Hedy graduates from Prescott High
8 February 2003—Hedy told her parents about the rape
July 2006—Townhouse incident
September 2006—The Mediation
2008 to 2020—Part Two

www.ingramcontent.com/pod-product-compliance
Lightning Source LLC
Chambersburg PA
CBHW030112240426
43673CB00002B/55